THE JOURNEY OF
CORONADO
1540–1542

THE JOURNEY OF
CORONADO
1540–1542

Translated and Edited by
George Parker Winship

Introduction by
Donald C. Cutter

Fulcrum Publishing
Golden, Colorado

Jacket and text design by Jody Chapel, Cover to Cover Design
Case design by Frederick R. Rinehart

Jacket art: Painting by Harold Wolfinbarger courtesy of the Denver Public Library
Western History Department, and map courtesy of the Denver Public Library,
Western History Department. Interior maps and facsimiles from George Parker
Winship's 1896 translation of the Spanish journals, published as part 1 of the
Fourteenth Annual Report (1892–93) of the United States Bureau of American
Ethnology. Courtesy of the Denver Public Library, Western History Collection.

Library of Congress Cataloging-in-Publication Data

Coronado expedition, 1540–1542.
    The journey of Coronado,1540–1542 / translated and edited by
George Parker Winship ; introduction by Donald C. Cutter.
        p.   cm.
    Reprint of George Parker Winship's 1904 translation of Spanish journals under title:
The journey of Coronado, 1540–1542, from the city of Mexico to the Grand Canon of
the Colorado and the Buffalo Plains of Texas, Kansas, and Nebraska, as told by himself
and his followers.
    Includes bibliographical references.
    ISBN 1-55591-066-1
    1. Southwest, New--Discovery and exploration. 2. Southwest, New--Description
and travel. 3. Vásquez de Coronado, Francisco, 1510–1549--Journeys--Southwest,
New. 4. Spaniards--Southwest, New--History--16th century. I. Vázquez de Coronado,
Francisco, 1510–1549. II. Title.
E125.V3C69   1990   90-39628
917.904'1--dc20   CIP

Printed in the United States of America

0   9   8   7   6   5   4   3   2   1

Fulcrum Publishing
350 Indiana Street
Golden, Colorado 80401

A Special Thank You to

Donald C. Cutter

Maxine Benson

Kay Baron

Denver Public Library Western History Collection

CONTENTS

Translation of the Narrative of Castañeda. Account of the Expedition to Cibola which Took Place in the Year 1540, in Which All Those Settlements, Their Ceremonies and Customes, are Described. Written by Pedro de Castañeda, of Najera.

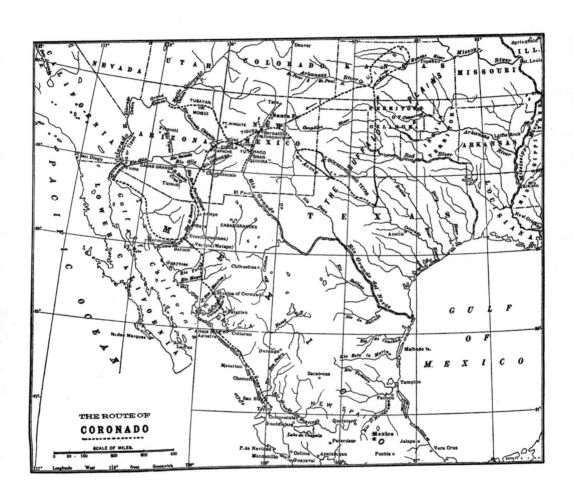

THE ROUTE OF
CORONADO

SCALE OF MILES.
0   50   100   200   300   400

PUBLISHER'S PREFACE

This book is dedicated to the memory of George Parker Winship, who translated and edited *The Journey of Coronado* almost a century ago.

George Parker Winship was born in Bridgewater, Massachusetts, on July 29, 1871, a son of Albert Edward and Ella R. (Parker) Winship. He graduated from Somerville High School, and went to Harvard College where he received an A.B. *cum laude* in 1893 and an A.M. in 1894.

In 1895, Winship was brought to Providence, Rhode Island, as librarian of the private collection of Americana formed by John Carter Brown and owned by his widow. Her son, John Nicholas Brown, made plans for the library's safekeeping and its use for scholars. Over the next ten years, under Winship's direction, the collections were doubled and the library was transformed into an independent research institution administered by Brown University. In addition, from 1904 to 1915 Winship had the honorary role of Curator of Mexican History in the Harvard College Library.

In 1915, after twenty years in Providence, Winship returned to Harvard as librarian of the Harry Elkins Widener collection and custodian of the rare books of the Harvard College Library, becoming Assistant Librarian in 1926. Winship was interested in the history of the book and as the first "rare book man" at Harvard, he began to gather a collection of the best of the written word. In the February 1923 *Harvard Library Notes* he wrote: "Certain books were more important for what they are, than for what they contain."

Winship was a lecturer on the history of printing and the history of culture.

His course, "History of the Printed Book," was taught in the library and dealt with the aesthetic appreciation and cultural background of books. His grandson, Michael, occasionally teaches a similar course at the American Antiquarian Society.

Winship was fascinated by the literature of discovery and exploration. He spent periods in Mexico and was attached to an expedition of the United States Bureau of American Ethnology. The breadth of his interest is shown in *The Coronado Expedition, 1540–1542*, published in 1896 in the *Fourteenth Annual Report* of the Bureau of American Ethnology; *Cabot Bibliography* (1900); *The Journey of Coronado, 1540–1542* (1904); and *Sailors Narratives of Voyages along the New England Coast, 1524–1624*, published in 1905.

George Parker Winship was also interested in fine printing. A prodigious writer of articles and an editor of early documents, he contributed such works as *The Literature of the History of Printing in the United States* (1923), *Gutenberg to Plantin: An Outline of the Early History of Printing* (1926), *Printing in the Fifteenth Century* (1940), and *The Cambridge Press, 1638–1692* (1945).

The breadth of his scholarship on both Spanish and English printing is indicated in a selection from his article *A Document Concerning the First Anglo-American Press* (1939): "English printing crossed the Atlantic in the late summer of 1638 and was at work the following spring. It was, however, a belated arrival in America, where the Spanish colonists had long enjoyed the benefits of typography, in Mexico since 1539 and in Peru since 1584, dates with which many North American writers on the subject have apparently been unacquainted."

Winship's accomplishments were recognized by his election to the American Antiquarian Society at the age of twenty-eight, and in 1905, he became a member of the Massachusetts Historical Society. Throughout his life, Winship was active in these organizations as well as in the Colonial Society of Massachusetts, the Club of Odd Volumes, and the Walpole Society.

In 1936 George Winship retired from Harvard to his Charles River Farm and his home in North Sandwich, New Hampshire. During his retirement he ran a private press, The Sign of the George. He died on June 22, 1952.

INTRODUCTION

by Donald C. Cutter

The words *conquistador* and *Coronado* evoke strong mental images of plumed knights in shining metal armor, involved in an almost medieval pageant, and ever hopeful that great discoveries would crown their efforts. To the local Indians, the sudden arrival of strange white men, some of whom were mounted on awe-inspiring animals, was a harbinger of great change. Recorded regional history of what is today the Southwest of the United States began with the arrival of Spanish explorers, most important of whom was Francisco Vásquez de Coronado.

The oft-told story of his expedition was first available in detail in English from an unlikely scholar, a young New England student who made the first important contribution to an imperfectly known and little-appreciated episode of American history. George Parker Winship published his translations of the key eyewitness accounts of a magnificent chapter in western history—the initial reconnaissance of much of the Southwest. A man in his mid-twenties who lived his entire life in Massachusetts, except for two decades of residence in nearby Rhode Island, became an important early contributor to what became known as the Spanish Borderlands. He made available, in both the original Spanish and in English translation, the contemporary accounts of one of the sixteenth century's greatest explorations, a story of great hope and of deep disappointment.

Winship's pioneer work appeared in 1896 as *The Coronado Expedition,*

1540–1542, in the *Fourteenth Annual Report* of the U.S. Bureau of American Ethnology, 1892–93, part 1. The tale that unfolds is that of a cavalcade of hopeful, young soldiers of fortune who in 1540 set out on a great adventure. Recruited somewhat haphazardly in Spain, almost all participants expected to better their status in life as a result of what lay ahead in a New World area of promise, the unknown North. Reports indicate that all went as volunteers and that they were assisted by ample support for the project from both private and viceregal sources. Leader and a major investor in the great exploratory effort was the governor of the frontier province of Nueva Galicia, Francisco Vásquez de Coronado. He was both psychologically prepared and personally well equipped for extensive yet comfortable operations, as was his retinue of motivated followers.

Vásquez de Coronado's march took him first west to Compostela (near Tepic) where final preparations were made. From there the group marched northward via Culiacán in Sinaloa, and finally eastward, during which time the party became the first organized European visitors to much of the American Southwest. It is a familiar story, known in detail by those interested in regional studies. Partly as a result of Winship's early work, there is no story of the Spanish Borderlands that is better known, even to the point of permitting the luxury of disagreement among scholars over minor points, but there is no controversy concerning the major point that the visit of an intrusive European army had a strong impact as a historical event.

The Coronado story has been told hundreds of times in books, articles, classrooms and even occasionally in popular drama. It keeps on contributing to placename geography, bequeathing a considerable legacy of toponyms. It has been recounted as high adventure, as a conflict of cultures, as a grand geography lesson, as evidence of the reputed Spanish zeal for mineral wealth, and as a major step in the northward political expansion of colonial New Spain, as the viceroyalty headquartered in Mexico City was called.

Brief accounts of the Coronado expedition appeared in some early history books, but the treatment hardly matched the material available in Winship's book. The appearance of two books over four decades after Winship's contribution did much for the dissemination of the Coronado story. Independently written, these were studies by A. Grove Day and Herbert E. Bolton, both prepared at about the same time.

Day's volume, *Coronado's Quest: The Discovery of the Southwestern States,* was published in 1940 by the University of California Press, the publication arm of the very institution at which Bolton was professor. *Coronado's Quest* was a biographical treatment written by an English professor who doubled as a historian. Day's book lacked some detail, but enjoyed the same clear narrative style later apparent in Day's work when he teamed with James A. Michener on *Rascals in Paradise*. Day pointed out that the modern history of the American Southwest opened with the epic of Francisco Vásquez de Coronado. He called him "soldier of Spain, crusader, gold-hunter, legend-chaser, the last of the great conquistadores." When, shortly after publication of his pioneer biography, Day left the Golden State for Hawaii, he also left behind Coronado and his "iron men of Iberia," and soon became one of Hawaii's best known experts. Grove Day, an engaging raconteur, "felt a keen obligation to the highest historical accuracy." Early in his bibliography and notes he placed in perspective one of his chief sources, Winship's documents, acknowledging his debt to those translations, though Day indicated that he had made alterations thereto. In Day's footnotes, the most frequent source cited is Winship.

A much better known contribution to Coronado studies is the second biography, that by Herbert E. Bolton, which appeared under two titles: *Coronado, Knight of Pueblos and Plains* and *Coronado on the Turquoise Trail: Knight of Pueblos and Plains*. Bolton, the master of Spanish Borderlands study, had access to more documentation than Day. This was due in part to his participation in the four-hundredth anniversary of Coronado's exploration, celebrated as the Coronado Cuarto Centennial. Part of that celebration was a planned multivolume series of which Bolton was scheduled to write the first volume. In a sense he did, since it was so numbered, but several of the later volumes predated the Coronado biography in appearance. Bolton's book was the best known contribution in the larger series, was awarded several literary prizes, and received a very favorable review in *Time* magazine.

The intervention of World War II, and a dispute over who had publication rights to Bolton's *Coronado*, resulted in the long delayed appearance of this detailed study. What had been intended as a commemoration of four hundred years appeared nine years late.

Whereas Day's *Coronado's Quest* has only been reprinted once, Bolton's *Coronado, Knight of Pueblos and Plains* has appeared from time to time in both hardback and paperback editions, the latest of which has been issued as recently as 1990. No change has been made in the original text, a study that made great use of the documents contained in the early Winship edition. In his acknowledgments, Bolton explained the relationship of his biography to Winship's work as follows: "Winship had laid the foundation of a study of the [Coronado] expedition to Cíbola and Quivira when in 1896 he published his monumental source book containing most of the essential documents at that time known." Bolton's use of documents was fully evident, though he did not annotate his work in the traditional manner,

Facsimile of Page of Castañeda's *Relacion*.

muchas tiendas y adobo muchas
telas y lastimo muchos cria
dos y quebro toda la loça dela mi
sa y cavallos que no pudo por
la necesidad porque por alli
no ay leña ni se hace ni calabaços
ni se sembra maiz ni comentos
salvo carne cruda o mal asada
y frutas

Des de alli embio el general
a descubrir y dieron en otras
rancherias a quatro jornadas
a manera de alixares e razon   Alixares
era muy poblada adonde avia
muchos frisoles y frutas como
las de castilla y pasaran dos a
barrestos pueblos de rancherias
tres jornadas de sia peccona
des de a priesa hizieron en el

but rather appended references for each chapter. With the confidence born of success, he privately asserted concerning footnotes that a master builder does not leave the scaffolding after completion of the edifice.

One of Bolton's contributions was to convert the early conquistador into a flesh-and-blood historical figure rather than simply a well-known name. Coronado as viewed by Bolton emerges as wise, skillful, intelligent, a noble nobleman. He was reputed to be a strict disciplinarian, personally both brave and soldierly.

Another major effort of Bolton's book, only lightly covered by Winship, was the detailed itinerary of the expedition, a subject which at present is a topic of possible reinterpretation. The latest change might have the expedition's terminal point in its Texas phase as considerably south of Bolton's estimates, as well as those of other interested parties.

Occasionally in the last half century researchers have attempted to reinterpret Winship's early comments, Day's account, and Bolton's *Coronado*. Some new light has been shed by these efforts, but by and large, the epic story has not changed significantly, mostly because the documentation first presented by Winship and interpreted into a narrative account by Day and Bolton, and augmented by some of the volumes of the Coronado Cuarto Centennial series, has not changed the basic picture. Reinterpretation is more frequently based on new insights into the sixteenth-century documentation as first made available in 1896. Reprinting at this time of Winship's early classic allows modern readers to see those basic documents without additions by Coronado's biographers and permits independent interpretations. It allows access to the unvarnished accounts of those who accompanied the "last of the Conquistadores."

Winship's purpose in making available the story, as told by the participants and presented by him, can become an advantage to the modern reader. Both Bolton and Day wrote from the perspective of the first half of the twentieth century. Another half century has passed, and references and allusions that were vital at that time are often less so today. Bolton died in early 1953 and Day, in his busy life as one of Hawaii's major literary figures, has given scant attention to a study done in his academic youth. Both of them, if writing today, would make changes. Other authors dealing briefly with Coronado have often altered the interpretation of his role and that of his expedition.

Winship made no attempt at biography and only very lightly edited the documentary record. The passage of nearly a century since his study has even eroded the validity of some of the few footnotes that he added, but it does give the reader an appreciation of the limited amount of material which the young New Englander had available to support his research efforts.

The value of the Winship documentary study is attested to in some measure by its partial or complete republication, and more so by its use by scholars interpreting or reinterpreting the sixteenth-century epic exploration. From the time of its first publication in 1896, there have been reprints, partial or complete, in 1904, 1907, 1922, 1933, 1964, 1966, 1969, and 1973. Only the original 1896 edition, and the 1964 facsimile reprint of it, presented both the Spanish originals and their translation into English.

Winship, as well as those who followed, fostered some misconceptions which may never be completely obliterated. The first is that involving the protagonist, who has become known as Coronado. Spanish surnames have often caused trouble for non-Spanish scholars, and even for some Spanish ones. In the case of the early explorer, his paternal surname was Vásquez de Coronado, a noble name proudly carried. Unlike some contemporaries, he did not use his mother's surname at all. In proper usage his name should be Francisco Vásquez de Coronado, perhaps even Francisco Vásquez would do, but never Francisco Coronado. The sixteenth-century documents make this point clear. This is not to suggest that Bolton and Day were ignorant of the usage. Perhaps as a person more removed from things Hispanic, the Yankee Winship was. However, they all bowed to Anglo usage rather than crusade for the correctness of Vásquez de Coronado. Both Bolton and Day even commented on the impropriety involved in calling their hero Coronado, but there is no likelihood that historians will ever speak of the epic Vásquez expedition.

A second, somewhat more complicated misconception, concerns the ethnic background of an important precursor to the 1540 exploration—Stephen, Estéban, Estevanico as he is variously called. Winship, Day, and Bolton all call him a Negro. The slave who accompanied Alvar Núñez Cabeza de Vaca and later was associated with Fray Marcos de Niza was probably *negro,* there being no doubt that his skin was black. The invention that he was Negro rests on poor translation. The early companion of other explorers was a Moor, which makes him a North African, Arab in culture, no matter how dark he may have been. Recent interpretation, based on his place of origin in Morocco and the use of the word *negro* as an adjective, suggests that all of the earlier writers were misled by a facile, cognate translation as Negro for the Spanish word *negro,* rather than merely "black." This concept is widespread, being both supported and refuted by modern scholars.

This is not to suggest that Winship alone was responsible for these doubtful interpretations, but as a precursor of later writings on Vásquez de Coronado, it is interesting to note the existing coincidence of usage. What is more evident is that

Winship's Coronado volume was a springboard for subsequent presentation of the story of the conquistador's epic journey, whether it is briefly told or recounted in detail.

Donald C. Cutter
Professor of Southwestern History, Emeritus
University of New Mexico, Albuquerque

SELECTED BIBLIOGRAPHY

Books

Bolton, Herbert E. *Coronado on the Turquoise Trail: Knight of Pueblos and Plains.* Coronado Cuarto Centennial Publications, 1540–1940, vol. 1. Albuquerque: University of New Mexico Press, 1949. Reprinted in 1949 jointly with Whittlesey House, New York, under the title *Coronado, Knight of Pueblos and Plains.*

———. *The Spanish Borderlands: A Chronicle of Old Florida and the Southwest.* Chronicles of America Series, vol. 23. New Haven: Yale University Press, 1921.

Chavez, Fray Angelico. *Coronado's Friars.* Washington, D.C.: Academy of American Franciscan History, 1968.

Day, A. Grove. *Coronado's Quest: The Discovery of the Southwestern States.* Berkeley: University of California Press, 1940.

De Voto, Bernard. *The Course of Empire.* Boston: Houghton, Mifflin, 1952.

Forbes, Jack D. *Apache, Navaho, and Spaniard.* Norman: University of Oklahoma Press, 1960.

Hammond, George P. *Coronado's Seven Cities.* Albuquerque: United States Coronado Exposition Commission, 1940.

Hammond, George P., and Edgar F. Goad. *The Adventure of Don Francisco Vásquez de Coronado.* Albuquerque: University of New Mexico Press, 1938.

Hammond, George P., and Agapito Rey, eds. *Narratives of the Coronado Expedition, 1540–1542*. Coronado Cuarto Centennial Publications, 1540–1940, vol. 2. Albuquerque: University of New Mexico Press, 1940.

Hewett, Edgar L. *Ancient Life in the American Southwest*. Indianapolis: Bobbs–Merrill, 1930.

Leonard, Irving A. *Books of the Brave, being an Account of Books and of Men in the Spanish Conquest and Settlement of the Sixteenth-Century New World*. Cambridge: Harvard University Press, 1949.

Prescott, William H. *History of the Conquest of Mexico, with a Preliminary View of the Ancient Mexican Civilization, and the Life of the Conqueror, Hernando Cortes*. New York: Harper, 1843.

Riley, Carroll L. *The Frontier People: The Greater Southwest in the Protohistoric Period*. Carbondale: Center for Archaeological Investigations, Southern Illinois University at Carbondale, 1982.

Thomas, Alfred B. *After Coronado: Spanish Exploration Northeast of New Mexico, 1696–1727*. Norman: University of Oklahoma Press, 1935.

Udall, Stewart L. *To the Inland Empire: Coronado and Our Spanish Legacy*. Garden City, NY: Doubleday, 1987.

Articles

Aiton, Arthur S. "Coronado's Commission as Captain-General." *Hispanic American Historical Review* 20 (February 1940):83–87.

———. "Coronado's First Report on the Government of New Galacia." *Hispanic American Historical Review* 19 (August 1939):306–13.

———. "Coronado's Muster Roll." *American Historical Review* 44 (April 1939):556–70.

———. "Report on the Residencia of the Coronado Government in New Galacia." *Panhandle-Plains Historical Review* 13 (1940):12–20.

Baskett, James Newton. "A Study of the Route of Coronado between the Rio Grande and Missouri Rivers." *Collections of the Kansas State Historical Society* 12 (1911–12):219–52.

Bryan, Frank. "The Llano Estacado: The Geographical Background of the Coronado Expedition." *Panhandle-Plains Historical Review* 13 (1940):21–37.

Day, A. Grove. "Coronado's Quest." *Panhandle-Plains Historical Review* 13 (1940):47–70.

———. "Mota Padilla on the Coronado Expedition." *Hispanic American Historical Review* 20 (February 1940):88–110.

Donoghue, David. "The Location of Quivira." *Panhandle-Plains Historical Review* 13 (1940):38–46.

Hodge, Frederick W. "The Six Cities of Cibola, 1581–1680." *New Mexico Historical Review* 1 (October 1926):478–88.

Inglis, G. Douglas. "The Men of Cibola: New Investigations on the Francisco Vásquez de Coronado Expedition." *Panhandle-Plains Historical Review* 55 (1982):1–24.

Mecham, J. Lloyd. "The Northern Expansion of New Spain, 1522–1822: A Selected Descriptive Bibliographical List." *Hispanic American Historical Review* 7 (May 1927):233–76.

Morgan, Lewis H. "The 'Seven Cities of Cibola.'" *North American Review* 108 (April 1869):457–98.

Reed, Erik K. "Southwestern Indians in Coronado's Time." *Region III Quarterly* (National Park Service) 2 (July 1940).

Robinson, Duncan. "Coronado and His Army." *Panhandle-Plains Historical Review* 13 (1940):71–79.

Sauer, Carl O. "The Road to Cibola." *Ibero-Americana* 3 (1932):1–58.

Strout, Clevy Lloyd. "The Coronado Expedition: Following the Geography Described in the Spanish Journals." *Great Plains Journal* 14 (Fall 1974):2–31.

———. "Flora and Fauna Mentioned in the Journals of the Coronado Expedition." *Great Plains Journal* 11 (Fall 1971):5–40.

Winship, George Parker. "Why Coronado Went to New Mexico in 1540." *Annual Report of the American Historical Association* (1894):83–92.

Zimmerman, James F. "The Coronado Cuarto Centennial." *Hispanic American Historical Review* 20 (February 1940):158–62.

A NOTE ON THIS EDITION

In 1896, George Parker Winship's *The Coronado Expedition, 1540–1542*, was published as part 1 of the *Fourteenth Annual Report* (1892–93) of the United States Bureau of American Ethnology. Featuring a Historical Introduction as well as the documents in the original Spanish and in English translation, the work was reissued in 1964 by the Rio Grande Press of Chicago.

Eight years after the appearance of the Bureau of American Ethnology report, Winship's translations of Castañeda's account and other documents were issued by A. S. Barnes and Company, New York, under the title *The Journey of Coronado, 1540–1542, from the City of Mexico to the Grand Canon of the Colorado and the Buffalo Plains of Texas, Kansas, and Nebraska, as Told by Himself and His Followers*. As Winship explained in his introduction, "many passages in these translations have been revised and corrected" since the first publication in 1896. The 1904 version was reprinted in 1922 by the Allerton Book Company, New York; in 1966 by University Microfilms, Ann Arbor, Michigan; in 1969 by Greenwood Press, New York; and in 1973 by AMS Press, New York.

Moreover, Frederick W. Hodge prepared additional notes and an introduction to Winship's 1904 work, which was published in a limited edition of 550 copies by the Grabhorn Press, San Francisco, in 1933 as *The Journey of Francisco Vázquez de Coronado, 1540–1542, as told by Pedro de Castañeda, Francisco Vázquez de Coronado, and Others*. Earlier, Hodge had edited and written an introduction to Winship's translations under the title *The Narrative of the Expedition of Coronado, by Pedro de Castañeda*, published in 1907 by Charles Scribner's Sons, New York.

For young readers, Robert K. Meredith and E. Brooks Smith "adapted and edited" Winship's translations for a book entitled *Riding with Coronado, from Pedro de Castañeda's Eyewitness Account of the Exploration of the Southwest, Called Relacion de la Jornada de Cibola, and Including Two of Coronado's Letters Sent from the Land of the Pueblos,* which was published by Little, Brown, and Company, Boston, in 1964. Winship himself had prepared a fifteen-page pamphlet, *Coronado's Journey to New Mexico and the Great Plains, 1540–42,* issued as part of the American History Leaflets series in 1894 by A. Lovell and Company, New York, and in 1906 and 1911 by Parker P. Simmons, New York.

The present work includes the Historical Introduction from the 1896 Bureau of American Ethnology report, followed by the translations of the documents as revised and introduced by George Parker Winship in 1904.

HISTORICAL INTRODUCTION

The Causes of the Coronado Expedition, 1528–1539

Alvar Nuñez Cabeza de Vaca

The American Indians are always on the move. Tribes shift the location of their homes from season to season and from year to year, while individuals wander at will, hunting, trading or gossiping. This is very largely true today, and when the Europeans first came in contact with the American aborigines, it was a characteristic feature of Indian life. The Shawnees, for example, have drifted from Georgia to the great lakes, and part of the way back, during the period since their peregrinations can first be traced. Traders from tribe to tribe, in the days when European commercial ideas were unknown in North America, carried bits of copper dug from the mines in which the aboriginal implements are still found, on the shores of Lake Superior, to the Atlantic coast on the one side and to the Rocky mountains on the other. The Indian gossips of central Mexico, in 1535, described to the Spaniards the villages of New Mexico and Arizona, with their many-storied houses of stone and adobe. The Spanish colonists were always eager to learn about unexplored regions

From George Parker Winship, *The Coronado Expedition, 1540–1542*, United States Bureau of American Ethnology, *Fourteenth Annual Report* (1896).

lying outside the limits of the white settlements, and their Indian neighbors and servants in the valley of Mexico told them many tales of the people who lived beyond the mountains which hemmed in New Spain on the north. One of these stories may be found in another part of this memoir, where it is preserved in the narrative of Pedro Castañeda, the historian of the Coronado expedition. Castañeda's hearsay report of the Indian story, which was related by an adventurous trader who had penetrated the country far to the north, compares not unfavorably with the somewhat similar stories which Marco Polo told to entertain his Venetian friends.[1] But whatever may have been known before, the information which led to the expedition of Friar Marcos de Niza and to that of Francisco Vazquez Coronado was brought to New Spain late in the spring of 1536 by Alvar Nuñez Cabeza de Vaca.

In 1520, before Cortes, the conqueror of Motecuhzoma, had made his peace with the Emperor Charles V and with the authorities at Cuba, Panfilo de Narvaez was dispatched to the Mexican mainland, at the head of a considerable force. He was sent to subdue and supersede the conqueror of Mexico, but when they met, Cortes quickly proved that he was a better general than his opponent, and a skillful politician as well. Narvaez was deserted by his soldiers and became a prisoner in the City of Mexico, where he was detained during the two years which followed. Cortes was at the height of his power, and Narvaez must have felt a longing to rival the successes of the conqueror, who had won the wealth of the Mexican empire. After Cortes resumed his dutiful obedience to the Spanish crown, friends at home obtained a royal order which effected the release of Narvaez, who returned to Spain at the earliest opportunity. Almost as soon as he had established himself anew in the favor of the court, he petitioned the King for a license which should permit him to conduct explorations in the New World. After some delay, the desired patent was granted. It authorized Narvaez to explore, conquer, and colonize the country between Florida and the Rio de Palmas, a grant comprising all that portion of North America bordering on the Gulf of Mexico, which is now included within the limits of the United States. Preparations were at once begun for the complete organization of an expedition suitable to the extent of this territory and to the power and dignity of its governor.

On June 17, 1527, Narvaez, governor of Florida, Rio de Palmas and Espiritu Santo—the Rio Grande and the Mississippi on our modern maps— sailed from Spain. He went first to Cuba, where he refitted his fleet and replaced one vessel which had been lost in a hurricane during the voyage. When everything was ready to start for the unexplored mainland, he ordered the pilots to conduct his fleet to the western limits of his jurisdiction—our Texas. They landed him, April 15, 1528, on the coast of the present Florida, at a bay which the Spaniards called Bahia de la Cruz, and which the map of Sebastian Cabot enables us to identify with Apalache bay. The pilots knew that a storm had driven them out of their course toward the east, but they could not calculate on the strong current of the gulf stream. They assured the commander that he was not far from the Rio de Palmas, the desired destination, and so he landed his force of 50 horses and 300 men—just half the number of the soldiers, mechanics, laborers, and priests who had started with him from Spain ten months before. He sent one of his vessels back to Cuba for recruits, and ordered the remaining three to sail along the coast toward the west and to wait for the army at the fine harbor of Panuco, which was reported to be near the mouth of Palmas river. The fate of these vessels is not known.

Narvaez, having completed these arrangements, made ready to lead his army overland to Panuco. The march began April 19. For a while, the Spaniards took a northerly direction, and then they turned toward the west. Progress was slow, for the men knew nothing of the country, and the forests and morasses presented many difficulties to the soldiers unused to woodcraft. Little help could be procured from the Indians, who soon became openly hostile wherever the Spaniards encountered them. Food grew scarce, and no persuasion could induce the natives to reveal hidden stores of corn, or of gold. On May 15, tired and discouraged, the Spaniards reached a large river with a strong current flowing toward the south. They rested here, while Cabeza de Vaca, the royal treasurer accompanying the expedition, took a small party of soldiers and followed the banks of the river down to the sea. The fleet was not waiting for them at the mouth of this stream, nor could anything be learned of the fine harbor for which they were searching. Disappointed anew by the report which Cabeza de Vaca made on his return to the main camp, the Spanish soldiers crossed the river and continued their march toward the west. They plodded on and on, and after awhile turned southward, to follow down the course of another large river which blocked their westward march. On the last day of July they reached a bay of considerable size, at the mouth of the river. They named this Bahia de los Cavallos, perhaps, as has been surmised, because it was here that they killed the last of their horses for food. The Spaniards, long before this, had become thoroughly disheartened. Neither food nor gold could be found. The capital cities, toward which the Indian captives had directed the wandering strangers, when reached, were mere groups of huts, situated in some cases on mounds of earth. Not a sign of anything which would reward their search, and hardly a thing to eat, had been discovered during the months of toilsome marching. The Spaniards determined to leave the country. They constructed forges in their camp near the seashore, and hammered their spurs, stirrups, and other iron implements of warfare into nails and saws and axes, with which to build the boats necessary for their escape from the country. Ropes were made of the tails and manes of the horses, whose hides, pieced out with the shirts of the men, were fashioned into sails. By September 22, five boats were ready, each large enough to hold between 45 and 50 men. In these the soldiers embarked. Scarcely a man among them knew anything of navigation, and they certainly knew nothing about the navigation of this coast. They steered westward, keeping near the land, and stopping occasionally for fresh water. Sometimes they obtained a little food.

Toward the end of October they came to the mouth of a large river which poured forth so strong a current that it drove the boats out to sea. Two, those which contained Narvaez and the friars, were lost. The men in the other three boats were driven ashore by a storm, somewhere on the coast of western Louisiana or eastern Texas.[2] This was in the winter of 1528–29. Toward the end of April, 1536, Cabeza de Vaca, Alonso del Castillo Maldonado, Andres Dorantes, and a negro named Estevan, met some Spanish slave catchers near the Rio de Petatlan, in Sinaloa, west of the mountains which border the Gulf of California. These four men, with a single exception,[3] were the only survivors of the three hundred who had entered the continent with Narvaez eight years before.

Cabeza de Vaca and his companions stayed in Mexico for several months, as the guests of the viceroy, Don Antonio de Mendoza. At first, it was probably the intention of the three Spaniards to return to Spain, in order to claim the due reward for their manifold sufferings. Mendoza says, in a letter dated December 10, 1537,[4] that he purchased the negro Estevan from Dorantes, so that there might be someone left in New Spain who could guide an expedition back into the countries about which the wanderers had heard. An earlier letter from the viceroy, dated February 11, 1537, commends Cabeza de Vaca and *Francisco* Dorantes—he must have meant Andres, and perhaps wrote it so in his original manuscript—as deserving the favor of the Empress. Maldonado is not mentioned in this letter, and no trace of him has been found after the arrival of the four survivors in Mexico. All that we know about him is that his home was in Salamanca.[5]

Cabeza de Vaca and Dorantes started from Vera Cruz for Spain in October, 1536, but their vessel was stranded before it got out of the harbor. This accident obliged them to postpone their departure until the following spring, when Cabeza de Vaca returned home alone. He told the story of his wanderings to the court and the King, and was rewarded, by 1540, with an appointment as adelantado, giving him the command over the recently occupied regions about the Rio de la Plata. The position was one for which he was unfitted, and his subordinates sent him back to Spain. The complaints against him were investigated by the Council for the Indies, but the judgment, if any was given, has never been published. He certainly was not punished, and soon settled down in Seville, where he was still living, apparently, twenty years later.[6]

While Dorantes was stopping at Vera Cruz during the winter of 1536–37, he received a letter from Mendoza, asking him to return to the City of Mexico. After several interviews, the viceroy induced Dorantes to remain in New Spain, agreeing to provide him with a party of horsemen and friars, in order to explore more thoroughly the country through which he had wandered. Mendoza explains the details of his plans in the letter written in December, 1537, and declares that he expected many advantages would be derived from this expedition which would redound to the glory of God and to the profit of His Majesty the King. The viceroy was prepared to expend a large sum—3,500 or 4,000 pesos—to insure a successful undertaking, but he promised to raise the whole amount, without taking a single maravedi from the royal treasury, by means of a more careful collection of dues, and especially by enforcing the payment of overdue sums, the collection of which hitherto had been considered impossible. This reform in the collection of rents and other royal exactions and the careful attention to all the details of the fiscal administration were among the most valuable of the many services rendered by Mendoza as viceroy. The expedition under Dorantes never started, though why nothing came of all the preparations, wrote Mendoza in his next letter to the King, "I never could find out."[7]

The three Spaniards wrote several narratives of their experiences on the expedition of Narvaez, and of their adventurous journey from the gulf coast of Texas to the Pacific coast of Mexico.[8] These travelers, who had lived a savage life for so long that they could wear no clothes, and were unable to sleep except upon the bare ground, had a strange tale to tell. The story of their eight years of wandering must have been often repeated—of their slavery, their buffalo-hunting expeditions, of the escape from their Indian masters, and their career as traders and as medicine men. These were wonderful and strange experiences, but the story contained little to arouse the eager interest of the colonists in New Spain, whose minds had been stirred by the accounts which came from Peru telling of the untold wealth of the Incas. A few things, however, had been seen and heard by the wanderers which suggested the possibility of lands worth conquering. "A copper hawks-bell, thick and large, figured with a face," had been given to Cabeza de Vaca, soon after he started on his journey toward Mexico. The natives who gave this to him said that they had received it from other Indians, "who had brought it from the north, where there was much copper, which was highly esteemed." After the travelers had crossed the Rio Grande, they showed this bell to some other Indians, who said that "there were many plates of this same metal buried in the ground in the place whence it had come, and that it was a thing which they esteemed highly, and that there were fixed habitations where it came from."[9] This was all the treasure which Cabeza de Vaca could say that he had seen. He had heard, however, of a better region than any he saw, for the Indians told him "that there are pearls and great riches on the coast of the South sea (the Pacific), and all the best and most opulent countries are near there." We may be sure that none of this was omitted whenever he told the Spanish colonists the story of the years of his residence in Texas and of the months of his journey across northern Mexico.[10]

The Governors of New Spain, 1530–1537

Don Antonio de Mendoza, "the good viceroy," had been at the head of the government of New Spain for two years when Cabeza de Vaca arrived in Mexico. The effects of his careful and intelligent administration were already beginning to appear in the increasing prosperity of the province and the improved condition of the colonists and of their lands. The authority of the viceroy was ample and extensive, although he was limited to some extent by the audiencia, the members of which had administered the government of the province since the retirement of Cortes. The viceroy was the president of this court, which had resumed more strictly judicial functions after his arrival, and he was officially advised by his instructions from the King to consult with his fellow members on all matters of importance.

Nuño de Guzman departed for New Spain in 1528, and became the head of the first audiencia. Within a year he had made himself so deservedly unpopular that when he heard that Cortes was coming back to Mexico from Spain, with the new title of marquis and fresh grants of power from the King, he thought it best to get out of the way of his rival. Without relinquishing the title to his position in the capital city, Guzman collected a considerable force and marched away toward the west and north, determined to win honor and security by new conquests. He explored and subdued the country for a considerable distance along the eastern shores of the Gulf of California, but he could find nothing there to rival the Mexico of Motecuhzoma. Meanwhile reports reached Charles V of the manner in which Guzman had been treating the Indians and the Spanish settlers, and so, March 17, 1536,[1] the King appointed the Licentiate Diego Perez de la Torre to take the residencia[2] of Guzman. At the same time Torre was commissioned to replace Guzman as governor of New Galicia, as this northwestern province had been named. The latter had already determined to return to Spain, leaving Don Christobal de Oñate, a model executive and administrative official, in charge of his province. Guzman almost succeeded in escaping, but his judge, who had landed at Vera Cruz by the end of 1536, met him at the viceroy's palace in Mexico city, and secured his arrest before he could depart. After his trial he was detained in Mexico until June 30, 1538, when he was enabled to leave New Spain by an order which directed him to surrender his person to the officers of the Casa de Contratacion,[3] at Seville. Guzman lost no time in going to Spain, where he spent the next four years in urging his claims to a right to participate in the northern conquests.

Torre, the licentiate, had barely begun to reform the abuses of Guzman's government when he was killed in a conflict with some revolted Indian tribes. Oñate again took charge of affairs until Mendoza appointed Luis Galindo chief justice for New Galicia. This was merely a temporary appointment, however, until a new governor could be selected. The viceroy's nomination for the position was confirmed by the King, in a cedula dated April 18, 1539, which commissioned Francisco Vazquez Coronado as governor.[4]

Cortes had been engaged, ever since his return from Spain, in fitting out expeditions which came to nothing,[5] but by which he hoped to accomplish his schemes for completing the exploration of the South sea. His leisure was more than occupied by his efforts to outwit the agents of the viceroy and the audiencia, who had received orders from the King to investigate the extent and condition of the estates held by Cortes. In the spring of 1535, Cortes established a colony on the opposite coast of California, the supposed Island of the Marquis, at Santa Cruz,[6] near the modern La Paz. Storms and shipwreck, hunger and surfeiting, reduced the numbers and the enthusiasm of the men whom he had conducted thither, and when his vessels returned from the mainland with the news that Mendoza had arrived in Mexico, and bringing letters from his wife urging him to return at once, Cortes went back to Mexico. A few months later he recalled the settlers whom he had left at Santa Cruz, in accordance, it may be, with the command or advice of Mendoza.[7] When the stories of Cabeza de Vaca suggested the possibility of making desirable conquests toward the north, Cortes possessed a better outfit for undertaking this work than any of the others who were likely to be rivals for the privilege of exploring and occupying that region.

Pedro de Alvarado was the least known of these rival claimants. He had been a lieutenant of Cortes until he secured an independent command in Guatemala, Yucatan and Honduras, where he subdued the natives, but discovered nothing except that there was nowhere in these regions any store of gold or treasures. Abandoning this field, he tried to win a share in the conquests of Pizarro and Almagro. He approached Peru from the north, and conducted his army across the mountains. This march, one of the most disastrous in colonial history, so completely destroyed the efficiency of his force that the conquerors of Peru easily compelled him to sell them what was left of his expedition. They paid a considerable sum, weighed out in bars of silver which he found, after his return to Panama, to be made of lead with a silver veneering.[8] Alvarado was ready to abandon the work of conquering America, and had forwarded a petition to the King, asking that he might be allowed to return to Spain, when Mendoza, or the audiencia which was controlled by the enemies of Alvarado, furthered his desires by ordering him to go to the mother country and present himself before the throne. This was in 1536. While at court Alvarado must have met Cabeza de Vaca. He changed his plans for making a voyage to the South seas, and secured from the King, whose favor he had easily regained, a commission which allowed him to build a fleet in Central America and explore the South sea—the Pacific—toward the west or the north. He returned to America early in 1539, bringing with him everything needed in the equipment of a large fleet.

Mendoza, meanwhile, 1536–1539, had been making plans and preparations. He had not come to the New World as an adventurer, and he lacked the spirit of eager, reckless, hopeful expectation of wealth and fame, which accomplished so much for the geographical unfolding of the two Americas. Mendoza appears to have arranged his plans as carefully as if he had been about to engage in some intrigue at court. He recognized his rivals and their strength. Nuño de Guzman was in disgrace and awaiting a trial, but he was at the court, where he could urge his claims persistently in person. Cortes was active, but he was where Mendoza could watch everything that he tried to do. He might succeed in anticipating the viceroy's plans, but his sea ventures heretofore had all been failures. So long as he kept to the water there seemed to be little danger. Mendoza's chief concern appears to have been to make sure that his rivals should have no chance of uniting their claims against him. Representing the Crown and its interests, he felt sure of everything else. The viceroy had no ambition to take the field in person as an explorer, and he selected Alvarado as the most available leader for the expedition which he had in mind, probably about the time that the latter came back to the New World. He wrote to Alvarado, suggesting an arrangement between them, and after due consideration on both sides, terms and conditions mutually satisfactory were agreed on. Mendoza succeeded in uniting Alvarado to his interests, and engaged that he should conduct an expedition into the country north of Mexico. This arrangement was completed, apparently, before the return of Friar Marcos from his reconnoissance, which added so largely to the probabilities of success.

The Reconnoissance of Friar Marcos de Niza

Mendoza did not confine himself to diplomatic measures for bringing about the exploration and conquest which he had in mind. In his undated "première lettre" the viceroy wrote that he was prepared to send Dorantes with forty or fifty horses and everything needed for an expedition into the interior; but nothing was done.

About this time, 1537–38, Friar Juan de la Asuncion seems to have visited the inland tribes north of the Spanish settlements. Mr Bandelier has presented all the evidence obtainable regarding the labors of this friar.[1] The most probable interpretation of the statements which refer to his wanderings is that Friar Juan went alone and without official assistance, and that he may have traveled as far north as the river Gila. The details of his journey are hopelessly confused. It is more than probable that there were a number of friars at work among the outlying Indian tribes, and there is no reason why one or more of them may not have wandered north for a considerable distance. During the same year the viceroy made an attempt, possibly in person, to penetrate into the country of Topira or Topia, in northwestern Durango,[2] but the mountains and the absence of provisions forced the party to return. It may be that this fruitless expedition was the same as that in which, according to Castañeda, Coronado took part, while Friar Marcos was on his way to Cibola. It is not unlikely, also, that Friar Marcos may have made a preliminary trip toward the north, during the same year, although this is hardly more than a guess to explain statements, made by the old chroniclers, which we can not understand.

As yet nothing had been found to verify the reports brought by Cabeza de Vaca, which, by themselves, were hardly sufficient to justify the equipment of an expedition on a large scale. But Mendoza was bent on discovering what lay beyond the northern mountains. He still had the negro Estevan, whom he had purchased of Dorantes, besides a number of Indians who had followed Cabeza de Vaca to Mexico and had been trained there to serve as interpreters. The experience which the negro had gained during the years he lived among the savages made him invaluable as a guide. He was used to dealing with the Indians, knew something of their languages, and was practiced in the all-important sign manual.

Friar Marcos de Niza was selected as the leader of the little party which was to find out what the viceroy wanted to know. Aside from his reconnoitering trip to Cibola, very little is known about this friar. Born in Nice, then a part of Savoy, he was called by his contemporaries a Frenchman. He had been with Pizarro in Peru, and had witnessed the death of Atahualpa. Returning to Central America, very likely with Pedro de Alvarado, he had walked from there barefooted, as was his custom, up to Mexico. He seems to have been somewhere in the northwestern provinces of New Spain, when Cabeza de Vaca appeared there after his wanderings. A member of the Franciscan brotherhood, he had already attained to some standing in the order, for he signs his report or personal narration of his explorations, as vice-commissary of the Franciscans. The father provincial of the order, Friar Antonio de Ciudad-Rodrigo, on August 26, 1539,[3] certified to the high esteem in which Friar Marcos was held, and stated that he was skilled in cosmography and in the arts of the sea, as well as in theology.

This choice of a leader was beyond question an excellent one, and Mendoza had every reason to feel confidence in the success of his undertaking. The viceroy drew up a set of instructions for Friar Marcos, which directed that the Indians whom he met on the way should receive the best of treatment, and provided for the scientific observations which all Spanish explorers were expected to record. Letters were to be left wherever it seemed advisable, in order to communicate with a possible sea expedition, and information of the progress of the party was to be sent back to the viceroy at convenient intervals. These instructions are a model of careful and explicit directions, and show the characteristic interest taken by Mendoza in the details of everything with which he was concerned. They supply to some extent, also, the loss of the similar instructions which Coronado must have received when he started on his journey in the following February.[4]

Friar Marcos, accompanied by a lay brother, Friar Onorato, according to Mendoza's "première lettre," left Culiacan on March 7, 1539. Coronado, now acting as governor of New Galicia, had escorted them as far as this town and had assured a quiet journey for a part of the way beyond by sending in advance six Indians, natives of this region, who had been "kept at Mexico to become proficient in the Spanish language and attached to the ways of the Christians."[5] The friars proceeded to Petatlan, where Friar Onorato fell sick, so that it was necessary to leave him behind. During the rest of the journey, Friar Marcos was the only white man in the party, which consisted of the negro Estevan, the Indian interpreters, and a large body of natives who followed him from the different villages near which he passed. The friar continued his journey to "Vacapa," which Mr Bandelier identifies with the Eudeve settlement of Matapa in central Sonora, where he arrived two days before Passion Sunday, which in 1539 fell on March 23.[6] At this place he waited until April 6, in order to send to the seacoast and summon some Indians, from whom he hoped to secure further information about the pearl islands of which Cabeza de Vaca had heard.

The negro Estevan had been ordered by the viceroy to obey Friar Marcos in everything, under pain of serious punishment. While the friar was waiting at Vacapa, he sent the negro toward the north, instructing him to proceed 50 or 60 leagues and see if he could find anything which might help them in their search.

If he found any signs of a rich and populous country, it was agreed that he was not to advance farther, but should return to meet the friar, or else wait where he heard the good news, sending some Indian messengers back to the friar, with a white cross the size of the palm of his hand. If the news was very promising, the cross was to be twice this size, and if the country about which he heard promised to be larger and better than New Spain, a cross still larger than this was to be sent back. Castañeda preserves a story that Estevan was sent ahead, not only to explore and pacify the country, but also because he did not get on well with his superior, who objected to his eagerness in collecting the turquoises and other things which the natives prized and to the moral effect of his relations with the women who followed him from the tribes which they met on their way. Friar Marcos says nothing about this in his narrative, but he had different and much more important ends to accomplish by his report, compared with those of Castañeda, who may easily have gathered the gossip from some native.

Estevan started on Passion Sunday, after dinner. Four days later messengers sent by him brought to the friar "a very large cross, as tall as a man." One of the Indians who had given the negro his information accompanied the messengers. This man said and affirmed, as the friar carefully recorded, "that there are seven very large cities in the first province, all under one lord, with large houses of stone and lime; the smallest one-story high, with a flat roof above, and others two and three stories high, and the house of the lord four stories high. They are all united under his rule. And on the portals of the principal houses there are many designs of turquoise stones, of which he says they have a great abundance. And the people in these cities are very well clothed. ... Concerning other provinces farther on, he said that each one of them amounted to much more than these seven cities." All this which the Indian told Friar Marcos was true; and, what is more, the Spanish friar seems to have correctly understood what the Indian meant, except that the Indian idea of several villages having a common allied form of government was interpreted as meaning the rule of a single lord, who lived in what was to the Indians the chief, because the most populous, village. These villages of stone and lime—or rather of stone and rolls or balls of adobe laid in mud mortar and sometimes whitened with a wash of gypsum[7]— were very large and wondrous affairs when compared with the huts and shelters of the Seri and some of the Piman Indians of Sonora.[8] The priest can hardly be blamed for translating a house entrance into a doorway instead of picturing it as a bulkhead or as the hatchway of a ship. The Spaniards—those who had seen service in the Indies—had outgrown their earlier custom of reading into the Indian stories the ideas of government and of civilization to which they were accustomed in Europe. But Friar Marcos was at a disadvantage hardly less than that of the companions of Cortes, when they first heard of Motecuhzoma, because his experience with the wealth of the New World had been in the realm of the Incas. He interpreted what he did not understand, of necessity, by what he had seen in Peru.

The story of this Indian did not convince the friar that what he heard about the grandeur of these seven cities was all true, and he decided not to believe anything until he had seen it for himself, or had at least received additional proof. The friar did not start immediately for the seven cities, as the negro had advised him to do, but waited until he could see the Indians who had been summoned from the seacoast. These told him about pearls, which were found near their homes. Some "painted" Indians, living to the eastward, having their faces, chests, and arms tattooed or decorated with pigments, who were perhaps the Pima or Sobaipuri Indians, also visited him while he was staying at Vacapa and gave him an extended account of the seven cities, very similar to that of the Indian sent by Estevan.

Friar Marcos started on the second day following Pascua Florida, or Easter, which came on April 6, 1539. He expected to find Estevan waiting at the village where he had first heard about the cities. A second cross, as big as the first, had been received from the negro, and the messengers who brought this gave a fuller and much more specific account of the cities, agreeing in every respect with what had previously been related. When the friar reached the village where the negro had obtained the first information about the cities, he secured many new details. He was told that it was thirty days' journey from this village to the city of Cibola, which was the first of the seven. Not one person alone, but many, described the houses very particularly and showed him the way in which they were built, just as the messengers had done. Besides these seven cities, he learned that there were other kingdoms, called Marata, Acus, and Totonteac. The linguistic students, and especially Mr Frank Hamilton Cushing, have identified the first of these with Matyata or Makyata, a cluster of pueblos about the salt lakes southeast of Zuñi, which were in ruins when Alvarado saw them in 1540, although they appeared to have been despoiled not very long before. Acus is the Acoma pueblo and Totonteac was in all probability the province of Tusayan, northwestward from Zuñi. The friar asked these people why they went so far away from their homes, and was told that they went to get turquoises and cow skins, besides other valuable things, of all of which he saw a considerable store in the village.

Friar Marcos tried to find out how these Indians bartered for the things they brought from the northern country, but all he could understand was that "with the sweat and service of their persons they went to the first city, which is called Cibola, and that they labored there by digging the earth and other services, and that for what they did they received turquoises and the skins of cows, such as those people had."

We now know, whatever Friar Marcos may have thought, that they doubtless obtained their turquoises by digging them out of the rocky ground in which they are still found in New Mexico, and this may easily have seemed to them perspiring labor. It is not clear just how they obtained the buffalo skins, although it was doubtless by barter. The friar noticed fine turquoises suspended in the ears and noses of many of the people whom he saw,[9] and he was again informed that the principal doorways of Cibola were ceremonially ornamented with designs made of these stones. Mr Cushing has since learned, through tradition, that this was their custom. The dress of these people of Cibola, including the belts of turquoises about the waist, as it was described to the friar, seemed to him to resemble that of the Bohemians, or gypsies. The cow skins, some of which were given to him, were tanned and finished so well that he thought it was evident that they had been prepared by men who were skilled in this work.

At this point in his narrative Friar Marcos first uses the word *pueblo*, village, in referring to the seven cities, a point which would be of some interest if only we could be sure that the report was written from notes made as he went along. He certainly implies that he kept some such record when he speaks of taking down the statements of the Indian who first told him about the seven cities. It looks as if the additional details which he was obtaining gradually dimmed his vision of cities comparable to those into which he had seen Pizarro gather the golden ransom of Atahualpa.

Friar Marcos had not heard from Estevan since leaving Vacapa, but the natives told him that the negro was advancing toward Cibola, and that he had been gone four or five days. The friar started at once to follow the negro, who had proceeded up Sonora valley, as Mr Bandelier traces the route. Estevan had planted several large crosses along the way, and soon began to send messengers to the friar, urging the latter to hasten, and promising to wait for him at the edge of the wilderness which lay between them and the country of Cibola. The friar followed as fast as he could, although constantly hindered by the natives, who were always ready to verify the stories he had already heard concerning Cibola. They pressed him to accept their offers of turquoises and of cow skins in spite of his persistent refusals. At one village, the lord of the place and his two brothers greeted the friar, having collars of turquoises about their necks, while the rest of the people were all *encaconados*, as they called it, with turquoises, which hung from their ears and noses. Here they supplied their visitor with deer, rabbits, and quail, besides a great abundance of corn and piñon seed. They also continued to offer him turquoises, skins, fine gourds, and other things which they valued. The Sobaipuri Indians, who were a branch of the Papago, among whom the friar was now traveling, according to Bandelier, seemed to be as well acquainted with Cibola as the natives of New Spain were with Mexico, or those of Peru with Cuzco. They had visited the place many times, and whatever they possessed which was made with any skill or neatness had been brought, so they told him, from that country.

Soon after he encountered these people, the friar met a native of Cibola. He was a well-favored man, rather old, and appeared to be much more intelligent than the natives of this valley or those of any of the districts through which the friar had passed in the course of his march. This man reported that the lord of Cibola lived and had his seat of government in one of the seven cities called Ahacus, and that he appointed men in the other cities who ruled for him. Ahacus is readily identified with Hawikuh, one of the present ruins near K'iapkwainakwin, or Ojo Caliente, about 15 miles southwest of Zuñi. On questioning this man closely, the friar learned that Cibola—by which, as Bandelier and Cushing maintain, the Indian meant the whole range occupied by the Zuñi people—was a large city, in which a great many people dwelt and which had streets and open squares or plazas. In some parts of it there were very large houses, which were ten stories high, and the leading men met together in these on certain days of the year. Possibly this is one of the rare references in the accounts of these early visits to Zuñi, to the ceremonials of the Pueblo Indians, which have been studied and described with so much care by later visitors, notably by Mrs M. C. Stevenson and by Dr J. Walter Fewkes of the Hemenway Southwestern Archeological Expedition.

This native of Cibola verified all the reports which the friar had already heard. Marata, he said, had been greatly reduced by the lord of Cibola during recent wars. Totonteac was a much larger and richer place, while Acus was an independent kingdom and province. The strange thing about all these reports is not that they are true, and that we can identify them by what is now known concerning these Indians, but the hard thing to understand is how the Spanish friar could have comprehended so well what the natives must have tried to tell him. When one considers the difficulties of language, with all its technicalities, and of radically different conceptions of every phase of life and of thought, the result must be an increased confidence in the common sense and the inherent intelligence of mankind.

On his way up this valley of Sonora, Friar Marcos heard that the seacoast turned toward the west. Realizing the importance of this point, he says that he "went in search of it and saw clearly that it turns to the west in 35 degrees." He was at the time between 31 and 31-1/2 degrees north, just opposite the head of the Gulf of California. If Bandelier's identification of the friar's route is accepted—and it has a great deal more in its favor than any other that can be proposed with any due regard to the topography of the country—Friar Marcos was then near the head of San Pedro valley, distant 200 miles in a direct line from the coast, across a rough and barren country. Although the Franciscan superior testified to Marcos' proficiency in the arts of the sea, the friar's calculation was 3-1/2 degrees out of the way, at a latitude where the usual error in the contemporary accounts of expeditions is on the average a degree and a half. The direction of the coast line does change almost due west of where the friar then was, and he may have gone to some point among the mountains from which he could satisfy himself that the report of the Indians was reliable. There is a week or ten days, during this part of the journey, for which his narrative gives no specific reckoning. He traveled rather slowly at times, making frequent stops, so that the side trip is not necessary to fill this gap. The point is a curious one; but, in the absence of any details, it is hardly likely that the friar did more than secure from other Indians stories confirming what he had already been told.

Friar Marcos soon reached the borders of the wilderness—the country in and about the present White Mountain Apache reservation in Arizona. He entered this region on May 9, and twelve days later a young man who had been with Estevan, the son of one of the Indian chiefs accompanying the friar, met him and told the story of the negro's death. Estevan had hastened to reach Cibola before the friar, and just prior to arriving at the first city he had sent a notice of his approach to the chief of the place. As evidence of his position or authority, he sent a gourd, to which were attached a few strings of rattles and two plumes, one of which was white and the other red.

While Cabeza de Vaca and his companions were traveling through Texas, the natives had flocked to see these strange white men and soon began to worship them, pressing about them for even a touch of their garments, from which the Indians trusted to receive some healing power. While taking advantage of the prestige which was thus obtained, Cabeza de Vaca says that he secured some gourds or rattles, which were greatly reverenced among these Indians and which never failed to produce a most respectful behavior whenever they were exhibited. It was also among these southern plains Indians that Cabeza de Vaca heard of the permanent settlements toward the north. Castañeda says that some of these plains Indians came each year to Cibola to pass the winter under the shelter of the adobe villages, but that they were distrusted and feared so much that they were not admitted into the villages unless unarmed, and under no conditions were they allowed to spend the night within the flat-roof houses. The connection between these Indian rattles and the gourd which Estevan prized so highly can not be proven, but it is not unlikely that the negro announced his arrival to the Cibola chiefs by sending them an important part of the paraphernalia of a medicine man of a tribe with which they were at enmity.

There are several versions of the story of Estevan's death, besides the one given in Friar Marcos' narrative, which were derived from the natives of Cibola. Castañeda, who lived among these people for a while the next year, states that the Indians kept the negro a prisoner for three days, "questioning him," before they killed him. He adds that Estevan had demanded from the Indians treasures and women, and this agrees with the legends still current among these people.[10] When Alarcon ascended Colorado river a year later, and tried to obtain news of Coronado, with whom he was endeavoring to cooperate, he heard of Estevan, who was described as a black man with a beard, wearing things that sounded, rattles, bells, and plumes, on his feet and arms—the regular outfit of a southwestern medicine man.[11] Friar Marcos was told that when the messengers bearing the gourd showed it to the chief of the Cibola village, he threw it on the ground and told the messengers that when their people reached the village they would find out what sort of men lived there, and that instead of entering the place they would all be killed. Estevan was not at all daunted when this answer was reported to him, saying that everything would be right when he reached the village in person. He proceeded thither at once, but instead of being admitted, he was placed under guard in a house near by.[12] All the turquoises and other gifts which he had received from the Indians during his journey were taken from him, and he was confined with the people who accompanied him, over night, without receiving anything to eat or drink. The next morning Estevan tried to run away, but was overtaken and killed. The fugitives who brought this news to Friar Marcos said that most of their companions also had been killed. The Indians who had followed the friar forthwith began to mourn for three hundred of their relations and friends, who had perished, they declared, as a result of their confidence in his forerunner. This number was undoubtedly an exaggeration. Castañeda heard that the natives of Cibola kept a few lads from among those who were with the negro, "and sent back all the rest, numbering about sixty." The story of Estevan's death is reputed to have been preserved among the legends of the Indians of Zuñi. According to this tradition, the village at which the "Black Mexican" was killed was K'iakima, a village now in ruins, situated on a bluff at the southwestern angle of Thunder mountain mesa; but this is totally at variance with the historical evidence, which seems to point quite conclusively to Hawikuh, the first village encountered from the southwest, as the scene of Estevan's death.[13] One of the Indian stories of Estevan's death is that their wise men took the negro out of the pueblo during the night, and "gave him a powerful kick, which sped him through the air back to the south, whence he came!"

The killing of Estevan made it impossible for Friar Marcos, alone and unprepared for fighting, to enter the Cibola region. The first reports of the disaster, as is usually the custom, told of the death of all who accompanied the negro, and in consequence there was much wailing among the Indians who had followed the friar. They threatened to desert him, but he pacified them by opening his bundles and distributing the trinkets brought from Mexico. While they were enjoying these, he withdrew a couple of stone-throws for an hour and a half to pray. Meanwhile, the Indians began again to think of their lost friends, and decided to kill the friar, as the indirect cause of the catastrophe. But when he returned from his devotions, reinvigorated, and learned of their determination, he diverted their thoughts by producing some of the things which had been kept back from the first distribution of the contents of his packs. He expounded to them the folly of killing him, since this would do him no hurt because he was a Christian and so would go at once to his home in the sky, while other Christians would come in search of him and kill all of them, in spite of his own desires to prevent, if possible, any such revenge. "With many other words" he succeeded at last in quieting them and in persuading two of the chief Indians to go with him to a point where he could obtain a view of the "city of Cibola." He proceeded to a small hill, from which he saw that it was situated on a plain on the slope of a round height. "It has a very fine appearance for a village," he writes, "the best that I have seen in these parts. The houses, as the Indians had told me, are all of stone, built in stories, and with flat roofs. Judging by what I could see from the height where I placed myself to observe it, the settlement is larger than the city of Mexico. ... It appears to me that this land is the best and largest of all those that have been discovered."

"With far more fright than food," the friar says he retraced his way toward New Spain, by hasty marches. During his journey to Cibola, he had heard of a large and level valley among the mountains, distant four or five days from the route which he followed, where he was told that there were many very large settlements in which the people wore clothes made of cotton. He showed his informants some metals which he had, in order to find out what there was in that region, and they picked out the gold, saying that the people in the valley had vessels made of this material and some round things which they hung from their ears and noses. They also had some little shovels of this same metal, with which they scraped themselves to get rid of their sweat. On his way back, although he had not recovered from his fright, the friar determined to see this valley. He did not dare to venture into it, because, as he says, he thought that those who should go to settle and rule the country of the seven cities could enter it more safely than he. He did not wish to risk his own life, lest he should be prevented from making the report of what he had already seen. He went as far as the entrance to the valley and saw seven good-looking settlements at a distance, in a very attractive country, from which arose a great deal of smoke. He understood from the Indians that there was much gold in the valley, and that the natives used it for vessels and ornaments, repeating in his narrative the reports which he had heard on his outward journey.

The friar then hastened down the coast to Culiacan, where he hoped, but failed, to find Coronado, the governor of the province. He went on to Compostela, where Coronado was staying. Here he wrote his report, and sent the announcement of his safe return to the viceroy. A similar notification to the provincial of his order contained a request for instructions as to what he should do next. He was still in Compostela on September 2, and as Mendoza and Coronado also were there, he took occasion to certify under oath before them to the truth of all that he had written in the report of his expedition to Cibola.

The Effect of Friar Marcos' Report

In his official report it is evident that Friar Marcos distinguished with care between what he had himself seen and what the Indians had told him. But Cortes began the practice of attacking the veracity and good faith of the friar, Castañeda continued it, and scarcely a writer on these events failed to follow their guidance until Mr Bandelier undertook to examine the facts of the case, and applied the rules of ordinary fairness to his historical judgment. This vigorous defender of the friar has successfully maintained his strenuous contention that Marcos neither lied nor exaggerated, even when he said that the Cibola pueblo appeared to him to be larger than the City of Mexico. All the witnesses agree that these light stone and adobe villages impress one who first sees them from a distance as being much larger than they really are. Mexico in 1539, on the other hand, was neither imposing nor populous. The great communal houses, the "palace of Montezuma," had been destroyed during or soon after the siege of 1521. The pueblo of Hawikuh, the one which the friar doubtless saw, contained about 200 houses, or between 700 and 1,000 inhabitants. There is something naïve in Mr Bandelier's comparison of this with Robert Tomson's report that the City of Mexico, in 1556, contained 1,500 Spanish households.[1] He ought to have added, what we may be quite sure was true, that the population of Mexico probably doubled in the fifteen years preceding Tomson's visit, a fact which makes Niza's comparison even more reasonable.[2]

The credit and esteem in which the friar was held by the viceroy, Mendoza, is as convincing proof of his integrity as that derived from a close scrutiny of the text of his narrative. Mendoza's testimony was given in a letter which he sent to the King in Spain, inclosing the report written by Friar Marcos, the "première lettre" which Ternaux translated from Ramusio. This letter spoke in laudatory terms of the friar, and of course is not wholly unbiased evidence. It is at least sufficient to counterbalance the hostile declarations of Cortes and Castañeda, both of whom had far less creditable reasons for traducing the friar than Mendoza had for praising him. "These friars," wrote Mendoza of Marcos and Onorato, "had lived for some time in the neighboring countries; they were used to hard labors, experienced in the ways of the Indies, conscientious, and of good habits." It is possible that Mendoza felt less confidence than is here expressed, for before he organized the Coronado expedition, late in the fall of this year 1539, he ordered Melchior Diaz to go and see if what he could discover agreed with the account which Friar Marcos gave.[3]

However careful the friar may have been, he presented to the viceroy a report in which gold and precious stones abounded, and which stopped just within sight of the goal—the Seven Cities of Nuño de Guzman and of the Indian traders and story tellers. Friar Marcos had something to tell which interested his readers vastly more than the painful, wonderful story of Cabeza de Vaca. The very fact that he took it for granted, as he says in his report, that they would go to populate and rule over this land of the Seven Cities, with its doorways studded with turquoises, was enough to insure interest. He must, indeed, have been a popular preacher, and when the position of father provincial to the Franciscans became vacant, just now, brother Marcos, already high in the order and with all the fresh prestige of his latest achievements, was evidently the subject for promotion. Castañeda, who is not the safest authority for events preceding the expedition, says that the promotion was arranged by the viceroy. This may have been so. His other statement is probable enough, that, as a result of the promotion, the pulpits of the order were filled with accounts of such marvels and wonders that large numbers were eager to join in the conquest of this new land. Whatever Friar Marcos may have sacrificed to careful truth was atoned for, we may be sure, by the zealous, loyal brethren of blessed Saint Francis.

Don Joan Suarez de Peralta was born, as Señor Zaragoza shows in his admirable edition of the Tratado del Descubrimiento de las Yndias y su Conquista, in Mexico between 1535 and 1540, and probably nearer the first of these five years. In the Tratado, Suarez de Peralta gives a most interesting description of the effect produced in Mexico by the departure and the return of the Coronado expedition. He can hardly have had very vivid personal recollections of the excitement produced by the reports of Friar Marcos, yet his account is so clear and circumstantial that it evidently must be the narrative of an eyewitness, though recorded, it may be, at secondhand. He tells us that "the country was so stirred up by the news which the friar had brought from the Seven Cities that nothing else was thought about. For he said that the city of Cibola was big enough to contain two Sevilles and over, and the other places were not much smaller; and that the houses were very fine edifices, four stories high; and in the country there are many of what they call wild cows, and sheep and goats and rich treasures. He exaggerated things so much, that everybody was for going there and leaving Mexico depopulated. ... The news from the Seven Cities inspired so eager a desire in every one that not only did the viceroy and the marquis (Cortes) make ready to start for there, but the whole country wanted to follow them so much that they traded for the licenses which permitted them to go as soldiers, and people sold these as a favor, and whoever obtained one of these thought that it was as good as a title of nobility at the least. For the friar who had come from there exaggerated and said that it was the best place in the world; the people in that country very prosperous, and all the Indians wearing clothes and the possessors of much cattle; the mountains like those of Spain, and the climate the same. For wood, they burnt very large walnut trees, which bear quantities of walnuts better than those of Spain. They have many mountain grapes, which are very good eating, chestnuts, and filberts. According to the way he painted it, this should have been the terrestrial paradise. For game, there were partridges, geese, cranes, and all the other winged creatures—it was marvelous what was there." And then Suarez adds, writing half a century later, "He told the truth in all this, because there are mountains in that country, as he said, and herds, especially of cows. ... There are grapes and game, without doubt, and a climate like that of Spain."[4]

Second-hand evidence, recorded fifty years after the occurrence, is far from conclusive. Fortunately, we are able to supplement it by legal testimony, taken down and recorded under oath, with all the formalities of the old Spanish law customs. When the news of Friar Marcos' journey reached Spain there was much rivalry among those who claimed the privilege of completing the discovery. Much evidence was presented and frequent pleas were entered by all the men who had an active part and leadership in the conquest of the northern portion of the New World. In the course of the litigation the representative of the adelantado Hernando de Soto, presented some testimony which had been given in the town of San Cristobal de la Habana de la Isla Fernandina—Habana and Cuba—dated November 12, 1539. There were seven witnesses, from a ship which had been obliged to put into this port in order to procure water and other supplies, and also because some persons aboard had become very sick. Each witness declared that a month or more before—Friar Marcos arrived back in Mexico before the end of August, 1539—he had heard, and that this was common talk in Mexico, Vera Cruz, and in Puebla de los Angeles, that a Franciscan friar named Fray Marcos, who had recently come from the inland regions, said that he had discovered a very rich and very populous country 400 to 500 leagues north of Mexico. "He said that the country is rich in gold, silver and other treasures, and that it contains very large villages; that the houses are built of stone, and terraced like those of Mexico, and that they are high and imposing. The people, so he said, are shrewd, and do not marry more than one wife at a time, and they wear coarse woolen cloth and ride on some animals," the name of which the witness did not know. Another testified that the common report was that this country "was very rich and populous and had great walled cities, and that the lords of the cities were called kings, and that the people were very shrewd and use the Mexican language." But the witness to whose deposition we are most indebted was Andrés Garcia. This man declared that he had a son-in-law who was a barber, who had shaved the friar after he came back from the new country. The son-in-law had told the witness that the friar, while being shaved, had talked about the country which he had discovered beyond the mountains. "After crossing the mountains, the friar said there was a river, and that many settlements were there, in cities and towns, and that the cities were surrounded by walls, with their gates guarded, and were very wealthy, having silversmiths, and that the women wore strings of gold beads and the men girdles of gold and white woolen dresses; and that they had sheep and cows and partridges and slaughterhouses and iron forges."[5]

Friar Marcos undoubtedly never willfully told an untruth about the country of Cibola, even in a barber's chair. But there seems to be little chance for doubting that the reports which he brought to New Spain were the cause of much talk as well as many sermons, which gave rise to a considerable amount of excitement among the settlers, whose old-world notions had been upset by the reputed glory of the Montezumas and the wealth of the Incas. Very many, though perhaps not all, of the colonists were stirred with an eager desire to participate in the rich harvest awaiting the conquerors of these new lands. Friar Marcos was not a liar, but it is impossible to ignore the charges against him quite as easily as Mr Bandelier has done.

Pedro Castañeda makes some very damaging statements, which are not conclusive proof of the facts. Like the statements of Suarez de Peralta, they represent the popular estimation of the father provincial, and they repeat the stories which passed current regarding him, when the later explorations had destroyed the vision that had been raised by the reports of the friar's exploration. The accusations made by Cortes deserve more careful consideration. Cortes returned to Spain about the time that the preparations for the Coronado expedition were definitely begun. Soon after his arrival at court, June 25, 1540,[6] he addressed a formal memorial to the King, setting forth in detail the ill treatment which he had received from Mendoza. In this he declared that after the viceroy had ordered him to withdraw his men from their station on the coast of the mainland toward the north—where they were engaged in making ready for extended inland explorations—he had a talk with Friar Marcos. "And I gave him," says Cortes, "an account of this said country and of its discovery, because I had determined to send him in my ships to follow up the said northern coast and conquer that country, because he seemed to understand something about matters of navigation. The said friar communicated this to the said viceroy, and he says that, with his permission, he went by land in search of the same coast and country as that which I had discovered, and which it was and is my right to conquer. And since his return, the said friar has published the statement that he came within sight of the said country, which I deny that he has either seen or discovered; but instead, in all that the said friar reports that he has seen, he only repeats the account I had given him regarding the information which I obtained from the Indians of the said country of Santa Cruz, because everything which the said friar says that he discovered is just the same as what these said Indians had told me: and in enlarging upon this and in pretending to report what he neither saw nor learned, the said Friar Marcos does nothing new, because he has done this many other times, and this was his regular habit, as is notorious in the provinces of Peru and Guatemala; and sufficient evidence regarding this will be given to the court whenever it is necessary."[7]

This is a serious charge, but so far as is known it was never substantiated. Cortes was anxious to enforce his point, and he was not always scrupulous in regard to the exact truth. The important point is that such charges were made by a man who was in the position to learn all the facts, and that the accusations were made before anyone knew how little basis there was for the stories which were the cause of the whole trouble. Without trying to clear the character of Cortes, it is possible to suggest the answer to the most evident reply to his accusations—that he never published the stories which he says he received from the Indians. Cortes certainly did persist in his endeavors to explore the country lying about the head of the Gulf of California. If he ever heard from the Indians anything concerning the Cibola region—which is doubtful, partly because Cortes himself complains that if Mendoza had not interfered with the efficiency of his expeditions, he would have secured this information—it would still have been the best policy for Cortes to keep the knowledge to himself, so that possible rivals might remain ignorant of it until he had perfected his own plans. It may be questioned how long such secrecy would have been possible, but we know how successfully the Spanish authorities managed to keep from the rest of the world the correct and complete cartographical information as to what was being accomplished in the New World, throughout the period of exploration and conquest.

The truce—it can hardly be called a friendship—between Mendoza and Cortes, which prevailed during the first years of the viceroy's administration, could not last long. Mendoza, as soon as he was fairly settled in his position in New Spain,[8] asked the King for a license to make explorations. Cortes still looked on every rival in the work of extending this portion of the Spanish world as an interloper, even though he must have recognized that his prestige at the court and in the New World was rapidly lessening. The distrust with which each of the two regarded the other increased the trouble which was inevitable so soon as the viceroy, urged on by the audiencia, undertook to execute the royal orders which instructed him to investigate the extent of the estates held by Cortes, and to enumerate the Indians held to service by the conqueror. Bad feeling was inevitable, and the squabbles over forms of address and of precedence, which Suarez de Peralta records, were only a few of many things which reveal the relations of the two leading men in New Spain.

We can not be certain what the plans of Cortes were, nor can we tell just how much he did to carry his schemes into execution, during the years from 1537 to 1540. Shortly after the men whom Cortes had established at Santa Cruz were recalled, a decree was issued, in the name of the audiencia, to forbid the sending of any expedition for exploration or conquest from New Spain. Cortes declared that he had at this time, September, 1538, nine good ships already built. He was naturally unwilling to give up all hope of deriving any benefit from his previous undertakings, as would be inevitable if Mendoza should succeed in his projects for taking advantage of whatever good things could be found toward the north. The danger must have seemed clear so soon as he learned of the departure of Friar Marcos and the negro on their journey toward the Seven Cities. There is no means of knowing whether Cortes had learned of the actual discovery of Cibola, when he suddenly ordered Francisco de Ulloa to take three vessels and sail up the coast toward the head of the Gulf of California. The friar may have sent Indian messengers to the viceroy so soon as he heard the native reports about the seven cities of Cibola, and it is possible that the news of his approaching return may have reached New Spain before the departure of Ulloa, which took place July 8, 1539, from Acapulco.[9] It seems clear that this action was unexpected, and that it was a successful anticipation of preventive measures. In the statement of his grievances, Cortes declares that Mendoza not only threw every possible obstacle in his way, seizing six or seven vessels which failed to get away with Ulloa, but that even after Ulloa had gone, the viceroy sent a strong force up the coast to prevent the ships from entering any of the ports. When stress of weather forced one of the ships to put into Guatulco, the pilot and sailors were imprisoned and the viceroy persistently refused to return the ship to its owner. About the same time, a messenger who had been sent to Cortes from Santiago in Colima was seized and tortured, in the hope of procuring from him information about the plans of Cortes.[10]

After Friar Marcos came back from the north and filled the people in New Spain with the desire of going to this new country, Cortes realized that he could do nothing, even in the city which he had won for his King and for Europe, to prevent the expedition which Mendoza was already organizing. Early in 1540—we know only that he was on his way when he wrote to Oviedo from Habana[11] on February 5—the conqueror of Motecuhzoma's empire left Mexico for the last time, and went to see what he could gain by a personal application at the court of His Majesty the Emperor, Charles V.

Mendoza had guarded against rival expeditions from his own territory, and so soon as he knew that Friar Marcos had succeeded in his quest, he took precautions to prevent the news of the discovery from reaching other portions of the New World. His chief fear, probably, was lest De Soto, who had recently received a license to explore the country between the Rio de las Palmas, in the present Texas, and Florida,[12] might direct his expedition toward the western limits of his territory, if he should learn of the rich prospects there. Although Mendoza probably did not know it, De Soto had sailed from Habana in May, 1539, and in July, sending back his largest ships, he began the long march through the everglades of Florida, which was to end in the Mississippi. Mendoza, with all the formality of the viceregal authority, ordered that no vessel sailing from New Spain should touch at any port in the New World on its way back to the home peninsula, and this notice was duly served on all departing shipmasters by the secretaries of the viceroy. By the middle of November, however, despite all this care, a ship from Vera Cruz sailed into the harbor of Habana. The master declared, on his oath, that he had been forced to put in there, because sickness had broken out aboard his vessel soon after the departure from New Spain and because he had discovered that his stock of provisions and water was insufficient for the voyage across the Atlantic. Curiously enough, one of the crew, possibly one of those who had been seized with the sickness, had in his possession some letters which he had been asked to deliver to Hernando De Soto, in Habana. Apparently the agent or friend of De Soto living in Mexico, one Francisco de Billegas, did not know that the adelantado had left Cuba, although he had arranged to have the letters carried to Spain and given to the representative of the adelantado there if De Soto was not found at Habana. De Soto had taken care that his interests should be watched and protected, in Spain as well as in the New World, when he started on his search for the land of wealth north of the Gulf of Mexico, the search on which Ayllon and Narvaez had failed so sadly.

It was the regular practice of all the governors and successful explorers in the colonies of the empire to maintain representatives in Spain who should look after their interests at court and before the administrative bureaus. When the news of Friar Marcos' discovery reached Europe, accompanied by reports of the preparations which Mendoza was making for an expedition to take possession of the new territory, protests and counterclaims were immediately presented in behalf of all those who could claim any right to participate in this new field of conquest. The first formal statements were filed with the Council for the Indies, March 3, 1540, and on June 10, 1541, the factor or representative of Cortes, whose petition is first among the papers relating to the case, asked for an extension of six days. This ends the documents concerning the litigation, so far as they have been printed.[13] Petitions, testimony, narratives of explorations and discoveries, acts taking possession of new lands, notifications and decisions, appeals and countercharges, were filed and referred, each claimant watching his rivals so closely and objecting to their claims so strenuously that the fiscal, Villalobos, in his report on the case, May 25, 1540, gives as one of the most conclusive reasons in favor of the advice which he offers to the Council, that each of the parties has clearly proved that none of the others have any right to claim a share in the newly discovered region by virtue of any grants, licenses, or achievements whatsoever.

Of the various claimants, the representative of the adelantado Hernando De Soto offered perhaps the best argument. The territory granted to De Soto extended on the west to the Rio de las Palmas, and this grant was the same as that previously made to Narvaez. The discovery had grown out of the expedition of Narvaez, to whose rights De Soto had succeeded, through the reports which Cabeza de Vaca carried to New Spain. The newly discovered region was evidently inland, and this fact disposed of the two prominent rivals, Cortes and Alvarado. The adelantado had expended large sums in preparing for this undertaking—a claim advanced with equal vigor by all the parties, and usually supported by specific accounts, which unfortunately are not printed—and it was only right that he should be given every opportunity to reap the full advantage from these outlays. Most important of all was the fact that De Soto was already in the country north of the gulf, in command of a large and well equipped force, and presumably on his way toward the region about which they were disputing. Because De Soto was there, urged his representative with strong and persistent emphasis, all other exploring expeditions ought to be kept away. It was clearly probable that great and notorious scandals would ensue unless this was guarded against, just as had happened in Peru. If this precaution was not taken, and two expeditions representing conflicting interests should be allowed to come together in the country beyond the reach of the royal restraint, many lives would inevitably be lost and great damage be done to the Spaniards, and to the souls of the Indians as well, while the enlargement of the royal patrimony would be hindered.[14]

Cortes reached Spain some time in April, 1540,[15] and was able to direct his case in person for much of the time. He urged the priority of his claims under the royal license, dating from 1529.[16] He told of his many efforts to enlarge the Spanish domain, undertaken at great expense, personal sacrifice and danger, and resulting in the loss of relations and friends. From all of this, as he carefully pointed out, neither His Majesty nor himself had received any proper benefit, though this was not the result of any fault or lack of diligence on his part, as he hastened to explain, but had been caused by the persistent and ill-concealed hostility of the audiencia and the viceroy in New Spain, "concerning all of which His Majesty must have been kept heretofore in ignorance."

Nuño de Guzman presented his case in person, though perhaps this was not so much because it was more effective as because his resources must have been limited and his time little occupied. He was able, indeed, to make out a very good argument, assuming his right to the governorship of New Galicia, a province which had been greatly enlarged by his conquests. These conquests were toward the north, and he had taken possession of all the land in that direction in behalf of His Catholic Majesty. He would have extended the Spanish territory much farther in the same direction, if only his zealous efforts had not been abruptly cut short by his persecutors, through whose malicious efforts he was even yet nominally under arrest. Nor was this all, for all future expeditions into the new region must go across the territory which was rightfully his, and they could only succeed by the assistance and resources which would be drawn from his country. Thus he was the possessor of the key to all that lay beyond.

The commission or license which Pedro de Alvarado took with him from Spain the year before these proceedings opened, granted him permission to explore toward the west and the north—the latter provision probably inserted as a result of the reports which Cabeza de Vaca brought to Spain. Alvarado had prepared an expedition at great expense, and since the new region lay within his grant, his advocate pleaded, it would evidently pertain to him to conquer it. Moreover, he was in very high favor at court, as is shown by the ease with which he regained his position, in spite of the attack by the Mexican audiencia, and also by the ease with which he obtained the papal permission allowing him to marry the sister of his former wife. But Alvarado figures only slightly in the litigation, and he may have appeared as a party in order to maintain an opposition, rather than with any hope or intention of establishing the justice of his claims. Everything seems to add to the probability of the theory that Mendoza effected an alliance with him very early. It is possible that the negotiations may have begun before Alvarado left Spain, although there is no certainty about anything which preceded the written articles of agreement. Some of the contemporary historians appear to have been ignorant even of these.

y enojan : finalmente es animal feo y fiero de ro-
ftro, y cuerpo. Huyē de los los cauallos por fu ma-
la catadura, o por nunca los auer vifto. No tienen
fus dueños otra riqueza , ni hazienda , dellos co-
men, beuen, viften, calçan , y hazen muchas cofas
de los cueros, cafas, calçado, veftido y fogas : delos
hueffos, punçones : delos neruios, y pelos, hilo : de
los cuernos, buches, y bexigas , vafos : delas boñi-
gas, lumbre : y delas terneras , odres , en que traen
y tienen agua : hazen en fin tantas cofas dellos
quantas han menefter , o quantas las baftan para
fu biuienda. Ay tambien otros animales, tan grandes como cauallos, que por tener cuernos , y lana
fina, los llaman carneros, y dizen , que cada cuer-
no pefa dos arrouas. Ay tambien grandes perros,
que

The Buffalo of Comara, 1554

The Council for the Indies referred the whole matter of the petitions and accompanying evidence to the fiscal, the licentiate Villalobos, April 21, 1540. He made a report, which virtually decided the case, May 25. The parties were given an opportunity of replying to this, and they continued to present evidence and petitions and countercharges for a year longer. The final decision, if any was made, has not been printed, so far as I know, but the Council could hardly have done anything beyond formally indorsing the report of Villalobos. The duty of the fiscal was plain, and his report advises His Majesty not to grant any of the things asked for by the petitioners. He states that this discovery ought to be made by and in behalf of His Majesty, since the region was not included in any previous grant. Although the Crown had forbidden any further unlicensed explorations, this would not prevent expeditions being undertaken on the part of the Crown, which is always at liberty to explore at will. In effect, of course, the report sanctioned the exploration by Mendoza, who represented the royal interests and power. An objection was at once entered in behalf of De Soto, using the very good argument that Mendoza's expedition would be sent out either at the expense of the Crown or of his private fortune. If the former, it was claimed that as the explorer would have the glory in any event, the Crown ought to save the expense by allowing De Soto, who had already undertaken the same thing at his own cost, to make these discoveries, which he promised should redound to as great an extent to the glory and advantage of the Emperor. If Mendoza was undertaking this at his own expense, it was evident that he would desire to recover his outlay. Here he was merely on the same footing as De Soto, who was prepared to make a better offer to his Royal Master than Mendoza could possibly afford. In either case there was the danger of scandal and disaster, in case the two expeditions should be allowed to come together beyond the range of the royal oversight. No answer to this appeal is recorded, and the parties continued to argue down their opponents' cases, while the viceroy in New Spain started the expedition which, under the command of Francisco Vazquez Coronado, discovered the Pueblo Indians of New Mexico, the Grand canyon of the Colorado, and the bison of the great plains.

The Expedition to
New Mexico and the Great Plains

The Organization of the Expedition

Two classes of colonists are essential to the security and the permanent prosperity of every newly opened country. In New Spain in the sixteenth century these two classes, sharply divided and almost antagonistic—the established settlers and the free soldiers of fortune—were both of considerable importance. Cortes, so soon as he had conquered the country, recognized the need of providing for its settlement by a stable population. In the petitions and memorials which he wrote in 1539 and 1540 he continually reiterates the declaration of the pains and losses sustained on account of his efforts to bring colonists from Spain to populate the New World. Whether he accomplished all that these memorials claim is doubtful, for there are comparatively few references to this class of immigrants during the years when Cortes was in a position to accomplish his designs. Mendoza declared that the increase of the European population in New Spain came largely after his own arrival there, in 1535, and this was probably true. The "good viceroy" unquestionably did more than anyone else to place the province on a permanent basis.[1]

Mendoza supervised with great care the assignment of land to the newcomers, and provided tools and stock for those who had not the means of equipping their farms. As a royal decree forbade the granting of land to unmarried men, besides directing an increase of royal favor and additional grants proportionate to the increase of children, the viceroy frequently advanced the money which enabled men who were desirous of settling down to get married. When he came from Spain in 1535, he brought with him a number of eligible spinsters, and it is quite probable that, after these had found husbands, he maintained the supply of maids suitable to become the wives of those colonists who wished to experience the royal bounty and favor. Alvarado engaged in a similar undertaking when he came out to Guatemala in 1539, but with less success than we may safely hope rewarded the thoughtfulness of Mendoza.[2] A royal order in 1538 had decreed that all who held encomiendas should marry within three years, if not already possessed of a wife, or else forfeit their estates to married men. Some of the bachelor landholders protested against the enforcement of this order in Guatemala, because eligible white women could not be found nearer than Mexico. To remove this objection, Alvarado brought twenty maidens from Spain. Soon after their arrival, a reception was held, at which they were given a chance to see their prospective husbands. During the evening, one of the girls declared to her companions that she never could marry one of these "old fellows, ... who were cut up as if they had just escaped from the infernal regions, ... for some of them are lame, some have only one hand, others have no ears or only one eye, and some of them have lost half their faces. The best of them have one or two scars across their foreheads." The story is that one of the "old fellows" overheard this outburst, reported it to his friends, and promptly went off and married the daughter of a powerful cacique.

Besides assisting his colonists to get wives, Mendoza did a great deal to foster the agricultural interests of the province. He continued the importation of cattle, which Cortes had begun, and also procured horses and sheep from Spain. He writes in one of his letters of the especial satisfaction that he felt because of the rapid increase of his merino sheep, in spite of the depredations of the natives and of wild animals. The chief concern of the officials of the audiencia had been the gold mines, which yielded a considerable revenue in certain districts; but Mendoza, without neglecting these, proved how large and reliable was the additional revenue which could be derived from other sources. The viceroy's success in developing the province can not be shown more clearly than by repeating the description of New Spain in 1555, written by Robert Tomson, an English merchant engaged in the Spanish trade. In the course of a business tour Tomson visited the City of Mexico. His commercial friends in the city entertained him most hospitably, and did their best to make his visit pleasant. He refused, however, to heed their warnings, and his indiscreet freedom of speech finally compelled the officials of the Inquisition to imprison him, thus adding considerably to the length of his residence in the city. After he returned home, he wrote a narrative of his tour, in which he says of New Spain:

"As for victuals in the said Citie, of beefe, mutton, and hennes, capons, quailes, Guiñy-cockes, and such like, all are very good cheape: To say, the whole quarter of an oxe, as much as a slaue can carry away from the Butchers, for fiue Tomynes, that is, fiue Royals of plate, which is just two shillings and sixe pence, and a fat sheepe at the Butchers for three Royals, which is 18. pence and no more. Bread is as good cheape as in Spaine, and all other kinde of fruites, as apples, peares, pomegranats, and quinces, at a reasonable rate. ... [The country] doth yeeld great store of very good silke, and Cochinilla. ... Also there are many goodly fruits, whereof we haue none such, as Plantanos, Guyaues, Sapotes, Tunas, and in the wildernes great store of blacke cheries, and other wholsome fruites. ... Also the Indico that doeth come from thence to die blew, is a certaine hearbe. ... Balme, Salsaperilla, cana fistula, suger, oxe hides, and many other good and seruiceable things the Countrey doeth yeeld, which are yeerely brought into Spaine, and there solde and distributed to many nations."[3]

The other class among the colonists of New Spain in the second quarter of the sixteenth century "floated like cork on the water" on those who had established their homes in the New World.[4] The men who made it possible to live in security on the farms and ranches of the province had rendered many and indispensable services, and there was much that they might still do to enlarge its boundaries and make the security more certain. They were, nevertheless, a serious hindrance to the prosperity of the settlements. For the most part they were young men of all sorts and degrees. Among them were many sons of Spanish noblemen, like Mendoza the viceroy, whose brother had just succeeded his father as Marquis de Mondejar. Very much of the extension of the Spanish world by discovery and conquest was due to the sons of men of rank, who had, perhaps generally, begun to sow their wild oats in Spain and were sent across the Atlantic in order to keep them out of mischief at home, or to atone, it may be, for mischief already done. In action, these young caballeros were most efficient. By personal valor and ability, they held the positions of leadership everywhere, among men who followed whom and when they chose, and always chose the man who led them most successfully. When inactive, these same cavaliers were a most trying annoyance to any community in which they happened to be. Armed with royal letters and comprehensive introductions, they had to be entertained, at heavy charges. Masters of their own movements, they came as they liked, and very often did not go away. Lovers of excitement, they secured it regardless of other men's wives or property.

There had been few attractions to draw these adventurers away from Mexico, the metropolis of the mainland, for some time previous to 1539. Peru still offered excitement for those who had nothing to gain or lose, but the purely personal struggle going on there between Pizarro and Almagro could not arouse the energies of those who were in search of glory as well as of employment. A considerable part of the rabble which followed Nuño de Guzman during the conquest of New Galicia went to Peru after their chief had been superseded by the Licentiate de la Torre, so that one town is said to have disappeared entirely from this cause; but among these there were few men of good birth and spirit. Mendoza had been able, at first, to accommodate and employ those who accompanied him from Spain, like Vazquez Coronado, "being chiefly young gentlemen." But every vessel coming from home brought some companion or friend of those who were already in New Spain, and after Cabeza de Vaca carried the reports of his discoveries to the Spanish court, an increasing number came each season to join the already burdensome body of useless members of the viceregal household. The viceroy recognized the necessity of relieving the community of this burden very soon after he had established himself in Mexico, and he was continually on the watch for some suitable means of freeing himself from these guests. By 1539 the problem of looking after these young gentlemen—whose number is determined quite accurately by the two hundred and fifty or three hundred "gentlemen on horseback" who left New Spain with Coronado in the spring of 1540—had become a serious one to the viceroy. The most desirable employment for all this idle energy would be, of course, the exploration and conquest of new country, or the opening of the border territory for permanent settlement. But no mere work for work's sake, no wild-goose chase, would do. These young gentlemen had many friends near to Charles V, who would have resented any abuse of privilege or of confidence. A suitable expedition could be undertaken only at considerable expense, and unless the cost could all be made good to the accountants in Spain, complaints were sure to be preferred against even the best of viceroys. So Mendoza entertained his guests as best he could, while they loafed about his court or visited his stock farms, and he anxiously watched the reports which came from the officials of the northwestern province of New Galicia and from the priests who were wandering and working among the outlying Indian tribes. When, late in the summer of 1539, Friar Marcos returned from the north, bringing the assurance that Cibola was a desirable field for conquest, the viceroy quickly improved the opportunity for which he had been waiting. Within a month and a half Mendoza had begun to organize the force which was to conquer this new country.

Compostela, on the Pacific coast, was announced as the place at which the force should assemble. The viceroy desired to have the army begin its march so soon as the roads were passable in the spring, and he wished also to relieve the Indians living in the districts between Mexico and the coast from as much as possible of the annoyance and loss which would be inevitable if the army started from Mexico and marched through this territory in a body. How much this forethought for the Indians was needed appears from Mendoza's reply to the accusations against him filed during the visita of 1547, which showed that all his care had not saved the Indians of Michoacan from needless injury at the hands of those who were on their way to join the gathering at Compostela. Incidentally, this arrangement also gave the capital city an earlier relief from its unwelcome guests.

Popular as was the expedition to the Seven Cities, there was a little opposition to the undertaking. When it became evident that a large force was about to leave the country, some of those who were to remain behind complained that all New Spain was being depopulated, and that no one would be left to defend the country in case of an Indian uprising. When Mendoza reached Compostela, by the middle of February, 1540, Coronado asked him to make an official investigation of these complaints. The formal request is dated February 21, and on the following day, Sunday, the viceroy held a grand review of the whole array, with everyone ready equipped for the march. As the men passed before the viceregal party the secretaries made an exact count and description of the force, but this document is not now known. Its loss is partly supplied by the sworn testimony of the officials who were best acquainted with the inhabitants of all parts of New Spain, recorded a few days after the departure of the expedition. They declare that in the whole army there were only two or three men who had ever been settled residents in the country; that these few were men who had failed to make a living as settlers, and that, in short, the whole force was a good riddance.[5]

The men who assembled at Compostela to start for the Seven Cities numbered, Mendoza stated at the time of the visita in 1547, "about two hundred and fifty Spaniards on horseback, ... and about three hundred Indians, a few more or less." Mota Padilla, who must have used documents of the very best authority, nearly all of which have since disappeared, gives the number of the force as "two hundred and sixty horsemen, ... seventy footmen, ... and more than a thousand friendly Indians and Indian servants." Herrera, who used official documents, says that there were one hundred and fifty horsemen and two hundred footmen. Mendoza's statement of the number of Indians may be explained, if we suppose him to have referred only to the friendly Indians who went on the expedition as native allies. His statement is made in the course of a defense of his administration, when he was naturally desirous of giving as small a number as possible. Castañeda says that there were three hundred horsemen, and this number occurs in other early narratives.

Mendoza spared neither pains nor expense to insure the success of the expedition. Arms, horses, and supplies were furnished in abundance; money was advanced from the royal chest to any who had debts to pay before they could depart, and provision was made for the support of those who were about to be left behind by fathers, brothers, or husbands. The equipment of the force was all that the viceroy could desire. Arms and military supplies had been among the things greatly needed in New Spain when Mendoza reported its condition in his first letters to the home government. In 1537 he repeated his request for these supplies with increased insistence. The subject is not again mentioned in his letters, and we may fairly suppose that he had received the weapons and munitions of war, fresh from the royal arsenals of Spain, with which he equipped the expedition on whose success he had staked so much. It was a splendid array as it passed in review before Mendoza and the officials who helped and watched him govern New Spain, on this Sunday in February, 1540. The young cavaliers curbed the picked horses from the large stock farms of the viceroy, each resplendent in long blankets flowing to the ground. Each rider held his lance erect, while his sword and other weapons hung in their proper places at his side. Some were arrayed in coats of mail, polished to shine like that of their general, whose gilded armor with its brilliant trappings was to bring him many hard blows a few months later. Others wore iron helmets or vizored headpieces of the tough bullhide for which the country has ever been famous. The footmen carried crossbows and harquebuses, while some of them were armed with sword and shield. Looking on at these white men with their weapons of European warfare was the crowd of native allies in their paint and holiday attire, armed with the club and the bow of an Indian warrior. When all these started off next morning, in duly ordered companies, with their banners flying, upward of a thousand servants and followers, black men and red men, went with them, leading the spare horses, driving the pack animals, bearing the extra baggage of their masters, or herding the large droves of "big and little cattle," of oxen and cows, sheep, and, maybe, swine,[6] which had been collected by the viceroy to assure fresh food for the army on its march. There were more than a thousand horses in the train of the force, besides the mules, loaded with camp supplies and provisions, and carrying half a dozen pieces of light artillery—the pedreros, or swivel guns of the period.

After the review, the army assembled before the viceroy, who addressed to them an exhortation befitting the occasion. Each man, whether captain or foot soldier, then swore obedience to his commander and officers, and promised to prove himself a loyal and faithful vassal to his Lord the King. During the preceding week the viceroy had divided the force into companies, and now he assigned to each its captain, as Castañeda relates, and announced the other officers of the army.

Francisco Vazquez Coronado—de Coronado it is sometimes written—was captain-general of the whole force. "Who he is, what he has already done, and his personal qualities and abilities, which may be made useful in the various affairs which arise in these parts of the Indies, I have already written to Your Majesty," writes Mendoza to the Emperor, in the letter of December 10, 1537. This previous letter is not known to exist, and there is very little to supply the place of its description of the character and antecedents of Vazquez Coronado. His home was in Salamanca,[7] and he came to America in the retinue of Mendoza in 1535. His relations with his patron, the viceroy, previous to the return of the expedition from Cibola, appear always to have been most cordial and intimate. In 1537 Coronado married Beatrice de Estrada, a cousin by blood, if gossip was true, of the Emperor, Charles V. Her father, Alonso, had been royal treasurer of New Spain. From his mother-in-law Coronado received as a marriage gift a considerable estate, "the half of Tlapa," which was confirmed to him by a royal grant. Cortez complained that the income from this estate was worth more than 3,000 ducados, and that it had been unduly and inconsiderately alienated from the Crown. Coronado obtained also the estate of one Juan de Búrgos, apparently one of those who forfeited their land because they persisted in the unmarried state. This arrangement likewise received the royal approval.[8] When, however, "the new laws and ordinances for the Indies" came out from Spain in 1544,[9] after Coronado's return from the northern expedition, one of the sections expressly ordered an investigation into the extent and value of the estates held by Francisco Vazquez de Coronado, since it had been reported to the King that the number of Indians held to service on these estates was very excessive. Mendoza had to answer the same charge at his visita in 1547.

Mendoza sent Coronado, in 1537, to the mines at Amatepeque, where the negroes had revolted and "elected a king," and where they threatened to cause considerable trouble. The revolt was quelled, after some fighting, with the help of the Indians of the district. A couple of dozen of the rebels were hung and quartered at the mines or in the City of Mexico.[10]

In the following August, Coronado was legally recognized as a citizen of the City of Mexico, where he was one of three witnesses chosen to testify to the formal recognition by Cortes of the royal order which permitted De Soto to explore and conquer Florida.[11] A month later, September 7, 1538, the representative of De Soto, Alvaro de Sanjurjo, summoned Coronado himself to recognize and promise obedience to the same royal order, "as governor, as the said Sanjurjo declared him to be, of New Galicia." Coronado readily promised his loyal and respectful obedience to all of His Majesty's commands, but observed that this matter did not concern him at all, "since he was not governor, nor did he know that His Majesty desired to have him serve in such a position; and if His Majesty should desire his services in that position, he would obey and submit to the royal provision for him whenever he was called on, and would do what was most serviceable to the royal interests." He adds that he knows nothing about the government of Ayllon or that of Narvaez, which were mentioned in the license to De Soto. This part of his statement can hardly have been strictly true. The answer was not satisfactory to Sanjurjo, who replied that he had received information that Coronado was to be appointed governor of New Galicia. The latter stated that he had already given his answer, and thereupon Sanjurjo formally protested that the blame for any expenditures, damages, or scandals which might result from a failure to observe the royal order must be laid at the door of the one to whom they rightfully belonged, and that they would not result from any fault or omission on the part of De Soto. Sanjurjo may have received some hint or suggestion of the intention to appoint Coronado, but it is quite certain that no definite steps had yet been taken to supplant the licentiate, De la Torre, as governor of New Galicia. Coronado's answer shows plainly that he intentionally refused to commit himself when so many things were uncertain, and when nothing was definitely known about the country of which Cabeza de Vaca had heard. Mendoza may have suggested his appointment at an earlier date, but the King apparently waited until he learned of De la Torre's untimely death before approving the selection. The confirmation was signed April 18, 1539, and at the same time Coronado was appointed to take the residencia of his predecessor. The King agreed to allow the new governor a salary of 1,000 ducats from the royal treasure chests and 1,500 more from the province, with the proviso that the royal revenues were not to be held responsible for this latter sum in case New Galicia proved too poor to yield so large an amount. Coronado probably went at once to his province when he received the notice of his nomination, for he was in Guadalajara on November 19, 1538, where he approved the selection of judges and magistrates for the ensuing year by the city of Compostela, which had held its election before his arrival. At the same time he appointed the judges for Guadalajara.

Coronado probably spent the winter of 1538–39 in New Galicia, arranging the administration and other affairs of his government. He entertained Friar Marcos, when the latter passed through his province in the spring of 1539, and accompanied the friar as far as Culiacan, the northernmost of the Spanish settlements. Here he provided the friar with Indians, provisions, and other things necessary for the journey to the Seven Cities. Later in the spring, the governor returned to Guadalajara, and devoted considerable attention to the improvement and extension of this city, so that it was able to claim and obtain from the King a coat of arms and the title of "city" during the following summer.[12] He was again here on January 9, 1540, when he promulgated the royal order, dated December 20, 1538, which decreed that inasmuch as it was reported that the cities in the Indies were not built with sufficient permanency, the houses being of wood and thatched with straw, so that fires and conflagrations were of frequent occurrence, therefore no settler should thereafter build a house of any material except stone, brick, or unbaked brick, and the houses should be built after the fashion of those in Spain, so that they might be permanent, and an adornment to the cities. Between these dates it is very likely that Coronado may have made some attempt to explore the mountainous regions north of the province, as Castañeda says, although his evidence is by no means conclusive.

About midsummer of 1539, Friar Marcos came back from Cibola. Coronado met him as he passed through New Galicia, and together they returned to Mexico to tell the viceroy what the friar had seen and heard. Coronado remained at the capital during the autumn and early winter, taking an active part in all the preparations for the expedition which he was to command. After the final review in Compostela, he was placed in command of the army, with the title of captain-general.

The Departure of the Expedition

Monday, February 23, 1540, the army which was to conquer the Seven Cities of Cibola started on its northward march from Compostela.[1] For 80 leagues the march was along the "much-used roads" which followed the coast up to Culiacan.[2]

Everyone was eager to reach the wonderful regions which were to be their destination, but it was impossible to make rapid progress. The cattle could not be hurried, while the baggage animals and the carriers were so heavily laden with equipment and provisions that it was necessary to allow them to take their own time. Several days were lost at the Centizpac river, across which the cattle had to be transported one at a time. At Chiametla there was another delay. Here the army camped in the remains of a village which Nuño de Guzman had established. The settlers had been driven away by a pestilence caught from the Indians, and by the fierce onslaught of the natives who came down upon them from the surrounding mountains. The food supply of Coronado's force was beginning to fail, and as the tribes here about were still in rebellion, it became necessary to send a force into the mountains to obtain provisions. The army master, Samaniego, who had been warden of one of the royal fortresses,[3] commanded the foraging party. The men found themselves buried in the thick underbrush as soon as they passed beyond the limits of the clearing. One of the soldiers inadvertently, but none the less in disregard of strict orders, became separated from the main party, and the Indians, who were nowhere to be seen, at once attacked him. In reply to his cries, the watchful commander hastened to his assistance. The Indians who had tried to seize him suddenly disappeared. When everything seemed to be safe, Samaniego raised his visor, and as he did so an arrow from among the bushes pierced his eye, passing through the skull. The death of Samaniego was a severe loss to the expedition. Brave and skillful, he was beloved by all who were with him or under him. He was buried in the little chapel of the deserted village. The army postponed its departure long enough to capture several natives of the district, whose bodies were left hanging on the trees in order to counteract the bad augury which followed from the loss of the first life.[4]

A much more serious presage was the arrival at Chiametla, as the army was preparing to leave, of Melchior Diaz and Juan de Saldivar, or Zaldivar, returning from their attempt to verify the stories told by Friar Marcos. Melchior Diaz went to New Galicia with Nuño de Guzman, and when Cabeza de Vaca appeared in that province, in May 1536, Diaz was in command of the outpost of Culiacan. He was still at Culiacan, in the autumn of 1539, when Mendoza directed him to take a mounted force and go into the country toward the north "to see if the account which Friar Marcos brought back agreed with what he could observe." He left Culiacan November 17, with fifteen horsemen, and traveled as far north as the wilderness beyond which Cibola was situated, following much the same route as the friar had taken, and questioning the Indians with great care. Many of the statements made by Friar Marcos were verified, and some new facts were obtained, but nowhere could he find any foundation for the tales of a wealthy and attractive country, except in the descriptions given by the Indians. The cold weather had begun to trouble his men seriously before he reached the limit of his explorations. He pushed on as far as Chichilticalli, however, but here the snows and fierce winds from across the wilderness forced him to turn back. At Chiametla he encountered Coronado's force. He joined the army, sending his lieutenant, Saldivar, with three other horsemen, to carry his report to the viceroy. This was delivered to Mendoza on March 20, and is embodied in the letter to the King, dated April 17, 1540.

Coronado did not allow Diaz to announce the results of his reconnoissance to the soldiers, but the rumor quickly spread that the visions inspired by Friar Marcos had not been substantiated. Fortunately, the friar was himself in the camp. Although he was now the father provincial of the Franciscan order in New Spain, he had determined to accompany the expedition, in order to carry the gospel to the savages whose salvation had been made possible by his heroic journey of the preceding spring. The mutterings of suspicion and discontent among the men grew rapidly louder. Friar Marcos felt obliged to exhort them in a special sermon to keep up a good courage, and by his eloquence he succeeded in persuading them that all their labors would soon be well repaid.

From Chiametla the army resumed its march, procuring provisions from the Indians along the way. Mendoza stated, in 1547, that he took every precaution to prevent any injury or injustice being done to the Indians at the time of Coronado's departure, and that he stationed officials, especially appointed for this purpose, at convenient points on the road to Culiacan, who were ordered to procure the necessary provisions for the expedition. There are no means of telling how well this plan was carried into execution.

A day or two before Easter, March 28, 1540, the army approached Culiacan. The journey had occupied a little over a month, but when Coronado, from his lodging in the Cibola village of Granada, three months later, recalled the slow and tedious marches, the continual waiting for the lazy cattle and the heavily loaded baggage trains, and the repeated vexatious delays, we can hardly wonder that it seemed to him to have been a period of fourscore days' journey.

The town of San Miguel de Culiacan, in the spring of 1540, was one of the most prosperous in New Spain. Nuño de Guzman had founded the settlement some years before, and had placed Melchior Diaz in charge of it. The appointment was a most admirable one. Diaz was not of gentle birth, but he had established his right to a position of considerable power and responsibility by virtue of much natural ability. He was a hard worker and a skillful organizer and leader. He inspired confidence in his companions and followers, and always maintained the best of order and of diligence among those who were under his charge. Rarely does one meet with a man whose record for every position and every duty assigned to him shows such uniform and thorough efficiency. The settlement increased rapidly in size and in wealth, and when Coronado's force encamped in the surrounding fields, the citizens of the town insisted on entertaining in their own homes all of the gentlemen who were with the expedition. The granaries of the place were filled with the surplus from the bountiful harvests of two preceding years, which sufficed to feed the whole army for three or four weeks, besides providing supplies sufficient for more than two months when the expedition resumed its march. These comfortable quarters and the abundant entertainment detained the general and his soldiers for some weeks.[5] This was the outpost of Spanish civilization, and Coronado made sure that his arrangements were as complete as possible, both for the army and for the administration of New Galicia during his absence.

The soldiers, and especially the gentlemen among them, had started from Compostela with an abundant supply of luxurious furnishings and extra equipment. Many of them were receiving their first rough lessons in the art of campaigning, and the experiences along the way before reaching Culiacan had already changed many of their notions of comfort and ease. When the preparations for leaving Culiacan began, the citizens of the town received from their guests much of the clothing and other surplus baggage, which was left behind in order that the expedition might advance more rapidly, or that the animals might be loaded with provisions. Aside from what was given to the people of the place, much of the heavier camp equipage, with some of the superfluous property of the soldiers, was put on board a ship, the *San Gabriel*, which was waiting in the harbor of Culiacan. An additional supply of corn and other provisions also was furnished for the vessel by the generous citizens.

The Expedition by Sea under Alarcon

A sea expedition, to cooperate with the land force, was a part of Mendoza's original plan. After the viceroy left Coronado, and probably while he was at Colima, on his way down the coast from Compostela, he completed the arrangements by appointing Hernando de Alarcon, his chamberlain according to Bernal Diaz, to command a fleet of two vessels. Alarcon was instructed to sail northward, following the coast as closely as possible. He was to keep near the army, and communicate with it at every opportunity, transporting the heavy baggage and holding himself ready at all times to render any assistance which Coronado might desire. Alarcon sailed May 9, 1540, probably from Acapulco.[1]

This port had been the seat of the shipbuilding operations of Cortes on the Pacific coast, and it is very probable that Alarcon's two ships were the same as those which the marquis claimed to have equipped for a projected expedition. Alarcon sailed north to Santiago, where he was obliged to stop, in order to refit his vessels and to replace some artillery and stores which had been thrown overboard from his companion ship during a storm. Thence he sailed to Aguaiauale, as Ramusio has it, the port of San Miguel de Culiacan. The army had already departed, and so Alarcon, after replenishing his store of provisions, added the *San Gabriel* to his fleet and continued his voyage. He followed the shore closely and explored many harbors "which the ships of the marquis had failed to observe," as he notes, but he nowhere succeeded in obtaining any news of the army of Coronado.

The Journey from Culiacan to Cibola

Melchior Diaz had met with so many difficulties in traveling through the country which the army was about to enter, on its march toward the Seven Cities, and the supply of food to be found there was everywhere so small, that Coronado decided to divide his force for this portion of the journey. He selected seventy-five or eighty horsemen, including his personal friends, and twenty-five or thirty foot soldiers. With these picked men, equipped for rapid marching, he hastened forward, clearing the way for the main body of the army, which was to follow more slowly, starting a fortnight after his own departure. With the footmen in the advance party were the four friars of the expedition, whose zealous eagerness to reach the unconverted natives of the Seven Cities was so great that they were willing to leave the main portion of the army without a spiritual guide. Fortunately for these followers, a broken leg compelled one of the brethren to remain behind. Coronado attempted to take some sheep with him, but these soon proved to be so great a hindrance that they were left at the river Yaquimi, in charge of four horsemen, who conducted them at a more moderate pace.

Leaving Culiacan on April 22, Coronado followed the coast, "bearing off to the left," as Mota Padilla says, by an extremely rough way, to the river Cinaloa. The configuration of the country made it necessary to follow up the valley of this stream until he could find a passage across the mountains to the course of the Yaquimi. He traveled alongside this stream for some distance, and then crossed to Sonora river.[1] The Sonora was followed nearly to its source before a pass was discovered. On the northern side of the mountains he found a stream—the Nexpa, he calls it—which may have been either the Santa Cruz or the San Pedro of modern maps. The party followed down this river valley until they reached the edge of the wilderness, where, as Friar Marcos had described it to them, they found Chichilticalli.[2]

Here the party camped for two days, which was as long as the general dared to delay, in order to rest the horses, who had begun to give out sometime before as a result of overloading, rough roads, and poor feed. The stock of provisions brought from Culiacan was already growing dangerously small, although the food supply had been eked out by the large cones or nuts of the pines of this country, which the soldiers found to be very good eating. The Indians who came to see him, told Coronado that the sea was ten days distant, and he expresses surprise, which Mr Bandelier has reëchoed, that Friar Marcos could have gone within sight of the sea from this part of the country.

Coronado entered the wilderness, the White Mountain Apache country of Arizona, on Saint John's eve, and in the quaint language of Hakluyt's translation of the general's letter, "to refresh our former trauailes, the first dayes we founde no grasse, but worser way of mountaines and badde passages."[3] Coronado, following very nearly the line of the present road from Fort Apache to Gila river, proceeded until he came within sight of the first of the Seven Cities. The first few days of the march were very trying. The discouragement of the men increased with the difficulties of the way. The horses were tired, and the slow progress became slower, as horses and Indian carriers fell down and died. The corn was almost gone, and as a result of eating the fruits and herbs which they found along the way, a Spaniard and some of the servants were poisoned so badly that they died. The skull and horns of a great mountain goat, which were lying on the ground, filled the Europeans with wonder, but this was hardly a sight to inspire them with hopes of abundant food and gold. There were 30 leagues of this travailing before the party reached the borders of the inhabited country, where they found "fresh grass and many nutte and mulberrie trees."

The day following that on which they left the wilderness, the advance guard was met, in a peaceable manner, by four Indians. The Spaniards treated them most kindly, gave them beads and clothing, and "willed them to return unto their city and bid them stay quiet in their houses fearing nothing." The general assured them that they need have no anxiety, because the newcomers had been sent by His Spanish Majesty, "to defend and ayde them."

The Capture of the Seven Cities

The provisions brought from Culiacan or collected along the way were now exhausted, and as a sudden attack by the Indians, during the last night before their arrival at the cities, had assured the Spaniards of a hostile reception, it was necessary to proceed rapidly. The inhabitants of the first city had assembled in a great crowd, at some distance in front of the place, awaiting the approach of the strangers. While the army advanced, Garcia Lopez de Cardenas, who had been appointed to Samaniego's position as field-master, and Hernando Vermizzo, apparently one of the "good fellows" whose name Castañeda forgot, rode forward and summoned the Indians to surrender, in approved Castilian fashion, as His Majesty commanded always to be done. The natives had drawn some lines on the ground, doubtless similar to those which they still mark with sacred meal in their ceremonial dramatizations, and across these they refused to let the Spaniards pass, answering the summons with a shower of arrows. The soldiers begged for the command to attack, but Coronado restrained them as long as he could. When the influence of the friars was added to the pleas of the men—perhaps without waiting for the command or permission—the whole company uttered the Santiago, the sacred war cry of Saint James, against the infidels, and rushed upon the crowd of Indians, who turned and fled. Coronado quickly recalled his men from the pursuit, and ordered them to prepare for an assault on the city. The force was divided into attacking parties, which immediately advanced against the walls from all sides. The crossbowmen and harquebusiers, who were expected to drive the enemy back from the tops of the walls, were unable to accomplish anything, on account of their physical weakness and of accidents to their weapons. The natives showered arrows against the advancing foes, and as the Spaniards approached the walls, stones of all sizes were thrown upon them with skillful aim and practiced strength. The general, in his glittering armor, was the especial target of the defenders, and twice he was knocked to the ground by heavy rocks. His good headpiece and the devotion of his companions saved him from serious injury, although his bruises confined him to the camp for several days. The courage and military skill of the white men, weak and tired as they were, proved too much for the Indians, who deserted their homes after a fierce, but not protracted, resistance. Most of the Spaniards had received many hard knocks, and Aganiez Suarez—possibly another of the gentlemen forgotten by Castañeda—was severely wounded by arrows, as were also three foot soldiers.

The Indians had been driven from the main portion of the town, and with this success the Spaniards were satisfied. Food—"that which we needed a great deal more than gold or silver," writes one member of the victorious force—was found in the rooms already secured. The Spaniards fortified themselves, stationed guards, and rested. During the night, the Indians, who had retired to the wings of the main building after the conflict, packed up what goods they could, and left the Spaniards in undisputed possession of the whole place.

The mystery of the Seven Cities was revealed at last. The Spanish conquerors had reached their goal. July 7, 1540, white men for the first time entered one of the communal villages of stone and mud, inhabited by the Zuñi Indians of New Mexico.[1] Granada was the name which the Spaniards gave to the first village—the Indian Hawikuh—in honor of the viceroy to whose birthplace they say it bore a fancied resemblance. Here they found, besides plenty of corn, beans and fowls, better than those of New Spain, and salt, "the best and whitest I have seen in all my life," writes one of those who had helped to win the town. But even the abundance of food could not wholly satisfy the men whose toilsome march of more than four months had been lightened by dreams of a golden haven. Friar Marcos was there to see the realization of the visions which the zealous sermons of his brethren and the prolific ardor of rumor and of common talk had raised from his truthful report. One does not wonder that he eagerly accepted the earliest opportunity of returning to New Spain, to escape from the not merely muttered complaints and upbraidings, in expressing which the general was chief.[2]

The Exploration of the Country

The Spaniards at Zuñi

Some of the inhabitants of Hawikuh-Granada returned to the village, bringing gifts, while Coronado was recovering from his wounds. The general faithfully exhorted them to become Christians and to submit themselves to the sovereign over-lordship of His Majesty the Spanish King. The interview failed to reassure the natives, for they packed all their provisions and property on the following day, and with their wives and children abandoned the villages in the valley and withdrew to their stronghold, the secure fastness on top of Taaiyalone or Thunder mountain.

As soon as he was able, Coronado visited the other villages of Cibola-Zuñi, observing the country carefully. He reassured the few Indians whom he found still living in the valley, and after some hesitation on their part succeeded in persuading the chiefs to come down from the mesa and talk with him. He urged them to return to their homes below, but without success. He was more fortunate in obtaining information regarding the surrounding country, which was of much use to him in directing further exploration. Then as now the rule held good that the Indians are much more likely to tell the truth when giving information about their neighbors than about themselves.

The Discovery of Tusayan and the Grand Canyon

A group of seven villages, similar to those at Cibola, was reported to be situated toward the west, "the chief of the towns whereof they have knowledge." Tucano was the name given to these, according to Ramusio's version of Coronado's letter, and it is not difficult to see in this name that of Tusayan, the Hopi or Moki settlements in northeastern Arizona.

As soon as everything was quiet in the Cibola country, about the middle of July, Don Pedro de Tovar was ordered to take a few horsemen and his company of footmen and visit this district. Don Pedro spent several days in the Tusayan villages, and after he had convinced the people of his peaceable designs, questioned them regarding the country farther west. Returning to the camp at Cibola within the thirty days to which his commission was limited, Tovar reported that the country contained nothing to attract the Spaniards. The houses, however, were better than those at Cibola. But he had heard stories of a mighty river and of giant peoples living toward the west, and so Don Garcia Lopez de Cardenas was instructed to go and verify these reports. Cardenas started, perhaps on August 25. He had authority for eighty days, and within this term he succeeded in reaching the Grand canyon of Colorado river, which baffled his most agile companions in their efforts to descend to the water or to discover some means of crossing to the opposite side. He returned with only the story of this hopeless barrier to exploration westward.

The Rio Grande and the Great Plains

The first expedition toward the east was sent out August 29 in charge of Don Hernando de Alvarado. Passing the rock of Acuco or Acoma—always a source of admiration—Alvarado reached the village and river of Tiguex—the Rio Grande—on September 7. Some time was spent in visiting the villages situated along the stream. The headquarters of the party were at Tiguex, at or near the site of the present town of Bernalillo, and here a list was drawn up and sent to the general giving the names of eighty villages of which he had learned from the natives of this place. At the same time Alvarado reported that these villages were the best that had yet been found, and advised that the winter quarters for the whole force should be established in this district. He then proceeded to Cicuye or Pecos, the most eastern of the walled villages, and from there crossed the mountains to the buffalo plains. Finding a stream which flowed toward the southeast—the Canadian river, perhaps—he followed its course for a hundred leagues or more. Many of the "humpback oxen" were seen, of which some of the men may have remembered Cabeza de Vaca's description.

On his return, Alvarado found the army-master, Garcia Lopez de Cardenas, at Tiguex, arranging winter quarters sufficient to accommodate the whole force in this region.[1] Coronado, who had made a trip to examine the villages farther south, along the Rio Grande, soon joined his lieutenants, leaving only a small force at Cibola to maintain the post. The whole of the advance party was now in Tiguex, and orders had been left at Cibola for the main body to proceed to the eastern settlements so soon as they should arrive from Culiacan and Corazones.

The March of the Army from Culiacan to Tiguex

The main portion of the army remained at Culiacan, under the command of Don Tristan de Arellano, when the general started for Cibola with his small party of companions. The soldiers completed the work of loading the *San Gabriel* with their surplus equipment and with provisions, and busied themselves about the town for a fortnight after the departure of their general. Some time between the first and middle of May, the army started to follow the route of the advance party. The whole force marched on foot, carrying their lances and other weapons, in order that the horses and other beasts, numbering more than six hundred, might all be loaded with provisions. It had taken Coronado and his party of horsemen, eager to push on toward their destination, more than a month to make the journey to Corazones or Hearts valley. We can only guess how much longer it took the slowly marching army to cover this first half of the distance to Cibola. The orders which the general had left with Arellano were that he should take the army to this valley, where a good store of provisions had been found by Melchior Diaz, and there wait for further instructions. Coronado promised to send for his soldiers as soon as he was sure that there was a country of the Seven Cities for them to conquer and settle.

In the valley of Corazones, which had been given its name by Cabeza de Vaca because the natives at this place offered him the hearts of animals for food, Arellano kept the soldiers busy by building a town on Suya river, naming it San Hieronimo de los Corazones—Saint Jerome of the Hearts. A small force was sent down the river to the seacoast, under the command of Don Rodrigo Maldonado, in the hope of communicating with the ships of Alarcon. Maldonado found neither signs nor news of the fleet, but he discovered a tribe of Indian "giants," one of whom accompanied the party back to the camp, where the soldiers were filled with amazement at his size and strength.

Thus the time passed until early in September, when Melchior Diaz and Juan Gallego brought the expected orders from the general. Gallego, who carried the letter which Coronado had written from Granada-Hawikuh on August 3, with the map and the exhibits of the country which it mentions, continued on to Mexico. He was accompanied by Friar Marcos. Diaz had been directed to stay in the new town of San Hieronimo, to maintain this post and to open communication with the seacoast. He selected seventy or eighty men—those least fitted for the hardships and struggles of exploration and conquest—who remained to settle the new town and to make an expedition toward the coast. The remainder of the army prepared to rejoin their general at Cibola, and by the middle of September the start was made.

After a long, rough march, in which little occurred to break the daily monotony, the soldiers reached the pueblo settlements. The bad weather had already begun, but the men were eager to continue their journey in spite of the snow and the fierce, cold winds. After a short rest, the force proceeded to Tiguex, where comfortable quarters were awaiting them, and in these they quickly settled for the winter.

The Winter of 1540–1541 along the Rio Grande

The Indian Revolt

The first winter spent by white men in the pueblos of New Mexico was a severe one. Fortunately for the strangers, however, they were comfortably domiciled in the best houses of the country, in which the owners had left a plentiful supply of food, and this was supplemented by the livestock brought from New Spain.

During the late autumn the Indians assumed a hostile attitude toward their visitors, and were reduced to peaceful inactivity only after a protracted struggle, which greatly aggravated the conquerors. The Spanish story of this revolt is clear—that the Indians suddenly surprised the Europeans by attacking the horses and mules of the army, killing or driving off a number of them, after which the natives collected their fighting force into two of the strongest villages, from one of which they were able to defy the soldiers until thirst compelled them to abandon the stronghold. The defenders attempted to escape by stealth, but the sentries of the besieging force discovered them and aroused the camp. Many of the Indians were killed by the soldiers during the flight which followed, while others perished in the icy waters of the Rio Grande. During an attack on the second village, a few of the Spaniards who had succeeded in making their way to the highest portion of the buildings, escaped from their perilous position by inducing the native warriors to surrender. The Indians received an ample promise of protection and safety, but the captain of the attacking party was not informed of this, and in obedience to the general's orders that no prisoners should be taken, he directed that the captives should be burned as a warning to the neighboring tribes. This affair is a terrible blot on the record of the expedition and of those who composed it. In condemning it most severely, however, English readers should remember that they are only repeating the condemnations which were uttered by most of the men of rank who witnessed it, which were repeated in New Spain and in old Spain, and which greeted the commander when he led his expedition back to Mexico, to receive the cold welcome of the viceroy.

The Spaniards have told us only one side of the story of what was happening along the Rio Grande in the fall of 1540. The other side will probably never be heard, for it disappeared with the traditions of the Indian villagers. Without pretending to supply the loss, it is at least possible to suggest that the preparations by which the army-master procured the excellent accommodations for the force must have appeared very differently to the people in whose homes Cardenas housed the soldiers, and to those who passed the winter in these snug quarters. Castañeda preserved one or two interesting details which are as significant as is the striking fact that the peaceful natives who entertained Alvarado most freely in September were the leaders of the rebellion three months later.

As soon as Coronado's men had completed the reduction of the refractory natives, and the whole country had been overawed by the terrible punishment, the general undertook to reestablish peaceful relations and confident intercourse between his camp and the surrounding villages. The Indians seem to have been ready to meet him almost half-way, although it is hardly surprising to find traces of an underlying suspicion, and a readiness for treacherous retaliation.

The Stories about Quivira

While this reconciliation was being effected, Coronado heard from one of the plains Indians,[1] held as a slave in the village of Cicuye or Pecos, the stories about Quivira, which were to add so much to the geographic extent of the expedition. When the Spaniards were about to kill this Indian—"The Turk," they called him[2]— he told them that his masters, the people of Cicuye, had induced him to lead the strangers away to the pathless plains, where water was scarce and corn was unknown, to perish there, or, if ever they should succeed in finding the way back to the village settlements, tired and weak, to fall an easy prey to their enemies.

This plan was shrewdly conceived, and it very nearly succeeded. There is little reason why we should doubt the truth of the confession, made when the Indian could scarcely have hoped to save his life, and it affords an easy explanation of the way in which the exaggerated stories of Quivira originated and expanded. The Turk may have accompanied Alvarado on the first visit to the great plains, and he

Toreau
sauuage.

tre ceste Floride & la riuiere de Palme se trouuent
diuerses especes de bestes monstrueuses: entre lesquel-
les lon peut voir vne espece de grands taureaux, por-

tans cornes longues seulement d'vn pié, & sur le dos
vne tumueur ou eminence, côme vn chameau: le poil
long par tout le corps, duquel la couleur s'approche fort
de celle d'vne mule fausse, & encores l'est plus celuy
qui est dessoubs le mentõ. Lon en amena vne sous deux
sous vifs en Espagne, de l'vn desquels j'ay veu la peau
& non autre chose, & n'y peurent viure long temps.
C'est animal ainsi que lon dit, est perpetuel ennemy du
cheual, & ne le peut endurer pres de luy. De la Floride tirant au promontoire de Baxe, se trouue quelque
petite riuiere, ou les esclaues vont pescher huitres, qui
portent perles. Or depuis que sommes venus iusque là,
que de toucher la collection des huitres, ne veux ou-
blier par quel moyen les parles en sont tirées, tant aux
Indes

Cap de
Baxe.

Huitres
portans
perles.

The Buffalo of Thevet, 1558

doubtless told the white men about his distant home and the roving life on the prairies. It was later, when the Spaniards began to question him about nations and rulers, gold and treasures, that he received, perhaps from the Spaniards themselves, the hints which led him to tell them what they were rejoiced to hear, and to develop the fanciful pictures which appealed so forcibly to all the desires of his hearers. The Turk, we can not doubt, told the Spaniards many things which were not true. But in trying to trace these early dealings of Europeans with the American aborigines, we must never forget how much may be explained by the possibilities of misinterpretation on the part of the white men, who so often heard of what they wished to find, and who learned, very gradually and in the end imperfectly, to understand only a few of the native languages and dialects. And besides this, the record of their observations, on which the students of today have to depend, was made in a language which knew nothing of the things which it was trying to describe. Much of what the Turk said was very likely true the first time he said it, although the memories of home were heightened, no doubt, by absence and distance. Moreover, Castañeda, who is the chief source for the stories of gold and lordly kings which are said to have been told by the Turk, in all probability did not know anything more than the reports of what the Turk was telling to the superior officers, which were passed about among the common foot soldiers.[3] The present narrative has already shown the wonderful power of gossip, and when it is gossip recorded twenty years afterward, we may properly be cautious in believing it.

Coronado wrote to the King from Tiguex, on April 20, 1541, as he says in his next letter, that of October 20. The April letter, written just before the start for Quivira, must have contained a full and official account of all that had been learned in regard to the country toward the east, as well as more reliable details than we now possess, of what had happened during the preceding fall and winter. But this April letter, which was an acknowledgment and answer to one from Charles V, dated in Madrid, June 11, 1540, has not been found by modern students. When the reply was dispatched, the messenger—probably Juan Gallego, who had perhaps brought the Emperor's letter from Mexico—was accompanied by Pedro de Tovar, who was going back to Corazones valley for reinforcements. Many mishaps had befallen the town of San Hieronimo during the year, and when the messengers arrived there they found it half deserted. Leaving Don Pedro here, Gallego hastened to Mexico, where he raised a small body of recruits. He was leading these men, whose number had been increased by some stragglers and deserters from the original force whom he picked up at Culiacan, toward Cibola and Quivira, when he met the expedition returning to New Spain. It was during this, probably his fifth trip over the road from Mexico to our New Mexico, that he performed the deeds of valor which Castañeda so enthusiastically recounts at the very end of his book.

The Journey Across the Buffalo Plains

April 23, 1541, Coronado left the Tiguex country and marched toward the northeast, to the plains where lay the rich land of Quivira. Every member of the army accompanied the general, for no one was willing to be left behind when such glorious prospects of fame and fortune lay before them. A few of the officers suggested the wisdom of verifying these Indian tales in some measure before setting the whole force in motion and abandoning their only sure base of supplies. It seems as if there must have been other reasons influencing Coronado beyond those revealed in Castañeda's narrative; but, if so, we do not know what they were. The fear lest he might fail to accomplish any of the things which had been hoped for, the absence of results on which to base a justification for all the expense and labor, the thought of what would await him if he should return empty handed, are perhaps enough to account for the determination to risk everything and to allow no possible lack of zeal or of strength to interfere with the realization of the hopes inspired by the stories of Quivira.

Guided by the Turk, the army proceeded to Cicuye, and in nine days more they reached the buffalo plains. Here began the long march which was to be without any guiding landmarks. Just where, or how, or how far the Spaniards went, I can not pretend to say. After a month and more of marching—very likely just thirty-five days—their patience became exhausted. A second native of the plains, who accompanied the Spaniards from the pueblo country, had declared from the first that the Turk was lying, but this had not made them trust the latter any less. When, however, the Indians whom they found living among the buffalo herds began to contradict the stories of their guide, suspicion was aroused. The Turk, after much persuasive cross-questioning, was at last induced to confess that he had lied. Quivira, he still insisted, existed, though it was not as he had described it. From the natives of the plains they learned that there were no settlements toward the east, the direction in which they had been traveling, but that toward the north, another good month's journey distant, there were permanent settlements. The corn which the soldiers had brought from Tiguex was almost gone, while the horses were tired and weak from the constant marching and buffalo chasing, with only grass for food. It was clearly impossible for the whole force to attempt this further journey, with the uncertain prospect of finding native tribes like those they had already seen as the only incentive. The general held a council of his officers and friends, and decided to select 30 of the best equipped horsemen, who should go with him and attempt to verify the new information.

After Coronado had chosen his companions, the rest of the force was sent back to Tiguex, as Castañeda relates. The Indians whom they met on the plains furnished guides, who led the soldiers to the Pueblo settlements by a more direct route than that which the Turk had taken. But the marches were short and slow, so that it was the middle of July before they were again encamped alongside the Rio Grande. So far as is known, nothing of interest happened while they were waiting there for the return of the general.

Coronado and his companion horsemen followed the compass needle for forty-two days after leaving the main force, or, as he writes, "after traveling across these deserts for seventy-seven days in all," they reached the country of Quivira. Here he found some people who lived in permanent settlements and raised a little corn, but whose sustenance came mainly from the buffalo herds, which they hunted at regular seasons, instead of continuously as the plains Indians encountered previously had done.[1]

Twenty-five days were spent among the villages at Quivira, so that Jaramillo, one of the party, doubtless remembered correctly when he said that they were there after the middle of August.[2] There was nothing here except a piece of copper hanging from the neck of a chief, and a piece of gold which one of the Spaniards was suspected of having given to the natives, which gave any promise of mineral wealth, and so Coronado determined to rejoin his main force. Although they had found no treasures, the explorers were fully aware of the agricultural advantages of this country, and of the possibilities for profitable farming, if only some market for the produce could be found.

Students of the Coronado expedition have very generally accepted the location of Quivira proposed by General Simpson, who put the northern point reached by Coronado somewhere in the eastern half of the border country of Kansas and Nebraska. If we take into account the expeditions which visited the outer limits of the Quivira settlements, this is not inconsistent with Bandelier's location of the main seat of these Indians "in northeastern Kansas, beyond the Arkansas river, and more than 100 miles northeast of Great Bend."[3]

It is impossible to ignore the question of the route taken by Coronado across the great plains, although the details chiefly concern local historians. The Spanish travelers spent the summer of 1541 on the prairies west of the Mississippi and south of the Missouri. They left descriptions of these plains, and of the people and animals inhabiting them, which are of as great interest and value as any which have since been written. Fortunately it is not of especial importance for us to know the exact section of the prairies to which various parts of the descriptions refer.

From Cicuye, the Pecos pueblo, Coronado marched northeast until he crossed Canadian river, probably a little to the east of the present river and settlement of Mora.[4] This was about the 1st of May, 1541. From this point General Simpson, whose intimate knowledge of the surface of the country thirty-five years ago makes his map of the route across the plains most valuable, carried the line of march nearly north, to a point halfway between Canadian and Arkansas rivers. Then it turned east, or a trifle north of east, until it reached one of the tributaries of the Arkansas, about 50 miles or so west of Wichita, Kansas. The army returned by a direct route to Cicuye or Pecos river, striking that stream nearly east of Bernalillo-Tiguex, while Coronado proceeded due north to Quivira on the Kansas-Nebraska boundary.

Mr Bandelier has traced a route for the march across the plains which corresponds with the statements of the contemporary narratives somewhat more closely than does that of General Simpson.[5] Crossing Canadian river by a bridge, just south of where Mora river enters it, the Spaniards, according to Bandelier, marched toward the northeast for ten days, until they met the first of the plains Indians, the Querecho or Tonkawa. Thence they turned almost directly toward the rising sun. Bandelier thinks that they very soon found out that the guides had lost their reckoning, which presumably means that it became evident that there was some difference of opinion among the Indians. After marching eastward for thirty-five days or so, the Spaniards halted on the banks of a stream which flowed in the bottom of a broad and deep ravine. Here it was computed that they had already traveled 250 leagues—650 miles—from Tiguex. They had crossed no other large river since leaving the bridge over the Canadian, and as the route had been south of east, as is distinctly stated by one member of the force, they had probably reached the Canadian again. There is a reference to crossing what may have been the North Fork of the Canadian, in which case the army would now be on the north bank of the main river, below the junction of the two forks, in the eastern part of Indian Territory. Here they divided. The Teya guides conducted the main force directly back to the Rio Grande settlements. Coronado went due north, and a month later he reached a larger river. He crossed to the north bank of this stream, and then followed its course for several days, the direction being northeast. This river, manifestly, must be the Arkansas, which makes a sharp turn toward the northeast at the Great Bend, east of Fort Dodge, flowing in that direction for 75 miles. Jaramillo states that they followed the current of the river. As he approached the settled country, Coronado turned toward the north and found Quivira, in northeastern Kansas, not far south of the Nebraska boundary.[6]

The two texts of the Relacion del Suceso differ on a vital point;[7] but in spite of this fact, I am inclined to accept the evidence of this anonymous document as the most reliable testimony concerning the direction of the army's march. According to this, the Spaniards traveled due east across the plains for 100 leagues—265 miles[8]—and then 50 leagues either south or southeast. The latter is the reading I should prefer to adopt, because it accommodates the other details somewhat better. This took them to the point of separation, which can hardly have been south of Red river, and was much more likely somewhere along the North Fork of the Canadian, not far above its junction with the main stream. From this point the army returned due west to Pecos river, while Coronado rode north "by the needle." From these premises, which are broad enough to be safe, I should be inclined to doubt if Coronado went much beyond the south branch of Kansas river, if he even reached that stream. Coronado probably spent more days on his march than General Simpson allowed for, but I do not think that he traveled nearly so far as General Simpson supposed. Coronado also returned to Cicuye by a direct route, which was about two-thirds as long as that of the outward march. The distances given for various portions of the journey have a real value, because each day's march was paced off by a soldier detailed for the purpose, who carefully recorded the distance covered.

The Winter of 1541–1542

By October 20, 1541, Coronado was back in Tiguex, writing his report to the King, in which he expressed his anxiety lest the failure to discover anything of immediate material profit might react unfavorably on his own prospects. Letters and dispatches from Mexico and Spain were awaiting him at Tiguex. One of these informed Don Garcia Lopez de Cardenas of the death of his brother, by which he became heir to the family estates. Cardenas had broken his arm on the plains, and this injury was still troubling him when he received permission to return to New Spain. He was accompanied by the messengers carrying letters to the viceroy and by ten or twelve other invalids, "not one of whom could have done any fighting." The party had no trouble, however, until they reached Suya, in Corazones valley, the settlement which had taken the place of San Hieronimo. Pedro de Tovar had reduced the already feeble garrison at the latter post by half, when he took away the reinforcements six months before. The town had been much weakened by desertions, as well as by the loss of its commander, the invaluable Melchior Diaz, before this. The Indians quickly discerned the condition of the town, and its defenders were unable to maintain friendly relations with the surrounding tribes. When Cardenas reached the place, he found everything burned to the ground, and the bodies of Spaniards, Indians, and horses lying about. Indeed, he seems barely to have saved the invalids accompanying him from being added to the number of the massacred. The party succeeded in making its way to Cibola in safety, and from there they returned to Tiguex, where they found the general seriously ill. By this time the winter was fairly begun, but the season, fortunately, was much less severe than the preceding one.

Two parties formed in the Spanish camp at Tiguex during the winter of 1541–52. The men who had seen Quivira can hardly have brought back from there much hope of finding gold or other treasure by further explorations in that country. But there were many who had not been there, who were unwilling to give up the ideas which had been formed during the preceding months. When the general parted from his army on the plains, he may have promised that he would return and lead the whole force to this land, if only it should prove to be such as their inclination pictured it. Many persisted in the belief that a more thorough exploration would discover some of the things about which they thought the Turk had told them. On the other hand, there were many besides the leader who were tired of this life of hardship, which had not even afforded the attractions of adventure and serious conflict. Few of them, doubtless, had wives and estates waiting to welcome them home, like their fortunate general, but most of the gentlemen, surely, were looking forward to the time when they could win wealth and glory, with which to return to old Spain, and add new luster to their family name. Castañeda gives a soldier's gossip of the intriguing and persuading which resulted in the abandonment of the Pueblo country, and Mota Padilla seems to support the main points in his story.

The Friars Remain in the Country

When it was determined that the army should return to Mexico, the friars who had accompanied the expedition[1] resolved to remain in the newly discovered regions and continue their labors among the people there. Friar Juan de Padilla was the leader of the three missionaries. Younger and more vigorous than his brethren, he had from the first been the most active in constantly maintaining the oversight and discipline of the church. He was with Tovar when the Tusayan country on the west was discovered, and with Alvarado during the first visit to the Rio Grande and the buffalo plains on the east. When Coronado and his companion horsemen visited the plains of Kansas, Friar Juan de Padilla went with him on foot. His brief experience in the Quivira country led him to decide to go back to that district, when Coronado was preparing to return to New Spain. If the Indians who guided Coronado from Quivira to Cicuye remained in the pueblo country during the winter, Padilla probably returned with them to their homes. He was accompanied by Andres Docampo, a Portuguese, mounted on a mare according to most accounts, besides five Indians, negroes or half-bloods, two "donados" or lay brethren, Indians engaged in the church service, who came from Michoacan and were named Lucas and Sebastian, a mestizo or half-blood boy and two other servants from Mexico.

The friar was successful in his labors until he endeavored to enlarge the sphere of his influence, when the jealousy, or possibly the cupidity, of the Indians led them to kill him, rather than permit the transference to some other tribe of the blessings which he had brought to them.[2]

Friar Juan de la Cruz is not mentioned by Castañeda nor by Jaramillo, but Mendieta and Mota Padilla are very clear in their accounts of him. He was an older man than the others, and had been engaged in missionary work among the natives of the Jalisco country before he joined this expedition. Coronado left him at Tiguex, where he was killed, according to Mota Padilla. The date, in the martyrologies, is November 25, 1542. Many natives of the Mexican provinces stayed in the Pueblo country when Coronado abandoned it. Some of these were still at Cibola when Antonio de Espejo visited it in 1583, while others doubtless made their way back to their old homes in New Spain, and they may have brought the information about the death of Friar Juan.

Friar Luis Descalona, or de Ubeda as Mota Padilla calls him, was a lay brother, who selected Cicuye or Pecos as the seat of his labors in New Mexico. Neither the Spanish chronicles nor the Indian traditions which Mr Bandelier was able to obtain give any hint as to his fate or the results of his devotion to the cause of Christianity.

The Return to New Spain

The army started on its return from Tiguex to Cibola and thence to Culiacan and Mexico early in the spring of 1542. The march was without interruption or diversion. As the soldiers reentered New Galicia and found themselves once more among settlements of their own race, beyond the reach of hostile natives, the ranks dwindled rapidly. The men stopped to rest and to recruit their strength at every opportunity, and it was only with the greatest difficulty that Coronado was able to keep together the semblance of a force with which to make his entry into the City of Mexico. Here he presented his personal report to the viceroy. He had little to tell which could interest the disappointed Mendoza, who had drawn so heavily on the royal treasure box two years before to furnish those who formed the expedition with everything that they might need. Besides the loss in his personal estate, there was this use of the royal funds which had to be accounted for to the officials in Spain. It is the best proof of the strength of Mendoza's able and economical administration that no opposition ever succeeded in influencing the home government against him, and that the failure of this expedition, with the attendant circumstances, furnished the most serious charge which those who had displayed hostility toward him were able to produce.

When Coronado reached the City of Mexico, "very sad and very weary, completely worn out and shamefaced," Suarez de Peralta was a boy on the streets. We catch a glimpse of him in the front rows of a crowd watching an execution, this same winter of 1542–43, and we may be sure that he saw all that was going on, and that he picked up and treasured the gossip of the city. His recollections give a vivid picture of the return of the expedition, when Coronado "came to kiss the hand of the viceroy and did not receive so good a reception as he would have liked, for he found him very sad." For many days after the general reached the city the men who had followed him came straggling in, all of them worn out with their toils, clothed in the skins of animals, and showing the marks of their misfortunes and sufferings. "The country had been very joyous when the news of the discovery of the Seven Cities spread abroad, and this was now supplanted by the greatest sadness on the part of all, for many had lost their friends and their fortunes, since those who remained behind had entered into partnerships with those who went, mortgaging their estates and their property in order to procure a share in what was to be gained, and drawing up papers so that those who were to be present should have power to take possession of mines and enter claims in the name of those who were left behind, in accordance with the custom and the ordinances which the viceroy had made for New Spain. Many sent their slaves also, since there were many of these in the country at this time. Thus the loss and the grief were general, but the viceroy felt it most of all, for two reasons: Because this was the outcome of something about which he had felt so sure, which he thought would make him more powerful than the greatest lord in Spain, and because his estates were ruined, for he had labored hard and spent much in sending off the army. Finally, as things go, he succeeded in forgetting about it, and devoted himself to the government of his province, and in this he became the best of governors, being trusted by the King and loved by all his subjects."

The End of Coronado

We do not know what became of Vazquez Coronado. The failure of the expedition was not his fault, and there is nothing to show that he ever sought the position which Mendoza intrusted to him. Neither is there any evidence that Mendoza treated him with any less marks of friendship after his return than before. The welcome home was not cordial, but there are no reports of upbraiding, nor any accusations of negligence or remissness. Coronado soon gave up his position as governor of New Galicia, but we need not suppose that he was compelled to resign. There was every reason why he should have desired to escape from a position which demanded much skill and unceasing active administration, but which carried with it no hope of reward or of honor. It is pleasant to believe that Coronado withdrew to his estates and lived happily ever after with his wife and children, spending his leisure in supervising the operations on his farm and ranch, and leading the uneventful life of a country gentleman. The only break in the monotony of which we happen to know—and this is the only part of this belief for which there is the slightest evidence that it is correct—came when he was accused, in 1544 and again in 1547, of holding more Indians to labor on his estates than were allowed by the royal regulations. We do not even know the outcome of this accusation. Vazquez Coronado sinks into oblivion after he made his report to the viceroy in the autumn of 1542.

Some Results of the Expedition —1540–1547

The Discovery of Colorado River

The Voyage of Alarcon

     Coronado found no gold in the land of the Seven Cities or in Quivira, but his search added very much to the geographical knowledge of the Spaniards.[1] In addition to the exploration of the Pueblo country of New Mexico and Arizona, and of the great plains as far north as Kansas or Nebraska, the most important subsidiary result of the expedition of 1540–1542 was the discovery of Colorado river. Hernando de Alarcon, who sailed from Acapulco May 9, 1540, continued his voyage northward along the coast, after stopping at the port of Culiacan to add the *San Gabriel* to his fleet, until he reached the shoals and sandbars at the head of the Gulf of California. The fleet which Cortes had sent out under the command of Ulloa the previous summer, turned back from these shoals, and Alarcon's sailors begged him not to venture among them. But the question of a passage by water through to the South, or Pacific, sea, which would make an island of the California peninsula, was still debated, and Alarcon refused to return until he had definitely determined the possibility of finding such a passage. His pilots ran the ships aground, but after a careful examination of the channel, the fleet was floated across the bar in safety, with the aid of the rising tide. Alarcon found that he was at the mouth of a large river, with so swift and strong a current that it was impossible for the large vessels to make any headway against it. He determined to explore the river, and, taking twenty men in two boats, started upstream on Thursday, August 26, 1540, when white men for the first time floated on the waters of the Colorado. Indians appeared on the river banks during the following day. The silence with which the strangers answered the threatening shouts of the natives, and the presence of the Indian interpreters in the boats, soon overcame the hostile attitude of the savages. The European trifles which had been brought for gifts and for trading completed the work of establishing friendly relations, and the Indians soon became so well disposed that they entirely relieved the Spaniards of the labor of dragging the boats up the stream. A crowd of Indians seized the ropes by which the boats were hauled against the current, and from this time on some of them were always ready to render this service to their visitors. In this fashion the Spaniards continued northward, receiving abundant supplies of corn from the natives, whose habits and customs they had many excellent opportunities for observing. Alarcon instructed these people dutifully in the worship of the cross, and continually questioned them about the places whose names Friar Marcos had heard. He met with no success until he had traveled a considerable distance up the river, when for the first time he found a man with whom his interpreter was able to converse.

This man said that he had visited Cibola, which was a month's journey distant. There was a good trail by which one might easily reach that country in forty days. The man said he had gone there merely to see the place, since it was quite a curiosity, with its houses three and four stories high, filled with people. Around the houses there was a wall half as high again as a man, having windows on each side. The inhabitants used the usual Indian weapons—bows and arrows, clubs, maces, and shields. They wore mantles and ox hides, which were painted. They had a single ruler, who wore a long shirt with a girdle, and various mantles over this. The women wore long white cloaks which completely covered them. There were always many Indians waiting about the door of their ruler, ready in case he should wish for anything. They also wore many blue stones which they dug out of a rock—the turquoises of the other narratives. They had but one wife, and when they died all their effects were buried with them. When their rulers ate, many men waited about the tables. They ate with napkins, and had baths—a natural inference from any attempt to describe the stuffy underground rooms, the estufas or kivas of the Pueblos.

Alarcon continued to question the Indian, and learned that the lord of Cibola had a dog like one which accompanied the Spaniards, and that when dinner was served, the lord of Cibola had four plates like those used by the Spaniards, except that they were green. He obtained these at the same time that he got the dog, with some other things, from a black man who wore a beard, whom the people of Cibola killed. A few days later, Alarcon obtained more details concerning the death of the negro "who wore certain things on his legs and arms which rattled." When asked about gold and silver, the Indians said that they had some metal of the same color as the bells which the Spaniards showed them. This was not made nor found in their country, but came "from a certain mountain where an old woman dwelt." The old woman was called Guatuzaca. One of Alarcon's informants told him about people who lived farther away than Cibola, in houses made of painted mantles or skins during the summer, and who passed the winter in houses made of wood two or three stories high. The Indian was asked about the leather shields, and in reply described a very great beast like an ox, but more than a hand longer, with broad feet, legs as big as a man's thigh, a head 7 hands long, and the forehead 3 spans across. The eyes of the beast were larger than one's fist, and the horns as long as a man's leg, "out of which grew sharp points an handful long, and the forefeet and hindfeet about seven handfuls big." The tail was large and bushy. To show how tall the animal was, the Indian stretched his arms above his head. In a note to his translation of this description, Hakluyt suggests, "This might be the crooke backed oxe of Quivira." Although the height and the horns are clearly those of a buck deer, the rest of the description is a very good account of the bison.

The man who told him all this was called ashore, and Alarcon noticed an excited discussion going on among the Indians, which ended in the return of his informant with the news that other white men like himself were at Cibola. Alarcon pretended to wonder at this, and was told that two men had just come from that country, where they had seen white men having "things which shot fire, and swords." These latest reports seemed to make the Indians doubt Alarcon's honesty, and especially his statements that he was a child of the Sun. He succeeded in quieting their suspicions, and learned more about Cibola, with which these people appeared to have quite frequent intercourse. He was told that the strangers at Cibola called themselves Christians, and that they brought with them many oxen like those at Cibola "and other little blacke beastes with wooll and hornes." Some of them also had animals upon which they rode, which ran very swiftly. Two of the party that had recently returned from Cibola, had fallen in with two of the Christians. The white men asked them where they lived and whether they possessed any fields sown with corn, and gave each of them little caps for themselves and for their companions. Alarcon did his best to induce some of his men to go to Cibola with a message to Coronado, but all refused except one negro slave, who did not at all want to go. The plan had to be given up, and the party returned to the ships. It had taken fifteen days and a half to ascend the river, but they descended with the swift current in two and a half. The men who had remained in the ships were asked to undertake the mission of opening communication with Coronado, but proved as unwilling as the others.

Much against the will of his subordinates, Alarcon determined to make a second trip up the river, hoping to obtain further information which might enable him to fulfill the purposes of his voyage. He took "three boats filled with wares of exchange, with corne and other seedes, hennes and cockes of Castille." Starting September 14, he found the Indians as friendly as before, and ascended the river, as he judged, about 85 leagues, which may have taken him to the point where the canyons begin. A cross was erected to inform Coronado, in case an expedition from Cibola should reach this part of the river,[2] that he had tried to fulfill his duty, but nothing more was accomplished.[3]

While Alarcon was exploring the river, one of the ships was careened and repaired and everything made ready for the return voyage. A chapel was built on the shore in honor of Nuestra Señora de Buenaguia, and the river was named the Buenaguia, out of regard for the viceroy, who carried this as his device.

The voyage back to Colima in New Spain was uneventful.

The Journey of Melchior Diaz

In September, 1540, seventy or eighty of the weakest and least reliable men in Coronado's army remained at the town of San Hieronimo, in the valley of Corazones or Hearts. Melchior Diaz was placed in command of the settlement, with orders to maintain this post and protect the road between Cibola and New Spain, and also to attempt to find some means of communicating with the fleet under Alarcon. After he had established everything in the town as satisfactorily as possible, Diaz selected twenty-five of these men to accompany him on an exploring expedition to the seacoast. He started before the end of September, going into the rough country west of Carazones valley, and finding only a few naked, weak-spirited Indians, who had come, as he understood, from the land on the farther side of the water, i.e., Lower California. He hurried across this region and descended the mountains on the west, where he encountered the Indian giants, some of whom the army had already seen. Turning toward the north, or northwest, he proceeded to the seacoast, and spent several days among Indians who fed him with the corn which they raised and with fish. He traveled slowly up the coast until he reached the mouth of a river which was large enough for vessels to enter. The country was cold, and the Spaniards observed that when the natives hereabouts wished to keep warm, they took a burning stick and held it to their abdomens and shoulders. This curious habit led the Spaniards to name the river Firebrand—Rio del Tizon. Near the mouth of the river was a tree on which was written, "A letter is at the foot of this." Diaz dug down and found a jar wrapped so carefully that it was not even moist. The inclosed papers stated that "Francisco de Alarcon reached this place in the year '40 with three ships, having been sent in search of Francisco Vazquez Coronado by the viceroy, D. Antonio de Mendoza; and after crossing the bar at the mouth of the river and waiting many days without obtaining any news, he was obliged to depart, because the ships were being eaten by worms," the terrible *Teredo navalis*.[4]

Diaz determined to cross the river, hoping that the country might become more attractive. The passage was accomplished, with considerable danger, by means of certain large wicker baskets, which the natives coated with a sort of bitumen, so that the water could not leak through. Five or six Indians caught hold of each of these and swam across, guiding it and transporting the Spaniards with their baggage, and being supported in turn by the raft. Diaz marched inland for four days, but not finding any people in the country, which became steadily more barren, he decided to return to Corazones valley. The party made its way back to the country of the giants without accident, and then one night while Diaz was watching the camp, a small dog began to bark and chase the flock of sheep which the men had taken with them for food. Unable to call the dog off, Diaz started after him on horseback and threw his lance while on the gallop. The weapon stuck up in the ground, and before Diaz could stop or turn his horse, which was running loose, the socket pierced his groin. The soldiers could do little to relieve his sufferings, and he died before they reached the settlement, where they arrived January 18, 1541. A few months later, Alcaraz, who had been placed in charge of the town when Diaz went away, abandoned Corazones valley for a more attractive situation on Suya river, some distance nearer Cibola. The post was maintained here until late in the summer, when it became so much weakened by dissensions and desertions that the Indians had little difficulty in destroying it. The defenders, with the exception of a few who were able to make their way back to Culiacan, were massacred.

The Indian Uprising in New Spain, 1540–1542

Of the arguments advanced by those who wished to hinder the expedition which Mendoza sent off under Coronado, none was urged more persistently than the claim that this undertaking would require all the men available for the protection of New Spain. It was suggested by all the parties to the litigation in Spain, was repeated by Cortes again and again, reappeared more than once during the visita of 1547, and was the cause of the depositions taken at Compostela on February 26,

1540. These last show the real state of affairs. The men who were withdrawn constituted a great resource in case of danger, but they were worse than useless to the community when things were peaceful. The Indians of New Spain had been quiet since the death of De la Torre, a few years before, but signs of danger, an increasing restlessness, unwilling obedience to the masters and encomenderos, and frequent gatherings, had been noticed by many besides Cortes. There were reasons enough to justify an Indian outbreak, some of them abuses which dated from the time of Nuño de Guzman, but there is every reason to suppose that the withdrawal of Coronado's force, following the irritation which was inevitably caused by the necessity of collecting a large food supply and many servants, probably brought matters to a crisis. Oñate, to whom the administration of New Galicia had again been intrusted during the absence of his superior, began to prepare for the trouble which he foresaw almost as soon as Coronado was gone from the province. In April he learned that two tribes had rebelled and murdered one of their encomenderos. A force was sent to put down the revolt. The rebels requested a conference, and then, early next morning, surprised the camp, which was wholly unprepared for defense. Ten Spaniards, including the unwary commander, and nearly two hundred native allies were killed. Thus began the last and the fiercest struggle of the Indians of New Spain against their European conquerors—the Mixton war.

Oñate prepared to march against the victorious rebels, as soon as the news of the disaster reached him, but when this was followed by additional information from the agents among the Indians, showing how widespread were the alliances of those who had begun the revolt, and that the Indians throughout the province of New Galicia were already in arms, he retired to Guadalajara. The defenses of this town were strengthened as much as possible, and messengers were dispatched to Mexico for reinforcements. The viceroy sent some soldiers and supplies, but this force was not sufficient to prevent the Indians—who were animated by their recent successes, by their numbers, by the knowledge of the weak points as well as of the strong ones in their oppressors, and who were guided by able leaders possessing all the prestige of religious authority—from attacking the frontier settlements and forcing the Spaniards to congregate in the larger towns.

There was much fighting during the early summer of 1540, in which the settlers barely held their own. In August, the adelantado Pedro de Alvarado sailed into the harbor of La Natividad. As the news of his arrival spread, requests were sent to him from many directions, asking for help against the natives. One of the most urgent came from those who were defending the town of Purificacion, and Alvarado was about to start to their assistance, when a message from Mendoza changed his plans. The two men arranged for a personal interview at Tiripitio in

Michoacan, where the estate of a relative afforded Alvarado a quasi neutral territory. After some difficulties had been overcome, the terms of an alliance were signed by both parties November 29, 1540. Each was to receive a small share in whatever had already been accomplished by the other, thus providing for any discoveries which might have rewarded Coronado's search before this date. In the future, all conquests and gains were to be divided equally. It was agreed that the expenses of equipping the fleet and the army should offset each other, and that all future expenses should be shared alike. Each partner was allowed to spend a thousand castellanos de minas yearly, and all expenditure in excess of this sum required the consent of the other party. All accounts were to be balanced yearly, and any surplus due from one to the other was to be paid at once, under penalty of a fine, which was assured by the fact that half of it was to go into the royal treasury.

Mendoza secured a half interest in the fleet of between nine and twelve vessels, which were then in the ports of Acapulco and of Santiago de Colima. Cortes accused the viceroy of driving a very sharp bargain in this item, declaring that Alvarado was forced to accept it because Mendoza made it the condition on which he would allow the ships to obtain provisions.[1] Mendoza, as matters turned out, certainly had the best of the bargain, although in the end it amounted to nothing. Whether this would have been true if Alvarado had lived to prosecute his schemes is another possibility. Alvarado took his chances on the results of Coronado's conquests, and it is very likely that, by the end of November, the discouraging news contained in Coronado's letter of August 3 was not generally known, if it had even reached the viceroy.

The contract signed, Alvarado and Mendoza went to Mexico, where they passed the winter in perfecting arrangements for carrying out their plans. The cold weather moderated the fury of the Indian war somewhat, without lessening the danger or the troubles of the settlers in New Galicia, all of whom were now shut up in the few large towns. Alvarado returned to the Pacific coast in the spring of 1541, and as soon as Oñate learned of this, he sent an urgent request for help, telling of the serious straits in which he had been placed. The security of the province was essential to the successful prosecution of the plans of the new alliance. Alvarado immediately sent reinforcements to the different garrisons, and at the head of his main force hastened to Guadalajara, where he arrived June 12, 1541. Oñate had received reports from the native allies and the Spanish outposts, who were best acquainted with the situation and plans of the hostile Indians, which led him to urge Alvarado to delay the attack until he could be certain of success. An additional force had been promised from Mexico, but Alvarado felt that the glory and the booty would both be greater if secured unaided. Scorning the advice of those who had been beaten by savages, he hastened to chastise the rebels. The campaign was a short one. On June 24 Alvarado reached the fortified height of Nochistlan, where he encountered such a deluge of men and of missiles that he was not able to maintain his ground, nor even to prevent the precipitate retreat of his soldiers. It was a terrible disaster, but one which reflected no discredit on Alvarado after the fighting began. The flight of the Spaniards continued after the Indians had grown tired of the chase. It was then that the adelantado tried to overtake his secretary, who had been one of those most eager to get away from the enemy. Alvarado was afoot, having dismounted in order to handle his men and control the retreat more easily, but he had almost caught up with his secretary, when the latter spurred his jaded horse up a rocky hill. The animal tried to respond, fell, and rolled backward down the hill, crushing the adelantado under him. Alvarado survived long enough to be carried to Guadalajara and to make his will, dying on the 4th of July.

This disaster did not fully convince the viceroy of the seriousness of the situation. Fifty men had already started from Mexico, arriving in Guadalajara in July, where they increased the garrison to eighty-five. Nothing more was done by Mendoza after he heard of the death of Alvarado. The Indians, emboldened by the complete failure of their enemies, renewed their efforts to drive the white men out of the land. They attacked Guadalajara on September 28, and easily destroyed all except the chief buildings in the center of the city, in which the garrison had fortified themselves as soon as they learned that an attack was about to be made. A fierce assault against these defenses was repulsed only after a hard struggle. The miraculous appearance of Saint Iago on his white steed and leading his army of allies, who blinded the idolatrous heathen, alone prevented the destruction of his faithful believers, according to the record of one contemporary chronicler. At last Mendoza realized that the situation was critical. A force of 450 Spaniards was raised, in addition to an auxiliary body of between 10,000 and 50,000 Aztec warriors. The native chieftains were rendered loyal by ample promises of wealth and honors, and the warriors were granted, for the first time, permission to use horses and Spanish weapons. With the help of these Indians, Mendoza eventually succeeded in destroying or reducing the revolted tribes. The campaign was a series of fiercely contested struggles, which culminated at the Mixton peñol, a strongly fortified height where the most bitter enemies of the Spanish conquerors had their headquarters. This place was surrendered during the Christmas holidays, and when Coronado returned in the autumn of 1542, the whole of New Spain was once more quiet.

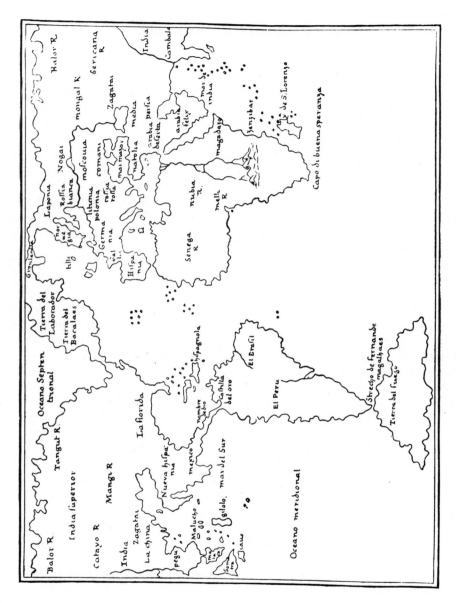

Map of the World by Ptolemy, 1548

Further Attempts at Discovery

The Voyage of Cabrillo

Mendoza took possession of the vessels belonging to Alvarado after the death of the latter. In accordance with the plans which the two partners had agreed on, apparently, the viceroy commissioned Juan Rodriguez Cabrillo to take command of two ships in the port of La Natividad and make an exploration of the coast on the western side of the peninsula of Lower California. Cabrillo started June 27, 1542, and sailed north, touching the land frequently. Much bad weather interfered with his plans, but he kept on till the end of December, when he landed on one of the San Lucas islands. Here Cabrillo died, January 3, 1543, leaving his chief pilot, Bartolome Ferrel or Ferrelo, "a native of the Levant," in command. Ferrel left the island of San Miguel, which he named Isla de Juan Rodriguez, on January 29, to continue the voyage. In a little more than a month the fleet had reached the southern part of Oregon or thereabouts, allowing for an error of a degree and a half in the observations, which said that they were 44° north. A severe storm forced the ships to turn back from this point.

The report of the expedition is little more than an outline of distances sailed and places named, although there are occasional statements which give us valuable information regarding the coast Indians.[1] Among the most interesting of these notes are those showing that the news of the expeditions to Colorado river, and perhaps of the occupancy of the Pueblo country by white men, had reached the Pacific coast. About September 1, 1542, a party from the fleet went ashore near the southern boundary of California. Five Indians met the Spanish sailors at a spring, where they were filling the water casks. "They appeared like intelligent Indians," and went on board the ships without hesitation. "They took note of the Spaniards and counted them, and made signs that they had seen other men like these, who had beards and who brought dogs and cross-bows and swords ... and showed by their signs that the other Spaniards were five days' journey distant. ... The captain gave them a letter, which he told them to carry to the Spaniards who they said were in the interior." September 28, at San Pedro bay, Ferrel again found Indians who told him by signs that "they had passed people like the Spaniards in the interior." Two days later, on Saturday morning, "three large Indians came to the ship, who told by signs that men like us were traveling in the interior, wearing beards, and armed and clothed like the people on the ships, and carrying cross-bows and swords. They made gestures with the right arm as if they were throwing lances, and went running in a posture as if riding on horseback. They showed that many of the native Indians had been killed, and that this was the reason they were afraid." A week later,

October 7, the ships anchored off the islands of Santa Cruz and Anacapa. The Indians of the islands and also of the mainland opposite, near Santa Barbara of the Santa Clara valley, gave the Spaniards additional descriptions of men like themselves in the interior.

The rest of the year 1542 was spent in this locality, off the coast of southern California, and then the voyage northward was resumed. Many points on the land were touched, although San Francisco bay quite escaped observation. Just before a severe storm, in which one of the vessels was lost, forcing him to turn back, Ferrel observed floating drift and recognized that it meant the neighborhood of a large river, but he was driven out to sea before reaching the mouth of the Columbia. The return voyage was uneventful, and the surviving vessel reached the harbor of Natividad in safety by April 14, 1543.

Villalobos Sails across the Pacific

Cortes and Alvarado had both conceived plans more than once to equip a great expedition in New Spain and cross the South sea to the isles of the Western ocean. After the death of Alvarado, Mendoza adopted this scheme, and commissioned Ruy Lopez de Villalobos to take command of some of the ships of Alvarado and sail westward. He started on All Saints day, the 1st of November, 1542, with 370 Spanish soldiers and sailors aboard his fleet. January 22, 1547, Friar Jeronimo de Santisteban wrote to Mendoza "from Cochin in the Indies of the King of Portugal." He stated that 117 of the men were still with the fleet, and that these intended to keep together and make their way as best they could home to Spain. Thirty members of the expedition had remained at Maluco, and twelve had been captured by the natives of various islands at which the party had landed. The rest, including Ruy Lopez, had succumbed to hunger and thirst, interminable labors and suffering, and unrelieved discouragement—the record of the previous months. This letter of Friar Jeronimo is the only published account of the fate of this expedition.

The brief and gloomy record of the voyage of Villalobos is a fit ending for this story of the Coronado expedition to Cibola and Quivira, of how it came about, of what it accomplished, and of what resulted from it. NOTHING is the epitome of the whole story. The lessons which it teaches are always warnings, but if one will read history rightly, every warning will be found to be an inspiration.

NOTES

THE CAUSES OF THE CORONADO EXPEDITION, 1528–1539

Alvar Nuñez Cabeza de Vaca

1   The Indian's story is in the first chapter of Castañeda's Narrative. Some additional information is given in Bandelier's Contributions to the History of the Southwest, the first chapter of which is entitled "Sketch of the knowledge which the Spaniards in Mexico possessed of the countries north of the province of New Galicia previous to the return of Cabeza de Vaca." For bibliographic references to this and other works referred to throughout this memoir, see the list at the end of the paper.

2   The most important source of information regarding the expedition of Narvaez is the Relation written by Cabeza de Vaca. This is best consulted in Buckingham Smith's translation. Mr Smith includes in his volume everything which he could find to supplement the main narration. The best study of the route followed by the survivors of the expedition, after they landed in Texas, is that of Bandelier in the second chapter of his Contributions to the History of the Southwest. In this essay Bandelier has brought together all the documentary evidence, and he writes with the knowledge obtained by traveling through the different portions of the country which Cabeza de Vaca must have traversed. Dr J. G. Shea, in his chapter in the Narrative and Critical History of America, vol. ii, p. 286, disagrees in some points with Mr Bandelier's interpretation of the route of Cabeza de Vaca west of Texas, and also with Mr Smith's identifications of the different points in the march of the main army before it embarked from the Bahia de los Cavallos. Other interesting conjectures are given in H. H. Bancroft's North Mexican States, vol. i, p. 63, and map at p. 67.

3   Buckingham Smith collected in his Letter of Hernando de Soto, pp. 57–61, and in his Narrative of the Career of Hernando de Soto (see index), all that is known in regard to Ortiz, one of the soldiers of Narvaez, who was found among the Indians by De Soto in 1540.

4   Mendoza to Charles V, 10 Diciembre, 1537. Cabeza de Vaca y Dorantes, ... despues de haber llegado aquí, determinaron de irse en España, y viendo que si V. M. era servido de enviar aquella tierra alguna gente para saber de cierto lo que era, no quedaba persona que pudiese ir con ella ni dar ninguna razon, compré á Dorantes para este efecto un negro que vino de allá y se halló con ellos en todo, que se llama Estéban, por ser persona de razon. Despues sucedió, como el navio en que Dorantes iba se volvió al puerto, y sabido esto, yo le escribí á la Vera-Cruz, rogándole que viniese aquí; y como llegó á esta ciudad, yo le hablé diciéndole que hubiese por bien de volver á esta tierra con algunos religiosos y gente de caballo, que yo le daria á calalla, y saber de cierto lo que en ella habia. Y él vista mi voluntad, y el servicio que yo le puse delantre que hacia con ello á Dios y á V. M., me respondió que holgaba dello, y así estoy

determinado de envialle allá con la gente de caballo y religiosos que digo. Pienso que ha de redundar dello gran servicio á Dios y á V. M.—From the text printed in Pacheco y Cardenas, Docs. de Indias, ii, 206.

5 Some recent writers have been misled by a chance comma inserted by the copyist or printer in one of the old narratives, which divides the name of Maldonado—Alonso del Castillo, Maldonado—making it appear as if there were five instead of four survivors of the Narvaez expedition who made their way to Mexico.

6 Besides the general historians, we have Cabeza de Vaca's own account of his career in Paraguay in his Comentarios, reprinted in Vedia, Historiadores Primitivos, vol. i. Ternaux translated this narrative into French for his Voyages, part vi.

7 The Spanish text of this letter has not been seen since Ramusio used it in making the translation for his Viaggi, vol. iii, fol. 355, ed. 1556. There is no date to the letter as Ramusio gives it. Ternaux-Compans translated it from Ramusio for his Cibola volume (Voyages, vol. ix, p. 287). It is usually cited from Ternaux's title as the "Première lettre de Mendoza." I quote from the French text the portion of the letter which explains my narrative: "... Andrès Dorantès, un de ceux qui firent partie de l'armée de Pamphilo Narvaez, vint près de moi. J'eus de fréquents entretiens avec lui; je pensai qu'il pouvait rendre un grand service à votre majesté; si je l'expédiais avec quarante ou cinquante chevaux et tous les objets nécessaires pour découvrir ce pays. Je dépensai beaucoup d'argent pour l'expédition, mais je ne sais pas comment il se fit que l'affaire n'eut pas de suite. De tous les préparatifs que j'avais faits, il ne me resta qu'un nègre qui est venu avec Dorantès, quelques esclaves que j'avais achetés, et des Indiens, naturels de ce pays, que j'avais fait rassembler."

8 Two of these are extant—the Relacion of Cabeza de Vaca and Oviedo's version of an account signed by the three Spaniards and sent to the Real Audiencia at Santo Domingo, in his Historia General de las Indias, lib. xxxv, vol. iii, p. 582, ed. 1853.

9 See Buckingham Smith's translation of Cabeza de Vaca's Narrative, p. 150.

10 The effect of the stories told by Cabeza de Vaca, and later by Friar Marcos, is considered in a paper printed in the Proceedings of the American Historical Association at Washington, 1894, "Why Coronado went to New Mexico in 1540."

The Governors of New Spain, 1530–1537

1 The best source for these proceedings is in Mota Padilla's Historia de la Nueva Galicia (ed. Icazbalceta, pp. 104-109). A more available account in English is in H. H. Bancroft's Mexico, vol. ii, p. 457.

2 An official investigation into the administration of an official who is about to be relieved of his duties.

3 The best account, in English, of the Casa de Contratacion is given by Professor Bernard Moses, of Berkeley, California, in the volume of papers read before the American Historical Association at its 1894 meeting.

4 See Fragmentos de una Historia de la Nueva Galicia, by Father Tello (Icazbalceta, Documentos de Mexico, vol. ii, p. 369).

5   Mendoza, in the "première lettre," gives a brief sketch of the efforts which Cortes had been making, and then adds: "Il ne put donc jamais en faire la conquête; il semblait même que Dieu voulût miraculeusement l'en éloigner." Ternaux, Cibola volume, p. 287.
6   On the maps it is usually designated as S. †.
7   The details of this episode are given in the relations and petitions of Cortes. H. H. Bancroft tells the story in his North Mexican States, vol. i, p. 77. The Cortes map of 1536 is reproduced, from a tracing, in Winsor's Narrative and Critical History of America, vol. ii, p. 442.
8   This is the story which Garcilaso de la Vega tells in his Commentales Reales, pt. II, lib. ii.

The Reconnoissance of Friar Marcos de Niza

1   Contributions to the History of the Southwest, pp. 79–103.
2   This region is identified by Bandelier in his Contributions, p. 104, note. The letter from which the details are obtained, written to accompany the report of Friar Marcos when this was transmitted to the King, is in Ramusio, and also in Ternaux, Cibola volume, p. 285.
3   This certification, with the report of Friar Marcos and other documents relating to him, is printed in the Pacheco y Cardenas Coleccion, vol. iii, pp. 325–351.
4   The instructions given to Friar Marcos have been translated by Bandelier in his Contributions, p. 109. The best account of Friar Marcos and his explorations is given in that volume.
5   Herrera, Historia General, dec. VI, lib. vii, cap. vii.
6   Bandelier, in his Contributions, p. 122, says this was "about the middle of April," but his chronology at this point must be at fault.
7   See F. W. Hodge, "Aboriginal Use of Adobes," The Archaeologist, Columbus, Ohio, August, 1895.
8   These are described in the Castañeda narrative.
9   In lieu of turquoises the Pima and Maricopa today frequently wear small beaded rings pendent from the ears and septum.
10 Bandelier, Contributions, pp. 154, 155.
11 There is an admirable and extended account, with many illustrations, of the Apache medicine men, by Captain John G. Bourke in the ninth report of the Bureau of Ethnology.
12 This is precisely the method pursued by the Zuñis today against any Mexicans who may be found in their vicinity during the performance of an outdoor ceremonial.
13 This question has been fully discussed by F. W. Hodge. See "The First Discovered City of Cibola," American Anthropologist, Washington, April, 1895.

The Effect of Friar Marcos' Report

1 Tomson's exceedingly interesting narrative of his experiences in Mexico is printed in Hakluyt, vol. iii, p. 447, ed. 1600.

2 Compare the ground plan of Hawikuh by Victor Mindeleff, in the eighth annual report of the Bureau of Ethnology, pl. XLVI, with the map of the city of Mexico (1550?), by Alonzo de Santa Cruz, pl. XLIII of this paper.

3 Diaz started November 17, 1539. The report of his trip is given in Mendoza's letter of April 17, 1540, in Pacheco y Cardenas, ii, p. 356, and translated herein.

4 The Spanish text from which I have translated may be found on pages 144 and 148 of Zaragoza's edition of Suarez de Peralta's Tratado. This edition is of the greatest usefulness to every student of early Mexican history.

5 The depositions as printed in the Pacheco y Cardenas Docs. de Indias, vol. XV., pp. 392–398, are as follows: Pedro Nuñez, testigo rescebido en la dicha razon, juró segun derecho, é dijo: … que estando en la ciudad de México, puede haber tres meses [the evidence being taken November 12, 1539], poco mas ó menos, oyó decir este testigo publicamente, que habia venido un fraile Francisco, que se dice Fray Marcos, que venia la tierra adentro, é que decia el dicho fraile que se habia descobierto una tierra muy rica é muy poblada; é que habia cuatrocientas leguas dende México allá; é que dice que han de ir allá por cerca del rio de Palmas; …

Garcia Navarro, … oyó decir publicamente, puede haber un mes ó mes y medio [and so all the remaining witnesses] que habia venido un fraile, nuevamente, de una tierra, nuevamente descobierta, que dicen ques quinientas leguas de México, en la tierra de la Florida, que dicen ques hácia la parte del Norte de la dicha tierra; la cual diz, que es tierra rica de oro é plata é otros resgates, é grandes pueblos; que las casas son de piedra é terrados á la manera de México, é que tienen peso é medida, é gente de razon, é que no casan mas de una vez, é que visten albornoces, é que andan cabalgando en unos animales, que no sabe cómo se llaman, … Francisco Serrano, … el fraile venia por tierra, por la via de Xalisco; é que muy rica é muy poblada é grandes ciudades cercadas; é que los señores dellas, se nombran Reyes; é que las casas son sobradas, é ques gente de mucha razon; que la lengua es mexicana, … Pero Sanchez, tinturero … una tierra nueva muy rica é muy poblada de ciudades é villas; … por la vía de Xalisco … hácia en medio de la tierra. … Francisco de Leyva … en la Vera-Cruz, oyó decir que habia venido un fraile de una tierra nueva muy rica é muy poblada de ciudades é villas, é ques á la banda del Sur, … Otrosí, dixo: que es verdad que no embargante que no toca en este puerto, dejaba de seguir su viaje; pero que entró en este puerto por necesidad que llevaba de agua é otros bastimentos é de ciertas personas que venian muy enfermos.

Hernando de Sotomayor … questando en la Puebla de los Angeles … públicamente se decia … é que las casas son de piedras sobradadas, é las ciudades cercadas, é gente de razon; … é questa dicha tierra es la parte donde vino Dorantes é Cabeza de Vaca, los cuales escaparon de la armada de Narvaez; é que sabe é vido este testigo, que fué mandado al maestre por mandado del Virey é con su mandamiento, que no tocase en parte ninguna, salvo que fuese derechamente á España, con la dicha nao, é quel secretario del Virey hizo un requirimiento al dicho maestre, viniendo por la mar, que no tocase en este puerto ni en otra parte destas islas. … [This statement appears in each deposition.]

Andrés Garcia, dixo: … questando en la ciudad de México, un Francisco de Billegas le dió cartas para dar en esta villa, para dar al Adelantado D. Hernando de Soto, é si no lo hallase, que las llevase á España é las diese al hacedor suyo; é queste testigo tiene un yerno barbero que afeitaba al fraile que vino de la dicha tierra; é quel dicho su yerno, le dixo este testigo, questando afeitando al dicho fraile, le dixo como antes que llegasen á la dicha tierra estaba una sierra, é que pasando la dicha sierra estaba un rio, é que habia muchas poblazones de ciudades é villas, é que las ciudades son cercades é guardadas á las puertas, é muy ricas; é que habia plateros; é que las mugeres traian sartas de oro é los hombres cintos de oro, é que habia albarnios é obejas é vacas é perdices é carnicerias é herreria, é peso é medida; é que un Bocanegra, dixo á esta testigo que se quedare, que se habia descobierto un nuevo mundo. …

6   The document, as printed in Doc. Inéd. Hist. España, vol. iv, pp. 209–217, is not dated. The date given in the text is taken from the heading or title to the petition, which, if not the original, has at least the authority of Señor Navarrete, the editor of this Coleccion when the earlier volumes were printed. This memorial appears, from the contents, to have been one of the documents submitted in the litigation then going on between the rival claimants for the privilege of exploring the country discovered by Friar Marcos, although the document is not printed with the other papers in the case.

7   Documentos Inéditos Hist. España, vol. iv, p. 211: Memorial que dió el Marqués del Valle en Madrid á 25 de Junio de 1540. … "Al tiempo que yo vine de la dicha tierra el dicho Fray Marcos habló conmigo … é yo le dí noticia de esta dicha tierra y descubrimiento de ella, porque tenia determinacion de enviarlo en mis navíos en proseguimiento y conquista de la dicha costa y tierra, porque parescia que se le entendia algo de cosas de navegacion: el cual dicho fraile lo comunicó con el dicho visorey, y con su licencia diz que fué por tierra en demanda de la misma costa y tierra que yo habia descubierto, y que era y es de mi conquista; y despues que volvió el dicho fraile ha publicado que diz que llegó á vista de la dicha tierra; lo cual yo niego haber él visto ni descubierto, antes lo que el dicho fraile refiere haber visto, lo ha dicho y dice por sola la relacion que yo le habia hecho de la noticia que tenia de los indios de la dicha tierra de Santa Cruz que yo truje, porque todo lo que el dicho fraile se dice que refiere, es lo mismo que los dichos indios á mí me dijeron; y en haberse en esto adelantado el dicho Fray Marcos fingiendo y refiriendo lo que no sabe ni vió, no hizo cosa nueva, porque otras muchas veces lo ha hecho y lo tiene por costumbre como es notorio en las provincias del Perú y Guatemala, y se dará de ello informacion bastante luego en esta corte, siendo necesario."

8   The request occurs in the earliest letters from the viceroy, and is repeated in that of

December 10, 1537. This privilege was withdrawn from all governors in the colonies by one of the New Laws of 1543. (Icazbalceta, Col. Hist. Mexico, ii, 204.) The ill success of Coronado's efforts did not weaken Mendoza's desire to enlarge his territory, for he begs his agent in Spain, Juan de Aguilar, to secure for him a fresh grant of the privilege in a later letter. (Pacheco y Cardenas, Doc. de Indias, vol. iii, p. 506; B. Smith, Florida, p. 7.)

9 Ulloa's Relation is translated from Ramusio in Hakluyt, vol. iii, p. 397, ed. 1600.

10 Memorial que dió al Rey el Marques del Valle, en Madrid, 25 de junio, 1540: Printed in Doc. Inéd. España, vol. iv, p. 209. Compare with this account that in H. H. Bancroft's Mexico, vol. ii, p. 425. Mr Bancroft is always a strong advocate of the cause of Cortes.

11 Oviedo, Historia General, vol. iv, p. 19.

12 The capitulacion or agreement with De Soto is printed in Pacheco y Cardenas, Doc. de Indias, vol. xv, pp. 354–363.

13 These documents fill 108 pages in volume xv of the Pacheco y Cardenas Documentos de Indias. At least one other document presented in the case, the Capitulacion ... que hizo Ayllon, is printed elsewhere in the same Coleccion. This, also, does not include the two long memorials which Cortes succeeded in presenting to the King in person.

14 This much feared conjunction came very near to being realized. A comparison of the various plottings of the routes De Soto and Coronado may have followed and of their respective itineraries shows that the two parties could not have been far apart in the present Oklahoma or Indian territory, or perhaps north of that region. This evidence is confirmed by the story of the Indian woman, related by Casteñada. Dr J. G. Shea, in Winsor's Narrative and Critical History, vol. ii, p. 292, states that Coronado heard of his countryman De Soto, and sent a letter to him. This is almost certainly a mistake, which probably originated in a misinterpretation of a statement made by Jaramillo.

15 See his Carta in Doc. Inéd. España, vol. civ, p. 491.

16 The Título, etc. dated 6 Julio, 1529, is in Pacheco y Cardenas, Coleccion de Documentos Inéditos de Indias, vol. iv, pp. 572–574.

THE EXPEDITION TO NEW MEXICO AND THE GREAT PLAINS

The Organization of the Expedition

1 Fragmento Visita: Mendoza, Icazbalceta's Mexico, vol. ii, p. 90, §86. "Porque antes que el dicho visorey viniese ... habia muy poca gente y los corregimientos bastaban para proveellos y sustentallos, y como despues de la venida del dicho visorey creció la gente y se aumentó, y de cada dia vienen gentes pobres á quien se ha de proveer de comer, con la dicha baja y vacaciones se han proveido y remediado, y sin ella hubieran padecido y padecieran gran necesidad, y no se poblara tanto la tierra, y dello se dió noticia á S. M. y lo aprobó y se tuvo por servido en ello. §194 (p. 117): Despues que el dicho visorey vino á esta Nueva España, continamente ha acogido en su casa á caballeros y otras personas que vienen necesitados de España y de otras partes,

dándoles de comer y vestir, caballos y armas con que sirvan á S. M." ...

2   Garcilaso de la Vega, Comentarios Reales, part II, cap. i, lib. ii, p. 58 (ed. 1722), tells the story of Alvarado's experiment. The picture of the life and character of the Spanish conquerors of America, in the eyes of a girl fresh from Europe, is so vivid and suggestive that its omission would be unjustifiable.

3   Tomson's whole narrative, in Hakluyt, Voyages, vol. iii, p. 447 (ed. 1600), is well worth reading. Considerable additional information in regard to the internal condition of New Spain, at a little later date, may be found in the "Discourses" which follow Tomson's Narrative, in the same volume of Hakluyt.

4   The proof text for this quotation, as for many of the following statements which are taken from Mota Padilla's Historia de la Nueva Galicia, may be found in footnotes to the passages which they illustrate in the translation of Castañeda's narrative. I hope this arrangement will prove most convenient for those who study the documents included in this memoir. I shall not attempt in the introductory narrative to make any further references showing my indebtedness to Mota Padilla's invaluable work.

5   The Testimonio contains so much that is of interest to the historical student that I have translated it in full herein.

6   Herrera, Historia General, dec. VI, lib. ix, cap. xi, vol. iii, p. 204 (ed. 1730), mentions pigs among the food supply of the army. For the above description, which is not so fanciful as it sounds, see notes from Mota Padilla, etc., accompanying the translation of Castañeda.

7   Castañeda's statement is supported by Herrera, Historia General, dec. VI, lib. v, cap. ix, vol. iii, p. 121 (ed. 1730), and by Tello, in Icazbalceta's Mexico, vol. ii, p. 370.

8   See the Fragmento de Visita, in Icazbalceta's Doc. Hist. Mexico, vol. ii, p. 95.

9   The laws were signed at Valladolid, June 4 and June 26, 1543, and the copy printed in Icazbalceta's Doc. Hist. Mexico, vol. ii, p. 214, was promulgated in New Spain, March 13, 1544.

10   See Mendoza's letter to the King, December 10, 1537.

11   The proceso which was served on Cortes is in Pacheco y Cardenas, Doc. de Indias, vol. xv, p. 371.

12   The grant, dated at Madrid, November 8, 1539, is given in Tello's Fragmento (Icazbalceta's Doc. Hist. Mexico, vol. ii, p. 371).

The Departure of the Expedition

1   Before the end of the month Mendoza wrote a letter to the King, in which he gave a detailed account of the preparations he had made to insure the success of the expedition, and of the departure of the army. This letter is not known to exist.

2   This march from Compostela to Culiacan, according to the letter which Coronado wrote from Granada-Zuñi on August 3, occupied eighty days. The same letter gives April 22 as the date when Coronado left Culiacan, after stopping for several days in that town, and this date is corroborated by another account, the Traslado de las Nuevas.

April 22 is only sixty days after February 23, the date of the departure, which is fixed almost beyond question by the legal formalities of the Testimonio of February 21–26. We have only Ramusio's Italian text of Coronado's August 3 letter, so that it is easy to suspect that a slip on the part of the translator causes the trouble. But to complicate matters, eighty days previous to April 22 is about the 1st of February. Mota Padilla, who used material of great value in his Historia de la Nueva Galicia, says that the army marched from Compostela "el 1º, de Febrero del año de 1540." Castañeda does not give much help, merely stating that the whole force was assembled at Compostela by "el dia de carnes tollendas," the carnival preceding Shrove tide, which in 1540 fell on February 10, Easter being March 28. Mendoza, who had spent the New Year's season at Pasquaro, the seat of the bishopric of Michoacan, did not hasten his journey across the country, and we know only that the whole force had assembled before he arrived at Compostela. At least a fortnight would have been necessary for completing the organization of the force, and for collecting and arranging all the supplies.

Another combination of dates makes it hard to decide how rapidly the army marched. Mendoza was at Compostela February 26. He presumably started on his return to Mexico very soon after that date. He went down the coast to Colima, where he was detained by an attack of fever for some days. Thence he proceeded to Jacona, where he wrote a letter to the King, April 17, 1540. March 20 Mendoza received the report of Melchior Diaz, who had spent the preceding winter in the country through which Friar Marcos had traveled, trying to verify the friar's report. Diaz, and Saldivar his lieutenant, on their return from the north, met the army at Chiametla as it was about to resume its march, after a few days' delay. Diaz stopped at Chiametla, while Saldivar carried the report to the viceroy, and he must have traveled very rapidly to deliver his packets on March 20, when Mendoza had left Colima, although he probably had not arrived at Jacona.

Everything points to the very slow progress of the force, hampered by the long baggage and provision trains. Castañeda says that they reached Culiacan just before Easter, March 28, less than thirty-five days after February 23. Here Coronado stopped for a fortnight's entertainment and rest, according to Castañeda, who was present. Mota Padilla says that the army stayed here a month, and this agrees with Castañeda's statement that the main body started a fortnight later than their general.

The attempt to arrange an itinerary of the expedition is perplexing, and has not been made easier by modern students. Professor Haynes, in his Early Explorations of New Mexico (Winsor's Narrative and Critical History, vol. ii, p. 481), following Bandelier's statement on page 26 of his Documentary History of Zuñi, says that the start from Compostela was made "in the last days of February, 1540." Mr Bandelier, however, who has given much more time to the study of everything connected with this expedition than has been possible for any other investigator, in his latest work— The Gilded Man, p. 164—adopts the date which is given by Mota Padilla. The best and the safest way out of this tangle in chronology is gained by accepting the three specific dates, February 23—or possibly 24—Easter, and April 22, disregarding every statement about the number of days intervening.

3   Mota Padilla says, "warden of one of the royal storehouses in Mexico," which may refer to some other position held by Samaniego, or may have arisen from some confusion of names.

4   This is taken from Mota Padilla's account of the incident, without any attempt to compare or to harmonize it with the story told by Castañeda. Mota Padilla's version seems much the more reasonable.

5   A note, almost as complicated as that which concerns the date of the army's departure, might be written regarding the length of the stay at Culiacan. Those who are curious can find the facts in Coronado's letter from Granada, in Castañeda, and in the footnotes to the translation of the latter.

The Expedition by Sea under Alarcon

1   The complete text of Alarcon's report was translated into Italian by Ramusio (vol. iii, fol. 363, ed. 1556), and the Spanish original is not known to exist. Herrera, however, gives an account which, from the close similarity to Ramusio's text and from the personality of the style, must have been copied from Alarcon's own narrative. The Ramusio text does not give the port of departure. Herrera says that the ships sailed from Acapulco. Castañeda implies that the start was made from La Natividad, but his information could hardly have been better than second hand. He may have known what the viceroy intended to do, when he bade the army farewell, two days north of Compostela. Alarcon reports that he put into the port of Santiago de Buena Esperanza, and as the only Santiago on the coast hereabout is south of La Natividad, which is on the coast of the district of Colima, H. H. Bancroft (North Mexican States, vol. i, p. 90) says the fleet probably started from Acapulco. Bancroft does not mention Herrera, who is, I suppose, the conclusive authority. Gen. J. H. Simpson (Smithsonian Report for 1869, p. 315), accepted the start from La Natividad, and then identified this Santiago with the port of Compostela, which was well known under the name of Xalisco. The distance of Acapulco from Colima would explain the considerable lapse of time before Alarcon was ready to start.

The Journey from Culiacan to Cibola

1   Coronado's description of this portion of the route in the letter of August 3 is abbreviated, he says, because it was accompanied by a map. As this is lost, I am following here, as I shall do throughout the Introduction, Bandelier's identification of the route in his Historical Introduction, p. 10, and in his Final Report, part II, pp. 407–409. The itinerary of Jaramillo, confused and perplexing as it is, is the chief guide for the earlier part of the route. There is no attempt in this introductory narrative to repeat the details of the journey, when these may be obtained, much more satisfactorily, from the translation of the contemporary narratives which form the main portion of this memoir.

2   This "Red House," in the Nahuatl tongue, has been identified with the Casa Grande ruins in Arizona ever since the revival of interest in Coronado's journey, which followed the explorations in the southwestern portion of the United States during the second quarter of the present century. Bandelier's study of the descriptions given by those who saw the "Red House" in 1539 and 1540, however, shows conclusively that the conditions at Casa Grande do not meet the requirements for Chichilticalli. Bandelier objects to Casa Grande because it is white, although he admits that it may once have been covered with the reddish paint of the Indians. This would suit Mota Padilla's explanation that the place was named from a house there which was daubed over with colored earth—almagre, as the natives called it. This is the Indian term for red ocher. Bandelier thinks that Coronado reached the edge of the wilderness, the White Mountain Apache reservation in Arizona, by way of San Pedro river and Arivaypa creek. This requires the location of Chichilticalli somewhere in the vicinity of the present Fort Grant, Arizona.

3   Hakluyt, Voyages, vol. iii, p. 375, ed. 1600.

The Capture of the Seven Cities

1   Hawikuh, near Ojo Caliente, was the first village captured by the Spaniards, as Bandelier has shown in his Contributions, p. 166, and Documentary History of Zuñi, p. 29. The definite location of this village is an important point, and the problem of its site was one over which a great deal of argument had been wasted before Mr Bandelier published the results of his critical study of the sources, which he was enabled to interpret by the aid of a careful exploration of the southwestern country, undertaken under the auspices of the Archaeological Institute of America. It was under the impetus of the friendly guidance and careful scrutiny of results by Professor Henry W. Haynes and the other members of the Institute that Mr Bandelier has done his best work. It is unfortunate that he did not use the letter which Coronado wrote from Granada-Hawikuh, August 3, 1540, which is the only official account of the march from Culiacan to Zuñi. The fact that Bandelier's results stand the tests supplied by this letter is the best proof of the exactness and accuracy of his work. (This note was written before the appearance of Mr Bandelier's Gilded Man, in which he states that Kiakima, instead of Hawikuh, is the Granada of Coronado. Mr F. W. Hodge, in an exhaustive paper on The First Discovered City of Cibola (American Anthropologist, Washington, April, 1895), has proved conclusively that Mr Bandelier's earlier position was the correct one.)

2   Marcos returned to Mexico with Juan de Gallego, who left Cibola-Zuñi soon after August 3. Bandelier, in his article on the friars, in the American Catholic Quarterly Review, vol. xv, p. 551, says that "the obvious reason" for Marcos's return "was the feeble health of the friar. Hardship and physical suffering had nearly paralyzed the body of the already aged man. He never recovered his vigor, and died at Mexico, after having in vain sought relief in the delightful climate of Jalapa, in the year 1558"—seventeen years later.

The Exploration of the Country

1 Alvarado's official report is probably the paper known as the Relacion de lo que . ... Alvarado y Fray Joan de Padilla descubrieron en demanda de la mar del Sur, which is translated herein. The title, evidently the work of some later editor, is a misnomer so far as the Mar del Sur is concerned, for this—the Pacific ocean—was west, and Alvarado's explorations were toward the east. This short report is of considerable value, but it is known only through a copy, lacking the list of villages which should have accompanied it. Muñoz judged that it was a contemporary official copy, which did not commend itself to that great collector and student of Spanish Americana. There is nothing about the document to show the century or the region to which it relates, so that one of Hubert H. Bancroft's scribes was misled into making a short abstract of it for his Central America, vol. ii, p. 185, as giving an account of an otherwise unknown expedition starting from another Granada, on the northern shore of Lake Nicaragua.

The Winter of 1540–1541 along the Rio Grande

1 Castañeda says that this Indian accompanied Alvarado on the first visit to the buffalo plains, and this may be true without disturbing the statement above.

2 He was called "The Turk" because the Spaniards thought that he looked like one. Bandelier, in American Catholic Quarterly Review, vol. xv, p. 555, thinks this was due to the manner in which he wore his hair, characteristic of certain branches of the Pawnee.

3 This probability is greatly strengthened by Mota Padilla's statement in relation to the Turk and Quivira, quoted in connection with Castañeda's narrative.

The Journey across the Buffalo Plains

1 The Spaniards had already observed two distinct branches of these pure nomads, whom they knew as Querechos and Teyas. Bandelier, in his Final Report, vol. i, p. 179, identified the Querechos with the Apaches of the plains, but later investigation by Mr James Mooney shows that Querecho is an old Comanche name of the Tonkawa of western central Texas (Hodge, Early Navajo and Apache, Am. Anthropologist, Washington, July, 1895, vol. iii, p. 235). I am unable to find any single tribal group among the Indians whom we know which can be identified with the Teyas, unless, as Mr Hodge has suggested, they may have been the Comanche, who roamed the plains from Yellowstone Park to Durango, Mexico.

2 I am inclined, also, to believe Jaramillo's statement that the day's marches on the journey to Quivira were short ones. But when he writes that the journey occupied "more than thirty days, or almost thirty days' journey, although not long day's marches,"—seguimos nuestro viaje ... más de treinta dias ú casi treinta dias de camino, aunque no de jornadas grandes—and again, that they decided to return "because it was already nearly the beginning of winter, ... and lest the winter might prevent the return,"—nos paresció á todos, que pues que hera ya casi la boca del inbierno, porque

si me acuerdo bien, jera media y más de Agosto, y por ser pocos para inbernar allí, ... y porque el invierno no nos cerrase los caminos de nieves y rios que no nos dexesen pasar (Pacheco y Cardenas, Doc. de Indias, vol. xiv, pp. 312, 314)—we experience some of the difficulties which make it hard to analyse the captain's recollections critically and satisfactorily.

3   Final Report, vol. i, p. 170.

4   Ibid., vol. i, p. 178.

5   Bandelier's best discussion of the route is in his article on Fray Juan de Padilla, in the American Catholic Quarterly Review, vol. xv, p. 551. The Gilded Man also contains an outline of the probable route. An element in his calculation, to which he gives much prominence, is the tendency of one who is lost to wander always toward the right. This is strongly emphasized in the Gilded Man; but it can, I think, hardly merit the importance which he gives to it. The emphasis appears, however, much more in Bandelier's words than in his results. I can not see that there is anything to show that the Indian guides ever really lost their reckoning.

6   Bandelier accounts for sixty-seven days of short marches and occasional delays between the separation of the force on Canadian river and the arrival at Quivira. It may be that the seventy-seven days of desert marching which Coronado mentions in his letter of October 20, 1541, refers to this part of the journey, instead of to the whole of the journey from the bridge (near Mora on the Canadian) to Quivira. But the number sixty-seven originated in a blunder of Ternaux-Compans, who substituted it for seventy-seven, in translating this letter. The mistake evidently influenced Bandelier to extend the journey over more time than it really took. But this need not affect his results materially, if we extend the amount of ground covered by each day's march and omit numerous halts, which were very unlikely, considering the condition of his party and the desire to solve the mystery of Quivira. If the Spaniards crossed the Arkansas somewhere below Fort Dodge, and followed it until the river turns toward the southeast, Quivira can hardly have been east of the middle part of the state of Kansas. It was much more probably somewhere between the main forks of Kansas river, in the central part of that state. Bandelier seems to have abandoned his documents as he approached the goal, and to have transported Coronado across several branches of Kansas river, in order to fill out his sixty-seven days—which should have been seventy-seven—and perhaps to reach the region fixed on by previous conceptions of the limit of exploration. He may have realized that the difficulty in his explanation of the route was that it required a reduction of about one-fourth of the distance covered by the army in the eastward march, as plotted by General Simpson. This can be accounted for by the wandering path which the army followed.

7   See the note at the end of the translation.

8   The Spanish (judicial) league was equivalent to 2.63 statute miles.

The Friars Remain in the Country

1   Castañeda implies that Friar Antonio Victoria, who broke his leg near Culiacan, accompanied the main force on its march to Cibola. This is the last heard of him, and it is much more probable that he remained in New Galicia.

2   Vetancurt, in the Menologia, gives the date of the martyrdom of Fray Juan de Padilla as November 30, 1544, and I see no reason to prefer the more general statements of Jaramillo, Castañeda, and Mota Padilla, which seem to imply that it took place in 1542. Docampo and the other companions of the friar brought the news to Mexico. They must have returned some time previous to 1552, for Gomara mentions their arrival in Tampico, on the Mexican gulf, in his Conquista de Mexico published in that year. Herrera and Gomara say that the fugitives had been captured by Indians and detained as slaves for ten months. These historians state also that a dog accompanied the fugitives. Further mention of dogs in connection with the Coronado expedition is in the stories of one accompanying Estevan which Alarcon heard along Colorado river, also in the account of the death of Melchior Diaz, and in the reference by Castañeda to the use of these animals as beasts of burden by certain plains tribes.

    Mendieta and Vetancurt say that, of the two donados, Sebastian died soon after his return, and the other lived long as a missionary among the Zacatecas.

SOME RESULTS OF THE EXPEDITION—1540–1547

The Discovery of Colorado River

1   The maps of the New World drawn and published between 1542 and 1600, reproductions of several of which accompany this memoir, give a better idea of the real value of the geographical discoveries made by Coronado than any bare statement could give. In 1540, European cartographers knew nothing about the country north of New Spain. Cortes had given them the name—Nueva España or Hispania Nova—and this, with the name of the continent, served to designate the inland region stretching toward the north and west. Such was the device which Mercator adopted when he drew his double cordiform map in 1538 (plates XLV, XLVI). Six years later, 1544, Sebastian Cabot published his elaborate map of the New World (see plate XL). He had heard of the explorations made by and for Cortes toward the head of the Gulf of California, very likely from the lips of the conqueror himself. He confined New Spain to its proper limits, and in the interior he pictured Indians and wild beasts. In 1548 the maps of America in Ptolemy's Geography for the first time show the results of Coronado's discoveries (see plate XLI). During the remainder of the century Granada, Cibola, Quivira, and the other places whose names occur in the various reports of the expedition, appear on the maps. Their location, relative to each other and to the different parts of the country, constantly changes. Quivira moves along the fortieth parallel from Espiritu Santo river to the Pacific coast. Tiguex and Totonteac are on any one of half a dozen rivers flowing into the Gulf of Mexico, the Espiritu Santo, or the

South sea. Acuco and Cicuye are sometimes placed west of Cibola, and so a contemporary map maker may be the cause of the mistaken title to the report of Alvarado's expedition to the Rio Grande. But many as were the mistakes, they are insignificant in comparison with the great fact that the people of Europe had learned that there was an inhabited country north of Mexico, and that the world was, by so much, larger than before.

2 See Castañeda's account of the finding of [a] similar message by the party under Diaz.

3 The account of this trip in Herrera (dec. VI, lib. ix, cap. xv, ed. 1728) is as follows: "Haviendo llegado à ciertas Montañas, adonde el Rio se estrechaba mucho, supo, que vn Encantador andaba preguntando por donde havia de pasar, y haviendo entendido, que por el Rio, puso desde vna Ribera à la otra algunas Cañas, que debian de ser hechiçadas; pero las Barcas pasaron sin daño; y haviendo llegado mui arriba, preguntando por cosas de la Tierra, para entender, si descubriria alguna noticia de Francisco Vazquez de Coronado ... Viendo Alarcon, que no hallaba lo que deseaba, i que havia subido por aquel Rio 85 Leguas, determinò de bolver." ...

4 Mota Padilla (p. 158, §1). "Los Indios, para resistir el frío, llevan en las manos un troncon ardiendo que les calienta el pecho, y del mismo modo la espalda; siendo esto tan comun en todos los indios, que por eso los nuestros pusieron á este rio el nombre del rio del Tison, cerca de él vieron un árbol en el cual estaban escritas unas letras, que decian: al pié está una carta: y con efecto; la hallaron en una olla, bien envuelta, porque no se humedeciese, y su contenido era: que el año de 40 llegó alli Francisco de Alarcon con tres navíos, y entrando por la barra de aquel rio, enviado por el virey D. Antonio de Mendoza, en busca de Francisco Vazquez Coronado: y que habiendo estado alli muchos dias sin noticia alguna le fué preciso salir porque los navíos se comian de broma."

The Indian Uprising of New Spain, 1540–1542

1 The accusation was made by others at the time. H. H. Bancroft repeats the charge in his Mexico, but it should always be remembered that Mr Bancroft, or his compilers, in everything connected with the conqueror, repeat whatever it may have pleased Cortes to write, without criticism or question.

Further Attempts at Discovery

1 The report or memorandum was written by Juan Paez, or more probably by the pilot Ferrel. It has been translated in the reports of the United States Geological Survey West of the One Hundredth Meridian. (Appendix to part i, vol. vii, Archaeology, pp. 293–314.) The translation is accompanied by notes identifying the places named, on which it is safe enough to rely, and by other notes of somewhat doubtful value.

INTRODUCTION

The narratives printed in the present volume tell the story of one of the most remarkable explorations recorded in the annals of American history. Seventy-five years before the English succeeded in establishing themselves on the northeastern coast of North America, a band of Spaniards, starting from what was already a populous and flourishing colony at the City of Mexico, penetrated the opposite extreme of the continent, and explored thoroughly a region as extensive as the coast line of the United States from Maine to Georgia.

The accounts of their experiences printed herewith were all written by members of the expedition. With two exceptions they were written during the journey, and were the official reports prepared by the general and sent to the viceroy in Mexico or the emperor-king in Spain, or by the lieutenants in charge of special explorations. The first and principal narrative was written for the purpose of providing a history of the expedition, by one of the common soldiers some time after his return to Mexico, when he apparently felt that there was danger that posterity would forget the deeds of those with whom he had toiled and suffered in the vain search for something which would reward their costly undertaking. All that is known of the author, Pedro Castañeda, beyond what he relates in this narrative, is that he was a native of the Biscayan town of Najera in northern Spain, who had established himself in the Spanish outpost at Culiacan, in northwestern Mexico, at the time Coronado organized his

From George Parker Winship, *The Journey of Coronado, 1540–1542* (1904).

expedition, and that he was the father of eight surviving children, who, with their mother, presented in 1554 a claim against the Mexican treasury, on account of the father's exploits. The Spanish text of Castañeda's history is preserved in the Lenox Library, now absorbed into the New York Public Library. It is printed, together with the translations reprinted herewith, in the Fourteenth Annual Report of the United States Bureau of Ethnology, Washington, D.C., 1896, a volume which has long been out of print. In the present book many passages in these translations have been revised and corrected. The editor is under obligations to Mr. F. W. Hodge of the Smithsonian Institution, Mr. W. M. Tipton of Santa Fé, Mr. Charles F. Lummis of Los Angeles, and Mr. Ripley Hitchcock and Mr. F. S. Dellenbaugh of New York, for suggestions and assistance in regard to these improvements in the text.

In February, 1540, the army whose fortunes are recounted in these narratives assembled at Compostela, on the Pacific coast west of Mexico city. When it passed in review before the viceroy Mendoza, who has provided the funds and equipment, the general in command, Francisco Vazquez Coronado, rode at the head of some two hundred and fifty horsemen and seventy Spanish foot soldiers armed with crossbows and harquebuses. Besides these there were three hundred or more native allies, and upward of a thousand negro and Indian servants and followers, to lead the spare horses, drive the pack mules, carry the extra luggage, and herd the droves of oxen and cows, sheep and swine.

The expedition started on February 23d, and a month later, on Easter day, it entered Culiacan, then the northwestern out-post of European civilization, half way up the mainland coast of the Gulf of California. Here Coronado reorganized his force and, toward the end of April, he started northward into the unknown country with a picked force of two hundred men equipped for rapid marching, leaving the rest to follow at the slower pace of the pack trains and the four-footed food supplies. Following the river courses up stream, the advance party was soon deep in the mountains. For two long months they persistently pushed ahead, the inhospitable country steadily growing worse. Eventually other streams showed them the way out on to a level district crossed by well-worn trails which led them toward the "Seven Cities of Cibola." These were the goal of whose fame they had heard from the Franciscan friar, Marcos of Nice, who had viewed them from a distant hilltop two years previously, and who now accompanied the expedition as guide and chaplain.

It was perhaps on July 4th, 1540, that Coronado drew up his force in front of the first of the "Seven Cities," and after a sharp fight forced his way into the stronghold, the stone and adobe-built pueblo of Hawikuh, whose ruins can still be traced on a low hillock a few miles southwest of the village now occupied by the New Mexican Zuñi Indians. Here the Europeans camped for several weeks, seeking rest, refreshment, and news of the land. A small party was sent off toward the northwest, where another group of seven villages was found in the region still occupied by the descendants of the people whom the Spaniards visited, the Moqui tribes of Tusayan. As a result of the information secured here, another party journeyed westward until its progress was stopped by the Grand Cañon of the Colorado, then seen for the first time by Europeans. Explorations were also made toward the east, where the river villages along the Rio Grande were found to be larger and better stocked with food supplies than the settlements at Cibola-Zuñi. Coronado therefore moved his headquarters to the largest of these river towns, Tiguex, near the modern Bernalillo, a short distance north of Albuquerque. Here, as the winter of 1540–41 was setting in, he was rejoined by the main body of the army, which had laboriously followed the trail of its general through the mountains and across the desert.

In one of the river villages Coronado found an Indian slave who said he was a native of Quivira, which he described as a rich and populous place far away in the east. Acting upon this information, with the Indian as a guide, Coronado started on April 23d, 1541, with his whole army to march to Quivira. From Cicuye or Pecos, whose ruins can still be seen by the traveller from the Atchison, Topeka and Santa Fé trains, the guide seems to have led the white men down the Pecos River until they were out of the mountains, and on to the vast plains where they soon met the countless herds of bison or "humpbacked oxen." For five weeks the Europeans plodded onward across what is now known as the "Staked Plains," following a generally easterly direction.

They had probably crossed the upper branches of the Colorado River of Texas and reached the head waters of the Nueces, when Coronado became convinced that his guide was endeavoring to lose him in this limitless expanse of rolling prairie. The food supplies were beginning to run low, and so the army was ordered to return to the villages on the Rio Grande. Some of the natives of the plains, met with on the march, had answered the questions about Quivira by pointing toward the north. That no chance might be left untried, the general selected thirty of the freshest and best-mounted of his men to accompany him in a search in that direction. For forty-two days they followed the compass needle, whose variation probably took them about three degrees west of a true northward course. At last their guides told them that they had reached Quivira, when they were not far from Great Bend on the Arkansas River, whose course they had followed from the neighborhood of Dodge City. It was a village of Wichita Indian tepees.

Coronado spent a month in exploring the surrounding country, moving his camp to a larger village further north, and sending out messengers and reconnoitering parties in all directions. Having assured himself that there was nothing to reward his search, he returned to the main body of his army, the Quiviran guides leading him by a much shorter route, along the line of the famous Santa Fé trail, to the Rio Grande. Every clew which promised anything of value to the Spaniards had been followed to its utmost, without revealing anything which they desired. In the spring of 1542 Coronado started back with his men to Cibola-Zuñi, through the rough mountain passages to the Gulf of California, and so on down to the city of Mexico, where he arrived in the early autumn, "very sad and very weary, completely worn out and shame-faced." He had failed to find any of the things for which he went in search. But he had added to the world as known to Europeans an extent of country bounded on the west by the Colorado River from its mouth to the Grand Cañon, on the east by the boundless prairies, and stretching northward to the upper waters of the Rio Grande and the southern boundary of Nebraska.

George Parker Winship

ITINERARY OF THE CORONADO EXPEDITIONS, 1527–1547

1527

June 17   Narvaez sails from Spain to explore the mainland north of the Gulf of Mexico.

1528

April 15   Narvaez lands in Florida.

Sept. 22   The failure of the Narvaez expedition is assured.

1535

Cortes makes a settlement in Lower California.

Mendoza comes to Mexico as viceroy of New Spain.

1536

April   Cabeza de Vaca and three other survivors of the Narvaez expedition arrive in New Spain.

The Licenciate de la Torre takes the residencia of Nuño de Guzman, who is imprisoned until June 30, 1538.

1537

Franciscan friars labor among the Indian tribes living north of New Spain. Coronado subdues the revolted miners of Amatepeque. The proposed expedition under Dorantes comes to naught.

| April 20 | De Soto receives a grant of the mainland of Florida. |

1538

| Sept. | It is rumored that Coronado has been nominated governor of New Galicia. |

1539

	Pedro de Alvarado returns from Spain to the New World.
March 7	Friar Marcos de Niza, accompanied by the negro Estevan, starts from Culiacan to find the Seven Cities.
April 18	The appointment of Coronado as governor of New Galicia is confirmed.
May	De Soto sails from Habana.
May 9	Friar Marcos enters the wilderness of Arizona.
May 21	Friar Marcos learns of the death of Estevan.
May 25	De Soto lands on the coast of Florida.
July 8	Ulloa sails from Acapulco nearly to the head of the Gulf of California in command of a fleet furnished by Cortes.
August	Friar Marcos returns from the north and certifies to the truth of his report before Mendoza and Coronado.
Sept. 2	
October	The news of Niza's discoveries spreads through New Spain.
Nov.	Mendoza begins to prepare for an expedition to conquer the Seven Cities of Cibola.
	Melchior Diaz is sent to verify the reports of Friar Marcos.
	De Soto finds the remains of the camp of Narvaez at Bahia de los Cavallos.
Nov. 12	Witnesses in Habana describe the effect of the friar's reports.

1540

Jan. 1	Mendoza celebrates the new year at Pasquaro.
Jan. 9	Coronado at Guadalajara.
Feb. 5	Cortes stops at Habana on his way to Spain.
Feb.	The members of the Cibola expedition assemble at Compostela, where the viceroy finds them on his arrival.
Feb. 22	Review of the army on Sunday.
Feb. 23	The army, under the command of Francisco Vazquez Coronado, starts for Cibola (not on February 1).

Feb. 26	Mendoza returns to Compostela, having left the army two days before, and examines witnesses to discover how many citizens of New Spain have accompanied Coronado. He writes a letter to King Charles V, which has been lost.
March	The army is delayed by the cattle in crossing the rivers.
	The death of the army master, Samaniego, at Chiametla.
	Return of Melchior Diaz and Juan de Saldivar from Chichilticalli.
March 3	Beginning of litigation in Spain over the right to explore and conquer the Cibola country.
March 28	Reception to the army at Culiacan, on Easter day.
April	The army is entertained by the citizens of Culiacan.
	Mendoza receives the report of Melchior Diaz' exploration, perhaps at Jacona.
	Coronado writes to Mendoza, giving an account of what has already happened, and of the arrangements which he has made for the rest of the journey. This letter has been lost.
April 17	Mendoza writes to the Emperor Charles V.
April 22	Coronado departs from Culiacan with about seventy-five horsemen and a few footmen.
April	Coronado passes through Petatlan,
May	Cinaloa, Los Cedros, Yaquemi, and other places mentioned by Jaramillo.
May 9	Alarcon sails from Acapulco to cooperate with Coronado. The army starts from Culiacan and marches toward the Corazones or Hearts valley.
May 26	Coronado leaves the valley of Corazones.
June	He proceeds to Chichilticalli, passing Señora or Sonora and Ispa, and thence crosses the Arizona wilderness, fording many rivers.
	The army builds the town of San Hieronimo in Corazones valley.
July 7	Coronado reaches Cibola and captures the first city, the pueblo of Hawikuh, which he calls Granada.
July 11	The Indians retire to their stronghold on Thunder mountain.
July 15	Pedro de Tovar goes to Tusayan or Moki, returning within thirty days.
July 19	Coronado goes to Thunder mountain and returns the same day.
Aug. 3	Coronado writes to Mendoza. He sends Juan Gallego to Mexico, and Melchior Diaz to Corazones with orders for the army. Friar Marcos accompanies them.

Aug. 25 (?)	Lopez de Cardenas starts to find the canyons of Colorado river, and is gone about eighty days.
Aug. 26	Alarcon enters the mouth of Colorado river.
Aug. 29	Hernando de Alvarado goes eastward to Tiguex, on the Rio Grande, and to the buffalo plains.
	Pedro de Alvarado arrives in New Spain.
Sept. 7	Hernando de Alvarado reaches Tiguex.
	Diaz and Gallego reach Corazones about the middle of September, and the army starts for Cibola.
	Coronado visits Tutahaco.
Sept. to January	The army reaches Cibola, and goes thence to Tiguex for its winter quarters. The natives in the Rio Grande pueblos revolt and are subjugated. The Turk tells the Spaniards about Quivira.
October	Diaz starts from Corazones before the end of September, with twenty-five men, and explores the country along the Gulf of California, going beyond Colorado river.
	Diego de Alcaraz is left in command of the town of San Hieronimo.
Nov. 29	Mendoza and Pedro de Alvarado sign an agreement in regard to common exploration and conquests.

1541

Jan. 8	Diaz dies on the return from the mouth of the Colorado, and his companions return to Corazones valley.
March	Alcaraz, during the spring, moves the village of San Hieronimo from Corazones valley to the valley of Suya river.
April 20	Beginning of the Mixton war in New Galicia.
	Coronado writes a letter to the King from Tiguex, which has been lost.
	Tovar and perhaps Gallego return to Mexico.
April 23	Coronado starts with all his force from Tiguex to cross the buffalo plains to Quivira.
May	The army is divided somewhere on the great plains, perhaps on Canadian river. The main body returns to Tiguex, arriving there by the middle or last of June.
	De Soto crosses the Mississippi.
June	Coronado, with thirty horsemen, rides north to Quivira, where he arrives forty-two (?) days later.

June 24	Pedro de Alvarado is killed at Nochistlan, in New Galicia.
August	Coronado spends about twenty-five days in the country of Quivira, leaving "the middle or last of August."
Sept. 28	The Indians in New Galicia attack the town of Guadalajara, but are repulsed.
Oct. 2	Coronado returns from Quivira to Tiguex and writes a letter to the King.
Nov.	Cardenas starts to return to Mexico with some other invalids from the army. He finds the village of Suya in ruins and hastily returns to Tiguex.
December	Coronado falls from his horse and is seriously injured.
	The Mixton peñol is surrendered by the revolted Indians during holiday week.

1542

Coronado and his soldiers determine to return to New Spain. They start in the spring, and reach Mexico probably late in the autumn. The general makes his report to the viceroy, who receives him coldly. Coronado not long after resigns his position as governor of New Galicia and retires to his estates.

April 17	De Soto reaches the mouth of Red river, where he dies, May 21.
June 27	Cabrillo starts on his voyage up the California coast. He dies in January, 1543, and the vessels return to New Spain by April, 1544.
Nov. 1	Villalobos starts across the Pacific. His fleet meets with many misfortunes and losses. The survivors, five years or more later, return to Spain.
Nov. 25	Friar Juan de la Cruz is killed at Tiguex, where he remained when the army departed for New Spain. Friar Luis also remained in the new country, at Cicuye, and Friar Juan de Padilla, at Quivira, where he is killed.
	The companions of Friar Juan de Padilla make their way back to Mexico, arriving before 1552.

1544

Nov. 30	Promulgation of the New Laws for the Indies.
	Sebastian Cabot publishes his map of the New World.

1547

Mendoza, before he leaves New Spain to become viceroy of Peru, answers the charges preferred against him by the officials appointed to investigate his administration.

TRANSLATION OF THE NARRATIVE OF CASTAÑEDA

Account of the expedition to Cibola
which took place in the year 1540, in which all those settlements,
their ceremonies and customes, are described.
Written by Pedro de Castañeda, of Najera.

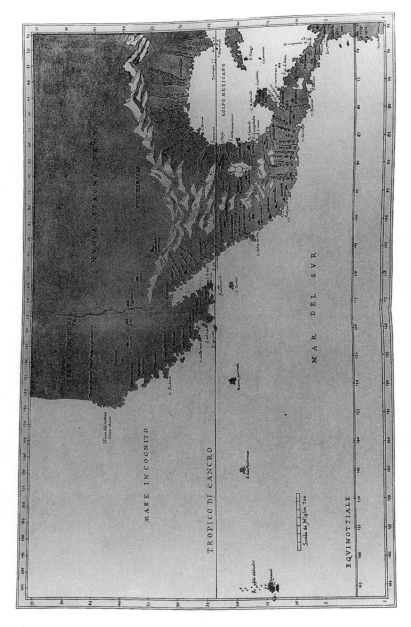

Battista Agnee's New Spain, Sixteenth Century

PREFACE

To me it seems very certain, my very noble lord, that it is a worthy ambition for great men to desire to know and wish to preserve for posterity correct information concerning the things that have happened in distant parts, about which little is known. I do not blame those inquisitive persons who, perchance with good intentions, have many times troubled me not a little with their requests that I clear up for them some doubts which they have had about different things that have been commonly related concerning the events and occurrences that took place during the expedition to Cibola, or the New Land, which the good viceroy—may he be with God in His glory[1]—Don Antonio de Mendoza, ordered and arranged, and on which he sent Francisco Vazquez de Coronado as captain-general.

In truth, they have reason for wishing to know the truth, because most people very often make things of which they have heard, and about which they have perchance no knowledge, appear either greater or less than they are. They make nothing of those things that amount to something, and those that do not they make so remarkable that they appear to be something impossible to believe. This may very well have been caused by the fact that, as that country was not permanently occupied, there has not been anyone who was willing to spend his time in writing about its peculiarities, because all knowledge was lost of that which it was not the pleasure of God—He alone knows the reason—that they should enjoy.

In truth, he who wishes to employ himself thus in writing out the things that happened on the expedition, and the things that were seen in those lands, and the ceremonies and customs of the natives, will have matter enough to test his judgment, and I believe that the result can not fail to be an account which, describing only the truth, will be so remarkable that it will seem incredible.

And besides, I think that the twenty years and more since that expedition took place have been the cause of some stories which are related. For example, some make it an uninhabitable country, others have it bordering on Florida, and still others on Greater India, which does not appear to be a slight difference. They are unable to give any basis upon which to found their statements. There are those who tell about some very peculiar animals, who are contradicted by others who were on the expedition, declaring that there was nothing of the sort seen. Others differ as to the limits of the provinces and even in regard to the ceremonies and customs, attributing what pertains to one people to others. All this has had a large part, my very noble lord, in making me wish to give now, although somewhat late, a short general account for all those who pride themselves on this noble curiosity, and to save myself the time taken up by these solicitations. Things enough will certainly be found here which are hard to believe. All or the most of these were seen with my own eyes, and the rest is from reliable information obtained by inquiry of the natives themselves.

Understanding as I do that this little work would be nothing in itself, lacking authority, unless it were favored and protected by a person whose authority would protect it from the boldness of those who, without reverence, give their murmuring tongues liberty, and knowing as I do how great are the obligations under which I have always been, and am, to your grace, I humbly beg to submit this little work to your protection. May it be received as from a faithful retainer and servant.

It will be divided into three parts, that it may be better understood. The first will tell of the discovery and the armament or army that was made ready, and of the whole journey, with the captains who were there; the second, of the villages and provinces which were found, and their limits, and ceremonies and customs, the animals, fruits, and vegetation, and in what parts of the country these are; the third, of the return of the army and the reasons for abandoning the country, although these were insufficient, because this is the best place there is for discoveries—the marrow of the land in these western parts, as will be seen. And after this has been made plain, some remarkable things which were seen will be described at the end, and the way by which one might more easily return to discover that better land which we did not see, since it would be no small advantage to enter the country through the land which the Marquis of the Valley, Don Fernando Cortes, went in search of under the Western star, and which cost him no small sea armament.

May it please our Lord to so favor me that with my slight knowledge and small abilities I may be able by relating the truth to make my little work pleasing to the learned and wise readers, when it has been accepted by your grace. For my intention is not to gain the fame of a good composer or rhetorician, but I desire to give a faithful account and to do this slight service to your grace, who will, I hope, receive it as from a faithful servant and soldier, who took part in it. Although not in a polished style, I write that which happened—that which I heard, experienced, saw, and did.

I always notice, and it is a fact, that for the most part when we have something valuable in our hands, and deal with it without hindrance, we do not value or prize it as highly as if we understood how much we would miss it after we had lost it, and the longer we continue to have it the less we value it; but after we have lost it and miss the advantages of it, we have a great pain in the heart, and we are all the time imagining and trying to find ways and means by which to get it back again. It seems to me that this has happened to all or most of those who went on the expedition which, in the year of our Savior Jesus Christ 1540, Francisco Vazquez Coronado led in search of the Seven Cities.

Granted that they did not find the riches of which they had been told, they found a place in which to search for them and the beginning of a good country to settle in, so as to go on farther from there. Since they came back from the country which they conquered and abandoned, time has given them a chance to understand the direction and locality in which they were, and the borders of the good country they had in their hands, and their hearts weep for having lost so favorable an opportunity. Just as men see more at the bull fight when they are upon the seats than when they are around in the ring, now when they know and understand the direction and situation in which they were, and see, indeed, that they can not enjoy it nor recover it, now when it is too late they enjoy telling about what they saw, and even of what they realize that they lost, especially those who are now as poor as when they went there. They have never ceased their labors and have spent their time to no advantage. I say this because I have known several of those who came back from there who amuse themselves now by talking of how it would be to go back and proceed to relate all that happened from the beginning.

FIRST PART

Chapter I

*Treats of the way we first came to know about
the Seven Cities, and of how Nuño de Guzman
made an expedition to discover them.*

In the year 1530 Nuño de Guzman, who was President of New Spain,[1] had in his possession an Indian, a native of the valley or valleys of Oxitipar, who was called Tejo by the Spaniards. This Indian said he was the son of a trader who was dead, but that when he was a little boy his father had gone into the back country with fine feathers to trade for ornaments, and that when he came back he brought a large amount of gold and silver, of which there is a good deal in the country. He went with him once or twice, and saw some very large villages, which he compared to Mexico and its environs. He had seen seven very large towns which had streets of silver workers. It took forty days to go there from his country, through a wilderness in which nothing grew, except some very small plants about a span high. The way they went was up through the country between the two seas, following the northern direction. Acting on this information, Nuño de Guzman got together nearly 400 Spaniards and 20,000 friendly Indians of New Spain, and, as he happened to be in Mexico, he crossed Tarasca, which is in the province of Michoacan, so as to get into the region which the Indian said was to be crossed toward the North sea, in this way getting to the country which they were looking for, which was already named "The Seven Cities." He thought, from the forty days of which the Tejo had spoken, that it would be found to be about 200 leagues, and that they would easily be able to cross the country.

Omitting several things that occurred on this journey, as soon as they had reached the province of Culiacan, where his government ended and where the New Kingdom of Galicia is now, they tried to cross the country, but found the difficulties very great, because the mountain chains which are near that sea are so rough that it was impossible, after great labor, to find a passageway in that region. His whole army had to stay in the district of Culiacan for so long on this account that some rich men who were with him, who had possessions in Mexico, changed their minds, and every day became more anxious to return. Besides this, Nuño de Guzman received word that the Marquis of the Valley, Don Fernando Cortes, had come from Spain with his new title,[2] and with great favors and estates, and as Nuño de Guzman had been a great rival of his at the time he was president,[3] and had done much damage to his property and to that of his friends, he feared that Don Fernando Cortes would want to pay him back in the same way, or worse. So he decided to establish the town of Culiacan there and to go back with the other men, without doing anything more.

After his return from this expedition, he founded Xalisco, where the city of Compostela is situated, and Tonala, which is called Guadalaxara,[4] and now this is the New Kingdom of Galicia. The guide they had, who was called Tejo, died about this time, and thus the name of these Seven Cities and the search for them remains until now, since they have not been discovered.[5]

Chapter II

*Of how Francisco Vazquez Coronado
came to be governor, and the second account
which Cabeza de Vaca gave.*

Eight years after Nuño de Guzman made this expedition, he was put in prison by a juez de residencia,[1] named the licentiate Diego de la Torre, who came from Spain with sufficient powers to do this.[2] After the death of the judge, who had also managed the government of that country himself, the good Don Antonio de

Mendoza, viceroy of New Spain, appointed as governor of that province Francisco Vazquez de Coronado, a gentleman from Salamanca, who had married a lady in the city of Mexico, the daughter of Alonso de Estrada, the treasurer and at one time governor of Mexico, and the son, most people said, of His Catholic Majesty Don Ferdinand, and many stated it as certain. As I was saying, at the time Francisco Vazquez was appointed governor, he was traveling through New Spain as an official inspector, and in this way he gained the friendship of many worthy men who afterward went on his expedition with him.

It happened that just at this time three Spaniards, named Cabeza de Vaca, Dorantes, and Castillo Maldonado, and a negro, who had been lost on the expedition which Pamfilo de Narvaez led into Florida, reached Mexico.[3] They came out through Culiacan, having crossed the country from sea to sea, as anyone who wishes may find out for himself by an account which this same Cabeza de Vaca wrote and dedicated to Prince Don Philip, who is now King of Spain and our sovereign.[4] They gave the good Don Antonio de Mendoza an extended account of some powerful villages, four and five stories high, of which they had heard a great deal in the countries they had crossed, and other things very different from what turned out to be the truth. The noble viceroy communicated this to the new governor, who gave up the visits he had in hand, on account of this, and hurried his departure for his government, taking with him the negro who had come [with Cabeza de Vaca] with the three friars of the order of Saint Francis, one of whom was named Friar Marcos of Nice, a regular priest, and another Friar Daniel, a lay brother, and the other Friar Antonio de Santa Maria. When he reached the province of Culiacan he sent the friars just mentioned and the negro, who was named Stephen, off in search of that country, because Friar Marcos offered to go and see it, because he had been in Peru at the time Don Pedro de Alvarado went there overland.

It seems that, after the friars I have mentioned and the negro had started, the negro did not get on well with the friars, because he took the women that were given him and collected turquoises, and got together a stock of everything. Besides, the Indians in those places through which they went got along with the negro better, because they had seen him before. This was the reason he was sent on ahead to open up the way and pacify the Indians, so that when the others came along they had nothing to do except to keep an account of the things for which they were looking.

Chapter III

Of how they killed the negro Stephen at Cibola,
and Friar Marcos returned in flight.

After Stephen had left the friars, he thought he could get all the reputation and honor himself, and that if he should discover those settlements with such famous high houses, alone, he would be considered bold and courageous. So he proceeded with the people who had followed him, and attempted to cross the wilderness which lies between the country he had passed through and Cibola. He was so far ahead of the friars that, when these reached Chichilticalli, which is on the edge of the wilderness, he was already at Cibola, which is 80 leagues beyond. It is 220 leagues from Culiacan to the edge of the wilderness, and 80 across the desert, which makes 300, or perhaps 10 more or less. As I said, Stephen reached Cibola loaded with the large quantity of turquoises they had given him and some beautiful women whom the Indians who followed him and carried his things were taking with them and had given him. These had followed him from all the settlements he had passed, believing that under his protection they could traverse the whole world without any danger.

But as the people in this country were more intelligent that those who followed Stephen, they lodged him in a little hut they had outside their village, and the older men and the governors heard his story and took steps to find out the reason he had come to that country. For three days they made inquiries about him and held a council. The account which the negro gave them of two white men who were following him, sent by a great lord, who knew about the things in the sky, and how these were coming to instruct them in divine matters, made them think that he must be a spy or a guide from some nations who wished to come and conquer them, because it seemed to them unreasonable to say that the people were white in the country from which he came and that he was sent by them, he being black. Besides these other reasons, they thought it was hard of him to ask them for turquoises and women, and so they decided to kill him. They did this, but they did not kill any of those who went with him, although they kept some young fellows and let the others, about 60 persons, return freely to their own country. As these, who were badly scared, were returning in flight, they happened to come upon the friars in the desert 60 leagues from Cibola, and told them the sad news, which frightened them so much that they would not even trust these folks who had been with the negro, but opened the packs they were carrying and gave away everything they had except the holy vestments for saying mass. They returned from here by double marches, prepared for anything, without seeing any more of the country except what the Indians told them.

Chapter IV

*Of how the noble Don Antonio de Mendoza
made an expedition to discover Cibola.*

After Francisco Vazquez Coronado had sent Friar Marcos of Nice and his party on the search already related, he was engaged in Culiacan about some business that related to his government, when he heard an account of a province called Topira,[1] which was to the north of the country of Culiacan. He started to explore this region with several of the conquerors and some friendly Indians, but he did not get very far, because the mountain chains which they had to cross were very difficult. He returned without finding the least signs of a good country, and when he got back, he found the friars who had just arrived, and who told such great things about what the negro Stephen had discovered and what they had heard from the Indians, and islands and other riches, that, without stopping for anything, the governor set off at once for the City of Mexico, taking Friar Marcos with him, to tell the viceroy about it. He made the things seem more important by not talking about them to anyone except his particular friends, under promise of the greatest secrecy, until after he had reached Mexico and seen Don Antonio de Mendoza. Then it began to be announced that they had really found the Seven Cities, for which Nuño de Guzman had searched, had already been discovered, and a beginning was made in collecting an armed force and in bringing together people to go to conquer them.

The noble viceroy arranged with the friars of the order of Saint Francis so that Friar Marcos was made father provincial, as a result of which the pulpits of that order were filled with such accounts of marvels and wonders that more than 300 Spaniards and about 800 natives of New Spain collected in a few days. There were so many men of such high quality among the Spaniards, that such a noble body was never collected in the Indies, nor so many men of quality in such a small body, there being 300 men. Francisco Vazquez Coronado, governor of New Galicia, was captain-general, because he had been the author of it all. The good viceroy Don

Antonio did this because at this time Francisco Vazquez was his closest and most intimate friend, and because he considered him to be wise, skillful, and intelligent, besides being a gentleman. Had he paid more attention and regard to the position in which he was placed and the charge over which he was placed, and less to the estates he left behind in New Spain, or, at least, more to the honor he had and might secure from having such gentlemen under his command, things would not have turned out as they did. When this narrative is ended, it will be seen that he did not know how to keep his position nor the government that he held.

Chapter V

Concerning the captains who went to Cibola.

When the viceroy, Don Antonio de Mendoza, saw what a noble company had come together, and the spirit and good will with which they had all presented themselves, knowing the worth of these men, he would have liked very well to make every one of them captain of an army; but as the whole number was small he could not do as he would have liked, and so he issued the commissions and captaincies as he saw fit, because it seemed to him that if they were appointed by him, as he was so well obeyed and loved, nobody would find fault with his arrangements. After everybody had heard who the general was, he made Don Pedro de Tovar ensign general, a young gentlemen who was the son of Don Fernando de Tovar, the guardian and lord high steward of the Queen Doña Juana, our demented mistress—may she be in glory—and Lope de Samaniego, the governor of the arsenal at Mexico,[1] a gentleman fully equal to the charge, army-master. The captains were Don Tristan de Arellano; Don Pedro de Guevara, the son of Don Juan de Guevara and nephew of the Count of Oñate; Don Garcia Lopez de Cardenas; Don Rodrigo Maldonado, brother-in-law of the Duke of the Infantado; Diego Lopez, alderman of Seville, and Diego Gutierres, for the cavalry.

All the other gentlemen were placed under the flag of the general, as being distinguished persons, and some of them became captains later, and their appointments were confirmed by order of the viceroy and by the general, Francisco Vazquez. To name some of them whom I happen to remember, there were Francisco de Barrionuevo, a gentleman from Granada; Juan de Saldivar, Francisco de Ovando, Juan Gallego, and Melchior Diaz—a captain who had been mayor of

Culiacan, who, although he was not a gentleman, merited the position he held. The other gentlemen, who were prominent, were Don Alonso Manrique de Lara; Don Lope de Urrea, a gentleman from Aragon; Gomez Suarez de Figueroa, Luis Ramirez de Vargas, Juan de Sotomayor, Francisco Gorbalan, the commissioner Riberos, and other gentlemen, men of high quality, whom I do not now recall. The infantry captain was Pablo de Melgosa of Burgos, and of the artillery, Hernando de Alvarado of the mountain district. As I say, since then I have forgotten the names of many gentleman. It would be well if I could name some of them, so that it might be clearly seen what cause I had for saying that they had on this expedition the most brilliant company ever collected in the Indies to go in search of new lands. But they were unfortunate in having a captain who left in New Spain estates and a pretty wife, a noble and excellent lady, which were not the least causes for what was to happen.

Chapter VI

Of how all the companies collected in
Compostela and set off on the journey in good order.

When the viceroy Don Antonio de Mendoza had fixed and arranged everything as we have related, and the companies and captaincies had been arranged, he advanced a part of their salaries from the chest of His Majesty to those in the army who were in greatest need. And as it seemed to him that it would be rather hard for the friendly Indians in the country if the army should start from Mexico, he ordered them to assemble at the city of Compostela, the chief city in the New Kingdom of Galicia, 110 leagues from Mexico, so that they could begin their journey there with everything in good order. There is nothing to tell about what happened on this trip, since they all finally assembled at Compostela by shrove-tide, in the year (fifteen hundred and) forty-one.[1]

After the whole force had left Mexico, he ordered Don Pedro de Alarcon to set sail with two ships that were in the port of La Natividad on the South seacoast, and go to the port of Xalisco to take the baggage which the soldiers were unable to carry,[2] and thence to sail along the coast near the army, because he had understood from the reports that they would have to go through the country near the seacoast, and that we could find the harbors by means of the rivers, and that the ships could always get news of the army, which turned out afterward to be false, and so all this stuff was lost, or, rather, those who owned it lost it, as will be told farther on. After the viceroy had completed all his arrangements, he set off for Compostela, accompanied by many noble and rich men. He kept the New Year of (fifteen hundred and) forty-one at Pasquaro, which is the chief place in the bishopric of Michoacan, and from there he crossed the whole of New Spain, taking much pleasure in enjoying the festivals and great receptions which were given him, till he reached Compostela, which is, as I have said, 110 leagues. There he found the whole company assembled, being well treated and entertained by Christobal de Oñate, who had the whole charge of that government for the time being. He had had the management of it and was in command of all that region when Francisco Vazquez was made governor.[3]

All were very glad when it arrived, and he made an examination of the company and found all those whom we have mentioned. He assigned the captains to their companies, and after this was done, on the next day, after they had all heard mass, captains and soldiers together, the viceroy made them a very eloquent short speech, telling them of the fidelity they owed to their general and showing them clearly the benefits which this expedition might afford, from the conversion of those peoples as well as in the profit of those who should conquer the territory, and the advantage to His Majesty and the claim which they would thus have on his favor and aid at all times. After he had finished, they all, both captains and soldiers, gave him their oaths upon the Gospels in a Missal that they would follow their general on this expedition and would obey him in everything he commanded them, which they faithfully performed, as will be seen. The next day after this was done, the army started off with its colors flying. The viceroy, Don Antonio, went with them for two days, and there he took leave of them, returning to New Spain with his friends.

Chapter VII

Of how the army reached Chiametla,
and the killing of the army-master, and the other things
that happened up to the arrival at Culiacan.

After the viceroy Don Antonio left them, the army continued its march. As each one was obliged to transport his own baggage and all did not know how to fasten the packs, and as the horses started off fat and plump, they had a good deal of difficulty and labor during the first few days, and many left many valuable things, giving them to anyone who wanted them, in order to get rid of carrying them. In the end necessity, which is all powerful, made them skillful, so that one could see many gentlemen become carriers, and anybody who despised this work was not considered a man.

With such labors, which they then thought severe, the army reached Chiametla, where it was obliged to delay several days to procure food. During this time the army-master, Lope de Samaniego, went off with some soldiers to find food, and at one village, a crossbowman having entered it indiscreetly in pursuit of the enemies, they shot him through the eye and it passed through his brain, so that he died on the spot. They also shot five or six of his companions before Diego Lopez, the alderman from Seville, since the commander was dead, collected the men and sent word to the general. He put a guard in the village and over the provisions. There was great confusion in the army when this news became known. He was buried here. Several sorties were made, by which food was obtained and several of the natives taken prisoners. They hanged those who seemed to belong to the district where the army-master was killed.

It seems that when the general, Francisco Vazquez, left Culiacan with Friar Marcos to tell the viceroy, Don Antonio de Mendoza, the news, as already related, he left orders for Captain Melchior Diaz and Juan de Saldivar to start off with a dozen good men from Culiacan and verify what Friar Marcos had seen and heard. They started and went as far as Chichilticalli, which is where the wilderness begins, 220 leagues from Culiacan, and there they turned back, not finding anything important. They reached Chiametla just as the army was ready to leave, and reported to the general. Although they were kept secret, the bad news leaked out, and there were some reports which, although they were exaggerated, did not fail to give an indication of what the facts were.[1] Friar Marcos, noticing that some were feeling disturbed, cleared away these clouds, promising that what they would see should be good, and that he would place the army in a country where their hands would be filled, and in this way he quieted them so that they appeared well satisfied. From there the army marched to Culiacan, making some detours into the country to seize provisions. They were two leagues from the town of Culiacan at Easter vespers, when the inhabitants came out to welcome their governor and begged him not to enter the town till the day after Easter.

Chapter VIII

*Of how the army entered the town of Culiacan
and the reception it received, and other things
which happened before the departure.*

When the day after Easter came, the army started in the morning to go to the town and, as they approached, the inhabitants of the town came out on to an open plain with foot and horse drawn up in ranks as if for a battle, and having its seven bronze pieces of artillery in position, making a show of defending their town. Some of our soldiers were with them. Our army drew up in the same way and began a skirmish with them, and after the artillery on both sides had been fired they were driven back, just as if the town had been taken by force of arms, which was a pleasant demonstration of welcome, except for the artilleryman who lost a hand by a shot, from having ordered them to fire before he had finished drawing out the ramrod.

After the town was taken, the army was well lodged and entertained by the townspeople, who, as they were all very well-to-do people, took all the gentlemen and people of quality who were with the army into their own apartments, although they had lodgings prepared for them all just outside the town. Some of the townspeople were not ill repaid for this hospitality, because all had started with fine clothes and accoutrements, and as they had to carry provisions on their animals after this, they were obliged to leave their fine stuff, so that many preferred giving it to their hosts instead of risking it on the sea by putting it in the ship that had followed the army along the coast to take the extra baggage, as I have said. After they arrived and were being entertained in the town, the general, by order of the viceroy Don Antonio, left Fernandarias de Saabedra, uncle of Hernandarias de Saabedra, count of Castellar, formerly mayor of Seville, as his lieutenant and captain in this town. The army rested here several days, because the inhabitants had gathered a good stock of provisions that year and each one shared his stock very gladly with his guests from our army. They not only had plenty to eat here, but they also had plenty to take away with them, so that when the departure came they started off with more than six hundred loaded animals, besides the friendly Indians and the servants— more than a thousand persons. After a fortnight had passed, the general started ahead with about fifty horsemen and a few foot soldiers and most of the Indian allies, leaving the army, which was to follow him a fortnight later, with Don Tristan de Arellano in command as his lieutenant.

At this time, before his departure, a pretty sort of thing happened to the general, which I will tell for what it is worth. A young soldier named Trugillo (Truxillo) pretended that he had seen a vision while he was bathing in the river. Feigning that he did not want to, he was brought before the general, whom he gave to understand that the devil had told him that if he would kill the general, he could marry his wife, Doña Beatris, and would receive great wealth and other very fine things. Friar Marcos of Nice preached several sermons on this, laying it all to the fact that the devil was jealous of the good which must result from this journey and so wished to break it up in this way. It did not end here, but the friars who were in the expedition wrote to their convents about it, and this was the reason the pulpits of Mexico proclaimed strange rumors about this affair.

The general ordered Truxillo to stay in that town and not to go on the expedition, which was what he was after when he made up that falsehood, judging from what afterward appeared to be the truth. The general started off with the force already described to continue his journey, and the army followed him, as will be related.

Chapter IX

*Of how the army started from Culiacan
and the arrival of the general at Cibola and
of the army at Señora and of other things that happened.*

The general, as has been said, started to continue his journey from the valley of Culiacan somewhat lightly equipped, taking with him the friars, since none of them wished to stay behind with the army. After they had gone three days, a regular friar who could say mass, named Friar Antonio Victoria, broke his leg, and they brought him back from the camp to have it doctored. He stayed with the army after this, which was no slight consolation for all. The general and his force crossed the country without trouble, as they found everything peaceful, because the Indians knew Friar Marcos and some of the others who had been with Melchior Diaz when he went with Juan de Saldibar to investigate.

After the general had crossed the inhabited region and came to Chichilticalli, where the wilderness begins, and saw nothing favorable, he could not help feeling somewhat downhearted, for, although the reports were fine about what was ahead, there was nobody who had seen it except the Indians who went with the negro, and these had already been caught in some lies. Besides all this, he was much affected by seeing that the fame of Chichilticalli was summed up in one tumble-down house without any roof, although it appeared to have been a strong place at some former time when it was inhabited, and it was very plain that it had been built by a civilized and warlike race of strangers who had come from a distance. This building was made of red earth. From here they went on through the wilderness, and in fifteen days came to a river about 8 leagues from Cibola, which they called Red River,[1] because its waters were muddy and reddish. In this river they found mullets like those of Spain. The first Indians from that country were seen here—two of them, who ran away to give the news. During the night following the next day, about 2 leagues from the village, some Indians in a safe place yelled so that, although the men were ready for anything, some were so excited that they put their saddles on hindside before; but these were the new fellows. When the veterans had mounted and ridden round the camp, the Indians fled. None of them could be caught because they knew the country.

The next day they entered the settled country in good order, and when they saw the first village, which was Cibola, such were the curses that some hurled at Friar Marcos that I pray God may protect him from them.

It is a little, crowded village, looking as if it had been crumpled all up together. There are ranch houses in New Spain which make a better appearance at a distance.[2] It is a village of about 200 warriors, is three and four stories high, with the houses small and having only a few rooms, and without a courtyard. One yard serves for each section. The people of the whole district had collected here, for there are seven villages in the province, and some of the others are even larger and stronger than Cibola. These folks waited for the army, drawn up by divisions in front of the village. When they refused to have peace on the terms the interpreters extended to them, but appeared defiant, the Santiago[3] was given, and they were at once put to flight. The Spaniards then attacked the village, which was taken with not a little difficulty, since they held the narrow and crooked entrance. During the attack they knocked the general down with a large stone, and would have killed him but for Don Garcia Lopez de Cardenas and Hernando de Alvarado, who threw themselves above him and drew him away, receiving the blows of the stones, which were not few. But the first fury of the Spaniards could not be resisted, and in less than an hour they entered the village and captured it. They discovered food there, which was the thing they were most in need of.[4] After this the whole province was at peace.

The army which had stayed with Don Tristan de Arellano started to follow their general, all loaded with provisions, with lances on their shoulders, and all on foot, so as to have the horses loaded. With no slight labor from day to day, they reached a province which Cabeza de Vaca had named Hearts (Corazones) because the people here offered him many hearts of animals. He founded a town here and named it San Hieronimo de los Corazones (Saint Jerome of the Hearts). After it had been started, it was seen that it could not be kept up here, and so it was afterward transferred to a valley which had been called Señora[5]. The Spaniards call it Señora, and so it will be known by this name.

From here a force went down the river to the seacoast to find the harbor and to find out about the ships. Don Rodrigo Maldonado, who was captain of those who went in search of the ships, did not find them, but he brought back with him an Indian so large and tall that the best man in the army reached only to his chest. It was said that other Indians were even taller on that coast. After the rains ceased the army went on to where the town of Señora was afterward located, because there were provisions in that region, so that they were able to wait there for orders from the general.

About the middle of the month of October[6] Captains Melchior Diaz and Juan Gallego came from Cibola, Juan Gallego on his way to New Spain and Melchior Diaz to stay in the new town of Hearts, in command of the men who remained there. He was to go along the coast in search of the ships.

Chapter X

Of how the army started from the town of Señora,
leaving it inhabited, and how it reached Cibola, and
of what happened to Captain Melchior Diaz on his expedition
in search of the ships and how he discovered the Tison (Firebrand) river.

After Melchior Diaz and Juan Gallego had arrived in the town of Señora, it was announced that the army was to depart for Cibola; that Melchior Diaz was to remain in charge of that town with 80 men; that Juan Gallego was going to New Spain with messages for the viceroy, and that Friar Marcos was going back with him, because he did not think it was safe for him to stay in Cibola, seeing that his report had turned out to be entirely false, because the kingdoms that he had told about had not been found, nor the populous cities, nor the wealth of gold, nor the precious stones which he had reported, nor the fine clothes, nor other things that had been proclaimed from the pulpits. When this had been announced, those who were to remain were selected and the rest loaded their provisions and set off in good order about the middle of September on the way to Cibola following their general.

Don Tristan de Arellano stayed in this new town with the weakest men, and from this time on there was nothing but mutinies and strife, because after the army had gone Captain Melchior Diaz took 25 of the most efficient men, leaving in his place one Diego de Alcaraz, a man unfitted to have people under his command. He took guides and went toward the north and west in search of the seacoast. After going about 150 leagues, they came to a province of exceedingly tall and strong men—like giants. They are naked and live in large straw cabins built underground like smoke houses, with only the straw roof above ground. They enter these at one end and come out at the other. More than a hundred persons, old and young, sleep in one cabin. When they carry anything, they can take a load of more than three or four hundredweight on their heads. Once when our men wished to fetch a log for the fire, and six men were unable to carry it, one of these Indians is reported to have come and raised it in his arms, put it on his head alone, and carried it very easily.[1] They eat bread cooked in the ashes, as big as the large two-pound loaves of Castile. On account of the great cold, they carry a firebrand (tison) in the hand when they go from one place to another, with which they warm the other hand and the body as well, and in this way they keep shifting it every now and then.[2] On this account the large river which is in that country was called Rio del Tison (Firebrand River). It is a very great river and is more than 2 leagues wide at its mouth; here it is half a league across. Here the captain heard that there had been ships at a point three days down toward the sea. When he reached the place where the ships had been, which was more than 15 leagues up the river from the mouth of the harbor, they found written on a tree: "Alarcon reached this place; there are letters at the foot of this tree." He dug up the letters and learned from that how long Alarcon had waited for news of the army and that he had gone back with the ships to New Spain, because he was unable to proceed farther, since this sea was a bay, which was formed by the Isle of the Marquis,[3] which is called California, and it was explained that California was not an island, but a point of the mainland forming the other side of that gulf.

After he had seen this, the captain turned back to go up the river, without going down to the sea to find a ford by which to cross to the other side, so as to follow the other bank. After they had gone five or six days, it seemed to them as if they could cross on rafts. For this purpose they called together a large number of the natives, who were waiting for a favorable opportunity to make an attack on our men, and when they saw that the strangers wanted to cross, they helped make the rafts with all zeal and diligence, so as to catch them in this way on the water and drown them or else so divide them that they could not help one another. While the rafts were being made, a soldier who had been out around the camp saw a large number of armed men go across to a mountain, where they were waiting till the soldiers should cross the river. He reported this, and an Indian was quietly shut up, in order to find out the truth, and when they tortured him he told all the arrangements that had been made. These were, that when our men were crossing and part of them had got over and part were on the river and part were waiting to cross, those who were on the rafts should drown those they were taking across and the rest of their force should make an attack on both sides of the river. If they had had as much discretion and courage as they had strength and power, the attempt would have succeeded.

When he knew their plan, the captain had the Indian who had confessed the affair killed secretly, and that night he was thrown into the river with a weight, so that the Indians would not suspect that they were found out. The next day they noticed that our men suspected them, and so they made an attack, shooting showers of arrows, but when the horses began to catch up with them and the lances wounded them without mercy and the musketeers likewise made good shots, they had to leave the plain and take to the mountain, until not a man of them was to be seen. The force then came back and crossed all right, the Indian allies and the Spaniards going across on the rafts and the horses swimming alongside the rafts, where we will leave them to continue their journey.

To relate how the army that was on its way to Cibola got on: Everything went along in good shape, since the general had left everything peaceful, because he wished the people in that region to be contented and without fear and willing to do what they were ordered. In a province called Vacapan there was a large quantity of prickly pears, of which the natives make a great deal of preserves.[4] They gave this preserve away freely, and as the men of the army ate much of it, they all fell sick with a headache and fever, so that the natives might have done much harm to the force if they had wished. This lasted regularly twenty-four hours. After this they continued their march until they reached Chichilticalli. The men in the advance guard saw a flock of sheep one day after leaving this place. I myself saw and followed them. They had extremely large bodies and long wool; their horns were very thick and large, and when they run they throw back their heads and put their horns on the ridge of their back. They are used to the rough country, so that we could not catch them and had to leave them.

Three days after we entered the wilderness we found a horn on the bank of a river that flows in the bottom of a very steep, deep gully, which the general had noticed and left there for his army to see, for it was six feet long and as thick at the base as a man's thigh. It seemed to be more like the horn of a goat than of any other animal. It was something worth seeing. The army proceeded and was about a day's march from Cibola when a very cold tornado came up in the afternoon, followed by a great fall of snow, which was a bad combination for the carriers. The army went on till it reached some caves in a rocky ridge, late in the evening. The Indian allies, who were from New Spain, and for the most part from warm countries, were in great danger. They felt the coldness of that day so much that it was hard work the next day taking care of them, for they suffered much pain and had to be carried on the horses, the soldiers walking. After this labor the army reached Cibola, where their general was waiting for them, with their quarters all ready, and here they were reunited, except some captains and men who had gone off to discover other provinces.

Chapter XI

How Don Pedro de Tovar discovered Tusayan or Tutahaco[1] and Don Garcia Lopez de Cardenas saw the Firebrand river and the other things that had happened.

While the things already described were taking place, Cibola being at peace, the General Francisco Vazquez found out from the people of the provinces that lay around it, and got them to tell their friends and neighbors that Christians had come into the country, whose only desire was to be their friends, and to find out about good lands to live in, and for them to come to see the strangers and talk with them. They did this, since they know how to communicate with one another in these regions, and they informed him about a province with seven villages of the same sort as theirs, although somewhat different. They had nothing to do with these people. This province is called Tusayan. It is twenty-five leagues from Cibola. The villages are high and the people are warlike.

The general had sent Don Pedro de Tovar to these villages with seventeen horsemen and three or four foot soldiers. Juan de Padilla, Franciscan friar, who had been a fighting man in his youth, went with them. When they reached the region, they entered the country so quietly that nobody observed them, because there were no settlements or farms between one village and another and the people do not leave the villages except to go to their farms, especially at this time, when they had heard that Cibola had been captured by very fierce people, who travelled on animals which ate people. This information was generally believed by those who had never seen horses, although it was so strange as to cause much wonder. Our men arrived after nightfall and were able to conceal themselves under the edge of the village, where they heard the natives talking in their houses. But in the morning they were discovered and drew up in regular order, while the natives came out to meet them, with bows, and shields, and wooden clubs, drawn up in lines without any confusion. The interpreter was given a chance to speak to them and give them due warning, for they were very intelligent people, but nevertheless they drew lines and insisted that our men should not go across these lines toward their village.[2]

While they were talking, some men acted as if they would cross the lines, and one of the natives lost control of himself and struck a horse a blow on the cheek of the bridle with his club. Friar Juan, fretted by the time that was being wasted in talking with them, said to the captain: "To tell the truth, I do not know why we came here." When the men heard this, they gave the Santiago so suddenly that they ran down many Indians and the others fled to the town in confusion. Some indeed did not have a chance to do this, so quickly did the people in the village come out with presents, asking for peace. The captain ordered his force to collect, and, as the natives did not do any more harm, he and those who were with him found a place to establish their headquarters near the village. They had dismounted here when the natives came peacefully, saying that they had come to give in the submission of the whole province and that they wanted him to be friends with them and to accept the presents which they gave him. This was some cotton cloth, although not much, because they do not make it in that district. They also gave him some dressed skins and corn meal, and pine nuts and corn and birds of the country. Afterward they presented some turquoises, but not many. The people of the whole district came together that day and submitted themselves, and they allowed him to enter their villages freely to visit, buy, sell, and barter with them.

It is governed like Cibola, by an assembly of the oldest men. They have their governors and generals. This was where they obtained the information about a large river, and that several days down the river there were some people with very large bodies.

As Don Pedro de Tovar was not commissioned to go farther, he returned from there and gave this information to the general, who dispatched Don Garcia Lopez de Cardenas with about twelve companions to go to see this river. He was well received when he reached Tusayan and was entertained by the natives, who gave him guides for his journey. They started from here loaded with provisions, for they had to go through a desert country before reaching the inhabited region, which the Indians said was more than twenty days' journey. After they had gone twenty days they came to the banks of the river. It seemed to be more than 3 or 4 leagues in an air line across to the other bank of the stream which flowed between them.

This country was elevated and full of low twisted pines, very cold, and lying open toward the north, so that, this being the warm season, no one could live there on account of the cold. They spent three days on this bank looking for a passage down to the river, which looked from above as if the water was 6 feet across, although the Indians said it was half a league wide. It was impossible to descend, for after these three days Captain Melgosa and one Juan Galeras and another companion, who were the three lightest and most agile men, made an attempt to go down at the least difficult place, and went down until those who were above were unable to keep sight of them. They returned about 4 o'clock in the afternoon, not having succeeded in reaching the bottom on account of the great difficulties which they found, because what seemed to be easy from above was not so, but instead very hard and difficult. They said that they had been down about a third of the way and that the river seemed very large from the place which they reached, and that from what they saw they thought the Indians had given the width correctly. Those who stayed above had estimated that some huge rocks on the sides of the cliffs seemed to be about as tall as a man, but those who went down swore that when they reached these rocks they were bigger than the great tower of Seville. They did not go farther up the river, because they could not get water.

Before this they had to go a league or two inland every day late in the evening in order to find water, and the guides said that if they should go four days farther it would not be possible to go on, because there was no water within three or four days, for when they travel across this region themselves they take with them women loaded with water in gourds, and bury the gourds of water along the way, to use when they return, and besides this, they travel in one day over what it takes us two days to accomplish.

This was the Tison (Firebrand) river, much nearer its source than where Melchior Diaz and his company crossed it. These were the same kind of Indians, judging from what was afterward learned. They came back from this point and the expedition did not have any other result. On the way they saw some water falling over a rock and learned from the guides that some bunches of crystals which were hanging there were salt. They went and gathered a quantity of this and brought it back to Cibola, dividing it among those who were there. They gave the general a written account of what they had seen, because one Pedro de Sotomayor had gone with Don Garcia Lopez as chronicler for the army. The villages of that province remained peaceful, since they were never visited again, nor was any attempt made to find other peoples in that direction.

Chapter XII

Of how people came from Cicuye to Cibola
to see the Christians, and how Hernando de Alvarado
went to see the cows.

While they were making these discoveries, some Indians came to Cibola from a village which was 70 leagues east of this province, called Cicuye. Among them was a captain who was called Bigotes (Whiskers) by our men, because he wore a long mustache. He was a tall, well-built young fellow, with a fine figure. He told the general that they had come in response to the notice which had been given, to offer themselves as friends, and that if we wanted to go through their country they would consider us as their friends. They brought a present of tanned hides and shields and headpieces, which were very gladly received, and the general gave them some glass dishes and a number of pearls and little bells which they prized highly, because these were things they had never seen. They described some cows which, from a picture that one of them had painted on his skin, seemed to be cows, although from the hides this did not seem possible, because the hair was woolly and snarled so that we could not tell what sort of skins they had. The general ordered Hernando de Alvarado to take 20 companions and go with them, and gave him a commission for eighty days, after which he should return to give an account of what he had found.[1]

Captain Alvarado started on this journey and in five days reached a village which was on a rock called Acuco,[2] having a population of about 200 men. These people were robbers, feared by the whole country round about. The village was very strong, because it was up on a rock out of reach, having steep sides in every direction, and so high that it was a very good musket that could throw a ball as high. There was only one entrance by a stairway built by hand, which began at the top of a slope which is around the foot of the rock. There was a broad stairway for about 200 steps, then a stretch of about 100 narrower steps, and at the top they had to go up about three times as high as a man by means of holes in the rock, in which they put the points of their feet, holding on at the same time by their hands. There was a wall of large and small stones at the top, which they could roll down without showing themselves, so that no army could possibly be strong enough to capture the village. On the top they had room to sow and store a large amount of corn, and cisterns to collect snow and water. These people came down to the plain ready to fight, and would not listen to any arguments. They drew lines on the ground and determined to prevent our men from crossing these, but when they saw that they would have to fight they offered to make peace before any harm had been done. They went through their forms of making peace, which is to touch the horses and take their sweat and rub themselves with it, and to make crosses with the fingers of the hands. But to make the most secure peace they put their hands across each other, and they keep this peace inviolably. They made a present of a large number of [turkey] cocks with very big wattles, much bread, tanned deerskins, pine [piñon] nuts, flour [corn meal], and corn.

From here they went to a province called Triguex,[3] three days distant. The people all came out peacefully, seeing that Whiskers was with them. These men are feared throughout all those provinces. Alvarado sent messengers back from here to advise the general to come and winter in this country. The general was not a little relieved to hear that the country was growing better. Five days from here he came to Cicuye,[4] a very strong village four stories high. The people came out from the village with signs of joy to welcome Hernando de Alvarado and their captain, and brought them into the town with drums and pipes something like flutes, of which they have a great many. They made many presents of cloth and turquoises, of which there are quantities in that region. The Spaniards enjoyed themselves here for several days and talked with an Indian slave, a native of the country toward Florida, which is the region Don Fernando de Soto discovered. This fellow said that there were large settlements in the farther part of that country. Hernando de Alvarado took him to guide them to the cows; but he told them so many and such great things about the wealth of gold and silver in his country that they did not care about looking for cows, but returned after they had seen some few, to report the rich news to the general. They called the Indian "Turk," because he looked like one.

Meanwhile the general had sent Don Garcia Lopez de Cardenas to Tiguex with men to get lodgings ready for the army, which had arrived from Señora about this time, before taking them there for the winter; and when Hernando de

Alvarado reached Tiguex, on his way back from Cicuye, he found Don Garcia Lopez de Cardenas there, and so there was no need for him to go farther. As it was necessary that the natives should give the Spaniards lodging places, the people in one village had to abandon it and go to others belonging to their friends, and they took with them nothing but themselves and the clothes they had on. Information was obtained here about many towns up toward the north, and I believe that it would have been much better to follow this direction than that of the Turk, who was the cause of all the misfortunes which followed.

Chapter XIII

Of how the general went toward Tutahaco
with a few men and left the army with Don Tristan,
who took it to Tiguex.

Everything already related had happened when Don Tristan de Arellano reached Cibola from Señora. Soon after he arrived, the general, who had received notice of a province containing eight villages, took 30 of the men who were most fully rested and went to see it, going from there directly to Tiguex with the skilled guides who conducted him. He left orders for Don Tristan de Arellano to proceed to Tiguex by the direct road, after the men had rested twenty days. On this journey, between one day when they left the camping place and midday of the third day, when they saw some snow-covered mountains, toward which they went in search of water, neither the Spaniards nor the horses nor the servants drank anything. They were able to stand it because of the severe cold, although with great difficulty. In eight days they reached Tutahaco,[1] where they learned that there were other towns down the river. These people were peaceful. The villages are terraced, like those at Tiguex, and of the same style.

The general went up the river from here, visiting the whole province, until he reached Tiguex, where he found Hernando de Alvarado and the Turk. He felt no slight joy at such good news, because the Turk said that in his country there was a river in the level country which was 2 leagues wide, in which there were fishes as big as horses, and large numbers of very big canoes, with more than 20 rowers on a side, and that they carried sails, and that their lords sat on the poop under awnings, and on the prow they had a great golden eagle. He said also that the lord of that country took his afternoon nap under a great tree on which were hung a great number of little gold bells, which put him to sleep as they swung in the air. He said also that everyone had their ordinary dishes made of wrought plate, and the jugs and bowls were of gold. He called gold acochis. For the present he was believed, on account of the ease with which he told it and because they showed him metal ornaments and he recognized them and said they were not gold, and he knew gold and silver very well and did not care anything about other metals.

The general sent Hernando de Alvarado back to Cicuye to demand some gold bracelets which this Turk said they had taken from him at the time they captured him. Alvarado went, and was received as a friend at the village, and when he demanded the bracelets they said they knew nothing at all about them, saying the Turk was deceiving him and was lying. Captain Alvarado, seeing that there were no other means, got the Captain Whiskers and the governor to come to his tent, and when they had come he put them in chains. The villagers prepared to fight, and let fly their arrows, denouncing Hernando de Alvarado, and saying that he was a man who had no respect for peace and friendship. Hernando de Alvarado started back to Tiguex, where the general kept them prisoners more than six months. This began the want of confidence in the word of the Spaniards whenever there was talk of peace from this time on, as will be seen by what happened afterward.

Chapter XIV

Of how the army went from Cibola to Tiguex
and what happened to them on the way,
on account of the snow.

We have already said that when the general started from Cibola, he left orders for Don Tristan de Arellano to start twenty days later. He did so as soon as he saw that the men were well rested and provided with food and eager to start off to find their general. He set off with his force toward Tiguex, and the first day they made their camp in the best, largest, and finest village of that (Cibola) province.[1] This is the only village that has houses with seven stories. In this village certain houses are used as fortresses; they are higher than the others and set up above them like towers, and there are embrasures and loopholes in them for defending the roofs of the different stories, because, like the other villages, they do not have streets, and the flat roofs are all of a height and are used in common. The roofs have to be reached first, and these upper houses are the means of defending them. It began to snow on us there, and the force took refuge under the wings of the village, which extend out like balconies, with wooden pillars beneath, because they generally use ladders to go up to those balconies, since they do not have any doors below.

The army continued its march from here after it stopped snowing, and as the season had already advanced into December, during the ten days that the army was delayed, it did not fail to snow during the evenings and nearly every night, so that they had to clear away a large amount of snow when they came to where they wanted to make a camp. The road could not be seen, but the guides managed to find it, as they knew the country. There are junipers and pines all over the country, which they used in making large brushwood fires, the smoke and heat of which melted the snow from 2 to 4 yards all around the fire. It was a dry snow, so that although it fell on the baggage and covered it for half a man's height it did not hurt it. It fell all night long, covering the baggage and the soldiers and their beds, piling up in the air, so that if any one had suddenly come upon the army nothing would have been seen but mountains of snow. The horses stood half buried in it. It kept those who were underneath warm instead of cold. The army passed by the great rock of Acuco, and the natives, who were peaceful, entertained our men well, giving them provisions and birds, although there are not many people here, as I have said. Many of the gentlemen went up to the top to see it, and they had great difficulty in going up the steps in the rock, because they were not used to them, for the natives go up and down so easily that they carry loads and the women carry water, and they do not seem even to touch their hands, although our men had to pass their weapons up from one to another.

From here they went on to Tiguex, where they were well received and taken care of, and the great good news of the Turk gave no little joy and helped lighten their hard labors, although when the army arrived we found the whole country or province in revolt, for reasons which were not slight in themselves, as will be shown, and our men had also burnt a village the day before the army arrived, and returned to the camp.

Chapter XV

Of why Tiguex revolted,
and how they were punished,
without being to blame for it.

It has been related how the general reached Tiguex, where he found Don Garcia Lopez de Cardenas and Hernando de Alvarado, and how he sent the latter back to Cicuye, where he took the Captain Whiskers and the governor of the village, who was an old man, prisoners. The people of Tiguex did not feel well about this seizure.

In addition to this, the general wished to obtain some clothing to divide among his soldiers, and for this purpose he summoned one of the chief Indians of Tiguex, with whom he had already had much intercourse and with whom he was on good terms, who was called Juan Aleman by our men, after a Juan gentleman who lived in Mexico, whom he was said to resemble. The general told him that he must furnish about three hundred or more pieces of cloth, which he needed to give his people. He said that he was not able to do this, but that it pertained to the governors; and that besides this, they would have to consult together and divide it among the villages, and that it was necessary to make the demand of each town separately. The general did this, and ordered certain of the gentlemen who were with him to go and make the demand; and as there were twelve villages, some of them went on one side of the river and some on the other. As they were in very great need, they did not give the natives a chance to consult about it, but when they came to a village they demanded what they had to give, so that they could proceed at once. Thus these people could do nothing except take off their own cloaks and give them to make up the number demanded of them. And some of the soldiers who were in these parties, when the collectors gave them some blankets or cloaks which were not such as they wanted, if they saw any Indian with a better one on, they exchanged with him without more ado, not stopping to find out the rank of the man they were stripping, which caused not a little hard feeling.

Besides what I have just said, one whom I will not name, out of regard for him, left the village where the camp was and went to another village about a league distant, and seeing a pretty woman there he called her husband down to hold his horse by the bridle while he went up; and as the village was entered by the upper story, the Indian supposed he was going to some other part of it. While he was there the Indian heard some slight noise, and then the Spaniard came down, took his horse, and went away. The Indian went up and learned that he had violated, or tried to violate, his wife, and so he came with the important men of the town to complain that a man had violated his wife, and he told how it happened. When the general made all the soldiers and the persons who were with him come together, the Indian did not recognize the man, either because he had changed his clothes or for whatever other reason there may have been, but he said that he could tell the horse, because he had held his bridle, and so he was taken to the stables, and found the horse, and said that the master of the horse must be the man. He denied doing it, seeing that he had not been recognized, and it may be that the Indian was mistaken in the horse; anyway, he went off without getting any satisfaction.[1] The next day one of the Indians, who was guarding the horses of the army, came running in, saying that a companion of his had been killed, and that the Indians of the country were driving off the horses toward their villages. The Spaniards tried to collect the horses again, but many were lost, besides seven of the general's mules.

The next day Don Garcia Lopez de Cardenas went to see the villages and talk with the natives. He found the villages closed by palisades and a great noise inside, the horses being chased as in a bull fight and shot with arrows. They were all ready for fighting. Nothing could be done, because they would not come down on to the plain and the villages are so strong that the Spaniards could not dislodge them. The general then ordered Don Garcia Lopez de Cardenas to go and surround one village with all the rest of the force. This village was the one where the greatest injury had been done and where the affair with the Indian woman occurred. Several captains who had gone on in advance with the general, Juan de Saldivar and Barrionuevo and Diego Lopez and Melgosa, took the Indians so much by surprise that they gained the upper story, with great danger, for they wounded many of our men from within the houses. Our men were on top of the houses in great danger for a day and a night and part of the next day, and they made some good shots with their crossbows and muskets. The horsemen on the plain with many of the Indian allies from New Spain smoked them out from the cellars[2] into which they had broken, so that they begged for peace.

Pablo de Melgosa and Diego Lopez, the alderman from Seville, were left on the roof and answered the Indians with the same signs they were making for peace, which was to make a cross. They then put down their arms and received pardon. They were taken to the tent of Don Garcia, who, according to what he said, did not know about the peace and thought that they had given themselves up of their own accord because they had been conquered. As he had been ordered by the general not to take them alive, but to make an example of them so that the other natives would fear the Spaniards, he ordered 200 stakes to be prepared at once to burn them alive. Nobody told him about the peace that had been granted them, for the soldiers knew as little as he, and those who should have told him about it remained silent, not thinking that it was any of their business. Then when the enemies saw that the Spaniards were binding them and beginning to roast them, about a hundred men who were in the tent began to struggle and defend themselves with what there was there and with the stakes they could seize. Our men who were on foot attacked the tent on all sides, so that there was great confusion around it, and then the horsemen chased those who escaped. As the country was level, not a man of them remained alive, unless it was some who remained hidden in the village and escaped that night to spread throughout the country the news that the strangers did not respect the peace they had made, which afterward proved a great misfortune. After this was over, it began to snow, and they abandoned the village and returned to the camp just as the army came from Cibola.

Chapter XVI

*Of how they besieged Tiguex and took it
and of what happened during the siege.*

As I have already related, it began to snow in that country just after they captured the village, and it snowed so much that for the next two months it was impossible to do anything except to go along the roads to advise them to make peace and tell them that they would be pardoned and might consider themselves safe, to which they replied that they did not trust those who did not know how to keep good faith after they had once given it, and that the Spaniards should remember that they were keeping Whiskers prisoner and that they did not keep their word when they burned those who surrendered in the village. Don Garcia Lopez de Cardenas was one of those who went to give this notice. He started out with about 30 companions and went to the village of Tiguex to talk with Juan Aleman. Although they were hostile, they talked with him and said that if he wished to talk with them he must dismount and they would come out and talk with him about a peace, and that if he would send away the horsemen and make his men keep away, Juan Aleman and another captain would come out of the village and meet him. Everything was done as they required, and then when they approached they said that they had no arms and that he must take his off. Don Garcia Lopez did this in order to give them confidence, on account of his great desire to get them to make peace. When he met them, Juan Aleman approached and embraced him vigorously, while the other two who had come with him drew two mallets[1] which they had hidden behind their backs and gave him two such blows over his helmet that they almost knocked him senseless. Two of the soldiers on horseback had been unwilling to go very far off, even when he ordered them, and so they were near by and rode up so quickly that they rescued him from their hands, although they were unable to catch the enemies because the meeting was so near the village that of the great shower of arrows which were shot at them one arrow hit a horse and went through his nose. The horsemen all rode up together and hurriedly carried off their captain, without being able to harm the enemy, while many of our men were dangerously wounded.

They then withdrew, leaving a number of men to continue the attack. Don Garcia Lopez de Cardenas went on with a part of the force to another village about half a league distant, because almost all the people in this region had collected into these two villages. As they paid no attention to the demands made on them except by shooting arrows from the upper stories with loud yells, and would not hear of peace, he returned to his companions whom he had left to keep up the attack of Tiguex. A large number of those in the village came out and our men rode off slowly, pretending to flee, so that they drew the enemy on to the plain, and then turned on them and caught several of their leaders. The rest collected on the roofs of the village and the captain returned to his camp.

After this affair the general ordered the army to go and surround the village. He set out with his men in good order, one day, with several scaling ladders. When he reached the village, he encamped his force near by, and then began the siege; but as the enemy had had several days to provide themselves with stores, they threw down such quantities of rocks upon our men that many of them were laid out, and they wounded nearly a hundred with arrows, several of whom afterward died on account of the bad treatment by an unskillful surgeon who was with the army. The siege lasted fifty days, during which time several assaults were made. The lack of water was what troubled the Indians most. They dug a very deep well inside the village, but were not able to get water, and while they were making it, it fell in and killed 30 persons. Two hundred of the besieged died in the fights. One day when there was a hard fight, they killed Francisco de Obando, a captain who had been army-master all the time that Don Garcia Lopez de Cardenas was away making the discoveries already described, and also Francisco Pobares, a fine gentleman. Our men were unable to prevent them from carrying Francisco de Obando inside the village, which was regretted not a little, because he was a distinguished person, besides being honored on his own account, affable and much beloved, which was noticeable.

One day, before the capture was completed, they asked to speak to us, and said that, since they knew we would not harm the women and children, they wished to surrender their women and sons, because they were using up their water. It was impossible to persuade them to make peace, as they said that the Spaniards would not keep an agreement made with them. So they gave up about a hundred persons, women and boys, who did not want to leave them. Don Lope de Urrea rode up in front of the town without his helmet and received the boys and girls in his arms, and when all of these had been surrendered, Don Lope begged them to make peace, giving them the strongest promises for their safety. They told him to go away, as they did not wish to trust themselves to people who had no regard for friendship or their own word which they had pledged. As he seemed unwilling to go away, one of them put an arrow in his bow ready to shoot, and threatened to shoot him with it unless he went off, and they warned him to put on his helmet, but he was unwilling to do so, saying that they would not hurt him as long as he stayed there. When the Indian saw that he did not want to go away, he shot and planted his arrow between the fore feet of the horse, and then put another arrow in his bow and repeated that if he did not go away he would really shoot him. Don Lope put on his helmet and slowly rode back to where the horsemen were, without receiving any harm from them. When they saw that he was really in safety, they began to shoot arrows in showers, with loud yells and cries. The general did not want to make an assault that day, in order to see if they could be brought in some way to make peace, which they would not consider.

Fifteen days later they decided to leave the village one night, and did so, taking the women in their midst. They started about the fourth watch, in the very early morning, on the side where the cavalry was. The alarm was given by those in the camp of Don Rodrigo Maldonado. The enemy attacked them and killed one Spaniard and a horse and wounded others, but they were driven back with great slaughter until they came to the river, where the water flowed swiftly and very cold. They threw themselves into this, and as the men had come quickly from the whole camp to assist the calvary, there were few who escaped being killed or wounded. Some men from the camp went across the river next day and found many of them who had been overcome by the great cold. They brought these back, cured them, and made servants of them. This ended that siege, and the town was captured, although there were a few who remained in one part of the town and were captured a few days later.

Two captains, Don Diego de Guevara and Juan de Saldivar, had captured the other large village after a siege. Having started out very early one morning to make an ambuscade in which to catch some warriors who used to come out every morning to try to frighten our camp, the spies, who had been placed where they could see when they were coming, saw the people come out and proceed toward the country. The soldiers left the ambuscade and went to the village and saw the people fleeing. They pursued and killed large numbers of them. At the same time those in the camp were ordered to go over the town, and they plundered it, making prisoners of all the people who were found in it, amounting to about a hundred women and children. This siege ended the last of March, in the year '42.[2] Other things had happened in the meantime, which would have been noticed, but that it would have cut the thread. I have omitted them, but will relate them now, so that it will be possible to understand what follows.

Chapter XVII

Of how messengers reached the army from the valley of Señora
and how Captain Melchior Diaz died on the expedition
to the Firebrand river.

We have already related how Captain Melchior Diaz crossed the Firebrand river on rafts, in order to continue his discoveries farther in that direction. About the time the siege ended, messengers reached the army from the city of San Hieronimo with letters from Diego de Alarcon,[1] who had remained there in the place of Melchior Diaz. These contained the news that Melchior Diaz had died while he was conducting his search, and that the force had returned without finding any of the things they were after. It all happened in this fashion:

After they had crossed the river they continued their search for the coast, which here turned back toward the south, or between south and east, because that arm of the sea enters the land due north and this river, which brings its waters down from the north, flowing toward the south, enters the head of the gulf. Continuing in the direction they had been going, they came to some sand banks of hot ashes which it was impossible to cross without being drowned as in the sea. The ground they were standing on trembled like a sheet of paper, so that it seemed as if there were lakes underneath them. It seemed wonderful and like something infernal, for the ashes to bubble up here in several places. After they had gone away from this place, on account of the danger they seemed to be in and of the lack of water, one day a greyhound belonging to one of the soldiers chased some sheep which they were taking along for food. When the captain noticed this, he threw his lance at the dog while his horse was running, so that it stuck up in the ground, and not being able to stop his horse he went over the lance so that it nailed him through the thighs and the iron came out behind, rupturing his bladder. After this the soldiers turned back with their captain, having to fight every day with the Indians, who had remained hostile. He lived about twenty days, during which they proceeded with great difficulty on account of the necessity of carrying him. They returned in good order without losing a man, until he died, and after that they were relieved of the greatest difficulty. When they reached Señora, Alcaraz dispatched the messengers already referred to, so that the general might know of this and also that some of the soldiers were ill disposed and had caused several mutinies, and that he had sentenced two of them to the gallows, but they had afterward escaped from the prison.

When the general learned this, he sent Don Pedro de Tovar to that city to sift out some of the men. He was accompanied by messengers whom the general sent to Don Antonio de Mendoza the viceroy, with an account of what had occurred and with the good news given by the Turk. When Don Pedro de Tovar arrived there, he found that the natives of that province had killed a soldier with a poisoned arrow, which had made only a very little wound in one hand. Several soldiers went to the place where this happened to see about it, and they were not very well received. Don Pedro de Tovar sent Diego de Alcaraz with a force to seize the chiefs and lords of a village in what they call the Valley of Knaves (de los Vellacos), which is in the hills. After getting there and taking these men prisoners, Diego de Alcaraz decided to let them go in exchange for some thread and cloth and other things which the soldiers needed. Finding themselves free, they renewed the war and attacked them, and as they were strong and had poison, they killed several Spaniards and wounded others so that they died on the way back. They retired toward the town, and if they had not had Indian allies from the country of the Hearts, it would have gone worse with them. They got back to the town, leaving 17 soldiers dead from the poison. They would die in agony from only a small wound, the bodies breaking out with an insupportable pestilential stink. When Don Pedro de Tovar saw the harm done, and as it seemed to them that they could not safely stay in that city, he moved 40 leagues toward Cibola into the valley of Suya, where we will leave them, in order to relate what happened to the general and his army after the siege of Tiguex.

Chapter XVIII

Of how the general managed to leave the country in peace
so as to go in search of Quivira,
where the Turk said there was the most wealth.

During the siege of Tiguex the general decided to go to Cicuye and take the governor with him, in order to give him his liberty and to promise them that he would give Whiskers his liberty and leave him in the village, as soon as he should start for Quivira. He was received peacefully when he reached Cicuye, and entered the village with several soldiers. They received their governor with much joy and gratitude. After looking over the village and speaking with the natives he returned to his army, leaving Cicuye at peace, in the hope of getting back their captain Whiskers.

After the siege was ended, as we have already related, he sent a captain to Chia, a fine village with many people, which had sent to offer its submission. It was 4 leagues distant to the west of the river. They found it peaceful and gave it four bronze cannon, which were in poor condition, to take care of. Six gentlemen also went to Quirix, a province with seven villages. At the first village, which had about a hundred inhabitants, the natives fled, not daring to wait for our men; but they headed them off by a short cut, riding at full speed, and then they returned to their houses in the village in perfect safety, and then told the other villagers about it and reassured them. In this way the entire region was reassured, little by little, by the time the ice in the river was broken up and it became possible to ford the river and so to continue the journey. The twelve villages of Tiguex, however, were not repopulated at all during the time the army was there, in spite of every promise of security that could possibly be given to them.

And when the river, which for almost four months had been frozen over so that they crossed the ice on horseback, had thawed out, orders were given for the start for Quivira, where the Turk said there was some gold and silver, although not so much as in Arche and the Guaes. There were already some in the army who suspected the Turk, because a Spaniard named Servantes,[1] who had charge of him during the siege, solemnly swore that he had seen the Turk talking with the devil in a pitcher of water, and also that while he had him under lock so that no one could speak to him, the Turk had asked him what Christians had been killed by the people at Tiguex. He told him "nobody" and then the Turk answered:

"You lie; five Christians are dead, including a captain." And as Cervantes knew that he told the truth, he confessed it so as to find out who had told him about it, and the Turk said he knew it all by himself and that he did not need to have anyone tell him in order to know it. And it was on account of this that he watched him and saw him speaking to the devil in the pitcher, as I have said.

While all this was going on, preparations were being made to start from Tiguex. At this time people came from Cibola to see the general, and he charged them to take good care of the Spaniards who were coming from Señora with Don Pedro de Tovar. He gave them letters to give to Don Pedro, informing him what he ought to do and how he should go to find the army, and that he would find letters under the crosses which the army would put up along the way. The army left Tiguex on the 5th of May[2] and returned to Cicuye, which, as I have said, is twenty-five marches, which means leagues, from there, taking Whiskers with them. Arrived there, he gave them their captain, who already went about freely with a guard. The village was very glad to see him, and the people were peaceful and offered food. The governor and Whiskers gave the general a young fellow called Xabe, a native of Quivira, who could give them information about the country. This fellow said that there was gold and silver, but not so much of it as the Turk had said. The Turk, however, continued to declare that it was as he had said. He went as a guide, and thus the army started off from here.

Chapter XIX

*Of how they started in search of Quivira
and of what happened on the way.*

The army started from Cicuye, leaving the village at peace and, as it seemed, contented, and under obligations to maintain the friendship because their governor and captain had been restored to them. Proceeding toward the plains, which are all on the other side of the mountains, after four days' journey they came to a river with a large, deep current, which flowed down toward Cicuye, and they named this the Cicuye river.[1] They had to stop here to make a bridge so as to cross it. It was finished in four days, by much diligence and rapid work, and as soon as it was done the whole army and the animals crossed. After ten days more they came to some settlements of people who lived like Arabs and who are called Querechos in that region. They had seen the cows for two days. These folks live in tents made of the tanned skins of the cows. They travel around near the cows, killing them for food.

They did nothing unusual when they saw our army, except to come out of their tents to look at us, after which they came to talk with the advance guard, and asked who we were. The general talked with them, but as they had already talked with the Turk, who was with the advance guard, they agreed with what he had said. That they were very intelligent is evident from the fact that although they conversed by means of signs they made themselves understood so well that there was no need of an interpreter.[2] They said that there was a very large river over toward where the sun came from, and that one could go along this river through an inhabited region for ninety days without a break from settlement to settlement. They said that the first of these settlements was called Haxa, and that the river was more than a league wide and that there were many canoes on it. These folks started off from here next day with a lot of dogs which dragged their possessions.

For two days, during which the army marched in the same direction as that in which they had come from the settlements—that is, between north and east, but more toward the north—they saw other roaming Querechos and such great numbers of cows that it already seemed something incredible. These people gave a great deal of information about settlements, all toward the east from where we were. Here Don Garcia broke his arm and a Spaniard got lost who went off hunting so far that he was unable to return to the camp, because the country is very level. The Turk said it was one or two days to Haya (Haxa). The general sent Captain Diego Lopez with ten companions lightly equipped and a guide to go at full speed toward the sunrise for two days and discover Haxa, and then return to meet the army, which set out in the same direction next day. They came across so many animals that those who were on the advance guard killed a large number of bulls. As these fled they trampled one another in their haste until they came to a ravine. So many of the animals fell into this that they filled it up, and the rest went across on top of them. The men who were chasing them on horseback fell in among the animals without noticing where they were going. Three of the horses that fell in among the cows, all saddled and bridled, were lost sight of completely.

As it seemed to the general that Diego Lopez ought to be on his way back, he sent six of his companions to follow up the banks of the little river, and as many more down the banks, to look for traces of the horses at the trails to and from the river. It was impossible to find tracks in this country, because the grass straightened up again as soon as it was trodden down. They were found by some Indians from the army who had gone to look for fruit. These got track of them a good league off, and soon came up with them. They followed the river down to the camp, and told the general that in the 20 leagues they had been over they had seen nothing but cows and the sky. There was another native of Quivira with the army, a painted

Indian named Ysopete. This Indian had always declared that the Turk was lying, and on account of this the army paid no attention to him, and even now, although he said that the Querechos had consulted with him, Ysopete was not believed.

The general sent Don Rodrigo Maldonado, with his company, forward from here. He traveled four days and reached a large ravine like those of Colima,[3] in the bottom of which he found a large settlement of people. Cabeza de Vaca and Dorantes had passed through this place, so that they presented Don Rodrigo with a pile of tanned skins and other things, and a tent as big as a house, which he directed them to keep until the army came up. He sent some of his companions to guide the army to that place, so that they should not get lost, although he had been making piles of stones and cow dung for the army to follow. This was the way in which the army was guided by the advance guard.

When the general came up with the army and saw the great quantity of skins, he thought he would divide them among the men, and placed guards so that they could look at them. But when the men arrived and saw that the general was sending some of his companions with orders for the guards to give them some of the skins, and that these were going to select the best, they were angry because they were not going to be divided evenly, and made a rush, and in less than a quarter of an hour nothing was left but the empty ground.

The natives who happened to see this also took a hand in it. The women and some others were left crying, because they thought that the strangers were not going to take anything, but would bless them as Cabeza de Vaca and Dorantes had done when they passed through here. They found an Indian girl here who was as white as a Castilian lady, except that she had her chin painted like a Moorish woman. In general they all paint themselves in this way here, and they decorate their eyes.

Chapter XX

*Of how great stones fell in the camp,
and how they discovered another ravine,
where the army was divided into two parts.*

While the army was resting in this ravine, as we have related, a tempest came up one afternoon with a very high wind and hail, and in a very short space of time a great quantity of hailstones, as big as bowls, or bigger, fell as thick as raindrops, so that in places they covered the ground two or three spans or more deep. And one hit the horse—or I should say, there was not a horse that did not break away, except two or three which the negroes protected by holding large sea nets over them, with the helmets and shields which all the rest wore; and some of them dashed up on to the sides of the ravine so that they got them down with great difficulty. If this had struck them while they were upon the plain, the army would have been in great danger of being left without its horses, as there were many which they were not able to cover. The hail broke many tents, and battered many helmets, and wounded many of the horses, and broke all the crockery of the army, and the gourds, which was no small loss, because they do not have any crockery in this region. They do not make gourds, nor sow corn, nor eat bread, but instead raw meat—or only half cooked—and fruit.

From here the general sent out to explore the country, and they found another settlement four days from there.[1] ... The country was well inhabited, and they had plenty of kidney beans and prunes like those of Castile, and tall vineyards. These village settlements extended for three days. This was called Cona. Some Teyas,[2] as these people are called, went with the army from here and traveled as far as the end of the other settlements with their packs of dogs and women and children, and then they gave them guides to proceed to a large ravine where the army was. They did not let these guides speak with the Turk and did not receive the same statements from these as they had from the others. These said that Quivira was toward the north, and that we would not find any good road thither. After this they began to believe Ysopete. The ravine which the army had now reached was a league wide from one side to the other, with a little bit of a river at the bottom, and there were many groves of mulberry trees near it, and rosebushes with the same sort of fruit that they have in France. They made verjuice from the unripe grapes at this ravine, although there were ripe ones. There were walnuts and the same kind of fowls as in New Spain, and large quantities of prunes like those of Castile. During this journey a Teya was seen to shoot a bull right through both shoulders with an arrow, which would be a good shot for a musket. These people are very intelligent; the women are well made and modest. They cover their whole body. They wear shoes and buskins made of tanned skin. The women wear cloaks over their small under petticoats, with sleeves gathered up at the shoulders, all of skin, and some wore something like little sanbenitos[3] with a fringe, which reached half-way down the thigh over the petticoat.

The army rested several days in this ravine and explored the country. Up to this point they had made thirty-seven days' marches, traveling 6 or 7 leagues a day. It had been the duty of one man to measure and count his steps. They found that it was 250 leagues to the settlements.[4] When the general Francisco Vazquez realized this, and saw that they had been deceived by the Turk heretofore, and as the provisions were giving out and there was no country around here where they could procure more, he called the captains and ensigns together to decide on what they thought ought to be done. They all agreed that the general should go in search of Quivira with thirty horsemen and half a dozen foot-soldiers, and that Don Tristan de Arellano should go back to Tiguex with all the army. When the men in the army learned of this decision, they begged their general not to leave them to conduct the further search, but declared that they all wanted to die with him and did not want to go back. This did not do any good, although the general agreed to send messengers to them within eight days saying whether it was best for them to follow him or not, and with this he set off with the guides he had and with Ysopete. The Turk was taken along in chains.

Chapter XXI

*Of how the army returned to Tiguex
and the general reached Quivira.*

The general started from the ravine with the guides that the Teyas had given him. He appointed the alderman Diego Lopez his army-master, and took with him the men who seemed to him to be most efficient, and the best horses. The army still had some hope that the general would send for them, and sent two horsemen, lightly equipped and riding post, to repeat their petition.

The general arrived—I mean, the guides ran away during the first few days and Diego Lopez had to return to the army for guides, bringing orders for the army to return to Tiguex to find food and wait there for the general. The Teyas, as before, willingly furnished him with new guides. The army waited for its messengers and spent a fortnight here, preparing jerked beef to take with them. It was estimated that during this fortnight they killed 500 bulls. The number of these that were there without any cows was something incredible. Many fellows were lost at this time who went out hunting and did not get back to the army for two or three days, wandering about the country as if they were crazy, in one direction or another, not knowing how to get back where they started from, although this ravine extended in either direction so that they could find it. Every night they took account of who was missing, fired guns and blew trumpets and beat drums and built great fires, but yet some of them went off so far and wandered about so much that all this did not give them any help, although it helped others. The only way was to go back where they had killed an animal and start from there in one direction and another until they struck the ravine or fell in with somebody who could put them on the right road. It is worth noting that the country there is so level that at midday, after one has wandered about in one direction and another in pursuit of game, the only thing to do is to stay near the game quietly until sunset, so as to see where it goes down, and even then they have to be men who are practiced to do it. Those who are not, had to trust themselves to others.

The general followed his guides until he reached Quivira, which took forty-eight days' marching, on account of the great detour they had made toward Florida. He was received peacefully on account of the guides whom he had. They asked the Turk why he had lied and had guided them so far out of their way. He said that his country was in that direction and that, besides this, the people at Cicuye had asked him to lead them off on to the plains and lose them, so that the horses would die when their provisions gave out, and they would be so weak if they ever returned that they would be killed without any trouble, and thus they could take revenge for what had been done to them. This was the reason why he had led them astray, supposing that they did not know how to hunt or to live without corn, while as for the gold, he did not know where there was any of it. He said this like one who had given up hope and who found that he was being persecuted, since they had begun to believe Ysopete, who had guided them better than he had, and fearing lest those who were there might give some advice by which some harm would come to him. They garroted him, which pleased Ysopete very much, because he had always said that Ysopete was a rascal and that he did not know what he was talking about and had always hindered his talking with anybody. Neither gold nor silver nor any trace of either was found among these people. Their lord wore a copper plate on his neck and prized it highly.

The messengers whom the army had sent to the general returned, as I said, and then, as they brought no news except what the alderman had delivered, the army left the ravine and returned to the Teyas, where they took guides who led them back by a more direct road. They readily furnished these, because these people are always roaming over this country in pursuit of the animals and so know it thoroughly. They keep their road in this way: In the morning they notice where the sun rises and observe the direction they are going to take, and then shoot an arrow in this direction. Before reaching this they shoot another over it, and in this way they go all day toward the water where they are to end the day. In this way they covered in 25 days what had taken them 37 days going, besides stopping to hunt cows on the way. They found many salt lakes on this road, and there was a great quantity of salt. There were thick pieces of it on top of the water bigger than tables, as thick as four or five fingers. Two or three spans down under water there was salt which tasted better than that in the floating pieces, because this was rather bitter. It was crystalline. All over these plains there were large numbers of animals like squirrels and a great number of their holes.

On its return the army reached the Cicuye river more than 30 leagues below there—I mean below the bridge they had made when they crossed it, and they followed it up to that place. In general, its banks are covered with a sort of rose bushes, the fruit of which tastes like muscatel grapes. They grow on little twigs about as high up as a man. It has the parsley leaf. There were unripe grapes and currants (?) and wild marjoram. The guides said this river joined that of Tiguex more than 20 days from here, and that its course turned toward the east. It is believed that it flows into the mighty river of the Holy Spirit (Espiritu Santo), which the men with Don Hernando de Soto discovered in Florida. A painted Indian woman ran away from Juan de Saldibar and hid in the ravines about this time, because she recognized the country of Tiguex where she had been a slave. She fell into the hands of some Spaniards who had entered the country from Florida to explore it in this direction. After I got back to New Spain I heard them say that the Indian told them that she had run away from other men like them nine days, and that she gave the names of some captains; from which we ought to believe that we were not far from the region they discovered, although they said they were more than 200 leagues inland. I believe the land at that point is more than 600 leagues across from sea to sea.

As I said, the army followed the river up as far as Cicuye, which it found ready for war and unwilling to make any advances toward peace or to give any food to the army. From there they went on to Tiguex where several villages had been reinhabited, but the people were afraid and left them again.

Chapter XXII

*Of how the general returned from Quivira
and of other expeditions toward the North.*

After Don Tristan de Arellano reached Tiguex, about the middle of July, in the year '42,[1] he had provisions collected for the coming winter. Captain Francisco de Barrionuevo was sent up the river toward the north with several men. He saw two provinces, one of which was called Hemes and had seven villages, and the other Yuqueyunque.[2] The other inhabitants of Hemes came out peaceably and furnished provisions. At Yuqueyunque the whole nation left two very fine villages which they had on either side of the river entirely vacant, and went into the mountains, where they had four very strong villages in a rough country, where it was impossible for horses to go. In the two villages there was a great deal of food and some very beautiful glazed earthenware with many figures and different shapes. Here they also found many bowls full of a carefully selected shining metal with which they glazed the earthenware. This shows that mines of silver would be found in that country if they should hunt for them.

There was a large and powerful river, I mean village, which was called Braba, 20 leagues farther up the river, which our men called Valladolid.[3] The river flowed through the middle of it. The natives crossed it by wooden bridges, made of very long, large, squared pines. At this village they saw the largest and finest hot rooms or estufas that there were in the entire country, for they had a dozen pillars, each one of which was twice as large around as one could reach and twice as tall as a man. Hernando de Alvarado visited this village when he discovered Cicuye. The country is very high and very cold. The river is deep and very swift, without any ford. Captain Barrionuevo returned from here, leaving the province at peace.

Another captain went down the river in search of the settlements which the people at Tutahaco had said were several days distant from there. This captain went down 80 leagues and found four large villages which he left at peace. He proceeded until he found that the river sank into the earth, like the Guadiana in Estremadura.[4] He did not go on to where the Indians said that it came out much larger, because his commission did not extend for more than 80 leagues march. After this captain got back, as the time had arrived which the captain had set for his return from Quivira, and as he had not come back, Don Tristan selected 40 companions and, leaving the army to Francisco de Barrionuevo, he started with them in search of the general.

When he reached Cicuye the people came out of the village to fight, which detained him there four days, while he punished them, which he did by firing some volleys into the village. These killed several men, so that they did not come out against the army, since two of their principal men had been killed on the first day. Just then word was brought that the general was coming, and so Don Tristan had to stay there on this account also, to keep the road open. Everybody welcomed the general on his arrival, with great joy. The Indian Xabe, who was the young fellow who had been given to the general at Cicuye when he started off in search of Quivira, was with Don Tristan de Arellano and when he learned that the general was coming he acted as if he was greatly pleased, and said, "Now when the general comes, you will see that there is gold and silver in Quivira, although not so much as the Turk said." When the general arrived, and Xabe saw that they had not found anything, he was sad and silent, and kept declaring that there was some. He made many believe that it was so, because the general had not dared to enter into the country on account of its being thickly settled and his force not very strong, and that he had returned to lead his army there after the rains, because it had begun to rain there already, as it was early in August when he left. It took him forty days to return, traveling lightly equipped. The Turk had said when they left Tiguex that they ought not to load the horses with too much provisions, which would tire them so that they could not afterward carry the gold and silver, from which it is very evident that he was deceiving them.

The general reached Cicuye with his force and at once set off for Tiguex, leaving the village more quiet, for they had met him peaceably and had talked with him. When he reached Tiguex, he made his plans to pass the winter there, so as to return with the whole army, because it was said that he brought information regarding large settlements and very large rivers, and that the country was very much like that of Spain in the fruits and vegetation and seasons. They were not ready to believe that there was no gold there, but instead had suspicions that there was some farther back in the country, because, although this was denied, they knew what the thing was and had a name for it among themselves—acochis. With this we end this first part, and now we will give an account of the provinces.

SECOND PART

*Which Treats of the High Villages and Provinces
and of their Habits and Customs,
as Collected by Pedro de Castañeda, Native of the City of Najara.*

Laus Deo

It does not seem to me that the reader will be satisfied with having seen and understood what I have already related about the expedition, although that has made it easy to see the difference between the report which told about vast treasures, and the places where nothing like this was either found or known. It is to be noted that in place of settlements great deserts were found, and instead of populous cities villages of 200 inhabitants and only 800 or 1,000 people in the largest. I do not know whether this will furnish grounds for pondering and considering the uncertainty of this life. To please these, I wish to give a detailed account of all the inhabited region seen and discovered by this expedition, and some of their ceremonies and habits, in accordance with what we came to know about them and the limits within which each province falls, so that hereafter it may be possible to understand in what direction Florida lies and in what direction Greater India; and this land of New Spain is part of the mainland with Peru, and with Greater India or China as well, there not being any strait between to separate them. On the other hand, the country is so wide that there is room for these vast deserts which lie between the two seas, for the coast of the North sea beyond Florida stretches toward the Bacallos[1] and then turns toward Norway, while that of the

139

South sea turns toward the west, making another bend down toward the south almost like a bow and stretches away toward India, leaving room for the lands that border on the mountains on both sides to stretch out in such a way as to have between them these great plains which are full of cattle and many other animals of different sorts, since they are not inhabited, as I will relate farther on. There is every sort of game and fowl there, but no snakes, for they are free from these. I will leave the account of the return of the army to New Spain until I have shown what slight occasion there was for this. We will begin our account with the city of Culiacan, and point out the differences between the one country and the other, on account of which one ought to be settled by Spaniards and the other not. It should be the reverse, however, with Christians, since there are intelligent men in one, and in the other wild animals and worse than beasts.

Chapter I

Of the province of Culiacan
and of its habits and customs.

Culiacan is the last place in the New Kingdom of Galicia, and was the first settlement made by Nuño de Guzman when he conquered this kingdom. It is 210 leagues west of Mexico. In this province there are three chief languages, besides other related dialects. The first is that of the Tahus, who are the best and most intelligent race. They are now the most settled and have received the most light from the faith. They worship idols and make presents to the devil of their goods and riches, consisting of cloth and turquoises. They do not eat human flesh nor sacrifice it. They are accustomed to keep very large snakes, which they venerate. Among them there are men dressed like women who marry other men and serve as their wives. At a great festival they consecrate the women who wish to live unmarried, with much singing and dancing, at which all the chiefs of the locality gather and dance naked, and after all have danced with her they put her in a hut that has been decorated for this event and the chiefs adorn her with clothes and bracelets of fine turquoises, and then the chiefs go in one by one to lie with her, and all the others who wish, follow them. From this time on these women can not refuse anyone who pays them a certain amount agreed on for this. Even if they take husbands, this does not exempt them from obliging anyone who pays them. The greatest festivals are on market days. The custom is for the husbands to buy the women whom they marry, of their fathers and relatives at a high price, and then to take them to a chief, who is considered to be a priest, to deflower them and see if she is a virgin; and if she is not, they have to return the whole price, and he can keep her for his wife or not, or let her be consecrated, as he chooses. At these times they all get drunk.

The second language is that of the Pacaxes, the people who live in the country between the plains and the mountains. These people are more barbarous. Some of them who live near the mountains eat human flesh. They are great sodomites, and have many wives, even when these are sisters. They worship painted and sculptured stones, and are much given to witchcraft and sorcery.

The third language is that of the Acaxes, who are in possession of a large part of the hilly country and all of the mountains. They go hunting for men just as they hunt animals. They all eat human flesh, and he who has the most human bones and skulls hung up around his house is most feared and respected. They live in settlements and in very rough country, avoiding the plains. In passing from one settlement to another, there is always a ravine in the way which they can not cross, although they can talk together across it. At the slightest call 500 men collect, and on any pretext kill and eat one another. Thus it has been very hard to subdue these people, on account of the roughness of the country, which is very great.

Many rich silver mines have been found in this country. They do not run deep, but soon give out. The gulf of the sea begins on the coast of this province, entering the land 250 leagues toward the north and ending at the mouth of the Firebrand (Tizon) river. This country forms its eastern limit, and California the western. From what I have been told by men who had navigated it, it is 30 leagues across from point to point, because they lose sight of this country when they see the other. They say the gulf is over 150 leagues broad (or deep), from shore to shore. The coast makes a turn toward the south at the Firebrand river, bending down to California, which turns toward the west, forming that peninsula which was formerly held to be an island, because it was a low sandy country. It is inhabited by brutish, bestial, naked people who eat their own offal. The men and women couple like animals, the female openly getting down on all fours.

Chapter II

Of the province of Petlatlan and
all the inhabited country as far as Chichilticalli.

Petlatlan is a settlement of houses covered with a sort of mats made of *plants*. These are collected into villages, extending along a river from the mountains to the sea. The people are of the same race and habits as the Culuacanian Tahues. There is much sodomy among them. In the mountain district there is a large population and more settlements. These people have a somewhat different language from the Tahues, although they understand each other. It is called Petlatlan because the houses are made of petates or palm-leaf mats.[1] Houses of this sort are found for more than 240 leagues in this region, to the beginning of the Cibola wilderness. The nature of the country changes here very greatly, because from this point on there are no trees except the pine, nor are there any fruits except a few tunas,[2] mesquites,[3] and pitahayas.[4]

Petlatlan is 20 leagues from Culiacan, and it is 130 leagues from here to the valley of Señora. There are many rivers between the two, with settlements of the same sort of people—for example, Sinoloa, Boyomo, Teocomo, Yaquimi, and other smaller ones. There is also the Corazones or Hearts, which is in our possession, down the valley of Señora.[5]

Senora is a river and valley thickly settled by able-bodied people. The women wear petticoats of tanned deerskin, and little san benitos reaching half way down the body. The chiefs of the villages go up on some little heights they have made for this purpose, like public criers, and there make proclamations for the space of an hour, regulating those things they have to attend to. They have some little huts for shrines, all over the outside of which they stick many arrows, like a hedgehog. They do this when they are eager for war. All about this province toward the mountains there is a large population in separate little provinces containing ten or twelve villages. Seven or eight of them, of which I know the names, are Comupatrico, Mochilagua, Arispa, and the Little Valley. There are others which we did not see.

It is 40 leagues from Señora to the valley of Suya. The town of Saint Jerome (San Hieronimo) was established in this valley, where there was a rebellion later, and part of the people who had settled there were killed, as will be seen in the third part. There are many villages in the neighborhood of this valley. The people are the same as those in Señora and have the same dress and language, habits, and customs, like all the rest as far as the desert of Chichilticalli. The women paint their chins and eyes like the Moorish women of Barbary. They are great sodomites. They drink wine made of the pitahaya, which is the fruit of a great thistle which opens like the pomegranate. The wine makes them stupid. They make a great quantity of preserves from the tuna; they preserve it in a large amount of its sap without other honey. They make bread of the mesquite, like cheese, which keeps good for a whole year.[6] There are native melons in this country so large that a person can carry only one of them. They cut these into slices and dry them in the sun. They are good to eat, and taste like figs, and are better than dried meat; they are very good and sweet, keeping for a whole year when prepared in this way.[7]

In this country there were also tame eagles, which the chiefs esteemed to be something fine.[8] No fowls of any sort were seen in any of these villages except in this valley of Suya, where fowls like those of Castile were found. Nobody could find out how they came to be so far inland, the people being all at war with one another. Between Suya and Chichilticalli there are many sheep and mountain goats with very large bodies and horns. Some Spaniards declare that they have seen flocks of more than a hundred together, which ran so fast that they disappeared very quickly.

At Chichilticalli the country changes its character again and the spiky vegetation ceases. The reason is that the gulf reaches as far up as this place, and the mountain chain changes its direction at the same time that the coast does. Here they had to cross and pass through the mountains in order to get into the level country.

Chapter III

Of Chichilticalli and the desert, of Cibola, its customs and habits, and of other things.

Chichilticalli is so called because the friars found a house at this place which was formerly inhabited by people who separated from Cibola. It was made of colored or reddish earth.[1] The house was large and appeared to have been a fortress. It must have been destroyed by the people of the district, who are the most barbarous people that have yet been seen. They live in separate cabins and not in settlements. They live by hunting. The rest of the country is all wilderness, covered with pine forests. There are great quantities of the pine nuts. The pines are two or three times as high as a man before they send out branches. There is a sort of oak with sweet acorns, of which they make cakes like sugar plums with dried coriander seeds. It is very sweet, like sugar. Watercress grows in many springs, and there are rosebushes, and pennyroyal, and wild marjoram.

There are barbels and picones, like those of Spain, in the rivers of this wilderness. Gray lions and leopards were seen.[2] The country rises continually from the beginning of the wilderness until Cibola is reached, which is 85 leagues, going north. From Culiacan to the edge of the wilderness the route had kept the north on the left hand.

Cibola[3] is seven villages. The largest is called Maçaque.[4] The houses are ordinarily three or four stories high, but in Maçaque there are houses with four and seven stories. These people are very intelligent. They cover their privy parts and all the immodest parts with cloths made like a sort of table napkin, with fringed edges and a tassel at each corner, which they tie over the hips. They wear long robes of feathers and of the skins of hares and cotton blankets.[5] The women wear blankets, which they tie or knot over the left shoulder, leaving the right arm out. These serve to cover the body. They wear a neat well-shaped outer garment of skin. They gather their hair over the two ears, making a frame which looks like an old-fashioned headdress.[6]

This country is in a valley between mountains in the form of isolated cliffs. They cultivate the corn, which does not grow very high, in patches. There are three or four large fat ears having each eight hundred grains on every stalk growing upward from the ground, something not seen before in these parts. There are large numbers of bears in this province, and lions, wild-cats, deer, and otter. There are very fine turquoises, although not so many as was reported. They collect the pine nuts each year, and store them up in advance. A man does not have more than one wife. There are estufas or hot rooms in the villages, which are the courtyards or places where they gather for consultation. They do not have chiefs as in New Spain, but are ruled by a council of the oldest men. They have priests who preach to them, whom they call papas.[7] These are the elders. They go up on the highest roof of the village and preach to the village from there, like public criers, in the morning while the sun is rising, the whole village being silent and sitting in the galleries to listen.[8] They tell them how they are to live, and I believe that they give certain commandments for them to keep, for there is no drunkenness among them nor sodomy nor sacrifices, neither do they eat human flesh, nor steal, but they are usually at work. The estufas belong to the whole village. It is a sacrilege for the women to go into the estufas to sleep.[9] They make the cross as a sign of peace. They burn their dead, and throw the implements used in their work into the fire with the bodies.[10]

It is 20 leagues to Tusayan, going northwest. This is a province with seven villages, of the same sort, dress, habits, and ceremonies as at Cibola. There may be as many as 3,000 or 4,000 men in the fourteen villages of these two provinces. It is 40 leagues or more to Tiguex, the road trending toward the north. The rock of Acuco, which we described in the first part, is between these.

Chapter IV

*Of how they live at Tiguex,
and of the province of Tiguex and its neighborhood.*

Tiguex is a province with twelve villages on the banks of a large, swift river; some villages on one side and some on the other. It is a spacious valley two leagues wide, and a very high, rough, snow-covered mountain chain lies east of it. There are seven villages in the ridges at the foot of this—four on the plain and three situated on the skirts of the mountain.

There are seven villages 7 leagues to the north [*i.e.* of Tiguex], at Quirix, and the seven villages of the province of Hemes are 40 leagues northeast. It is four leagues north or east to Acha.[1] Tutahaco, a province with eight villages, is toward the southeast. In general, these villages all have the same habits and customs, although some have some things in particular which the others have not.[2] They are governed by the opinions of the elders. They all work together to build the villages, the women being engaged in making the mixture and the walls, while the men bring the wood and put it in place.[3] They have no lime, but they make a mixture of ashes, coals, and dirt which is almost as good as mortar, for when the house is to have four stories, they do not make the walls more than half a yard thick. They gather a great pile of twigs of thyme and sedge grass and set it afire, and when it is half coals and ashes they throw a quantity of dirt and water on it and mix it all together. They make round balls of this, which they use instead of stones after they are dry, fixing them with the same mixture, which comes to be like a stiff clay. Before they are married the young men serve the whole village in general, and fetch the wood that is needed for use, putting it in a pile in the courtyard of the villages, from which the women take it to carry to their houses.

The young men live in the estufas, which are in the yards of the village.[4] They are underground, square or round, with pine pillars. Some were seen with twelve pillars and with four in the center as large as two men could stretch around. They usually had three or four pillars. The floor was made of large, smooth stones, like the baths which they have in Europe. They have a hearth made like the binnacle or compass box of a ship, in which they burn a handful of thyme at a time to keep up the heat, and they can stay in there just as in a bath. The top was on a level with the ground. Some that were seen were large enough for a game of ball. When any man wishes to marry, it has to be arranged by those who govern. The man has to spin and weave a blanket and place it before the woman, who covers herself with it and becomes his wife. The houses belong to the women, the estufas to the men. If a man repudiates his woman, he has to go to the estufa. It is forbidden for women to sleep in the estufas, or to enter these for any purpose except to give their husbands or sons something to eat. The men spin and weave. The women bring up the children and prepare the food. The country is so fertile that they do not have to break up the ground the year round, but only have to sow the seed, which is presently covered by the fall of snow, and the ears come up under the snow. In one year they gather enough for seven. A very large number of cranes and wild geese and crows and starlings live on what is sown, and for all this, when they come to sow for another year, the fields are covered with corn which they have not been able to finish gathering.

There are a great many native fowl in these provinces, and cocks with great hanging chins.[5] When dead, these keep for sixty days, and longer in winter, without losing their feathers or opening, and without any bad smell, and the same is true of dead men.

The villages are free from nuisances, because they go outside to excrete, and they pass their water into clay vessels, which they empty at a distance from the village.[6]

They keep the separate houses where they prepare the food for eating and where they grind the meal, very clean. This is a separate room or closet, where they have a trough with three stones fixed in stiff clay. Three women go in here, each one having a stone, with which one of them breaks the corn, the next grinds it, and the third grinds it again.[7] They take off their shoes, do up their hair, shake their clothes, and cover their heads before they enter the door. A man sits at the door playing on a fife while they grind, moving the stones to the music and singing together. They grind a large quantity at one time, because they make all their bread of meal soaked in warm water, like wafers. They gather a great quantity of brushwood and dry it to use for cooking all through the year. There are no fruits good to eat in the country, except the pine nuts. They have their preachers. Sodomy is not found among them. They do not eat human flesh nor make sacrifices of it. The people are not cruel, for they had Francisco de Ovando in Tiguex about forty days, after he was dead, and when the village was captured, he was found among their dead, whole and without any other wound except the one which killed him, white as snow, without any bad smell. I found out several things about them from one of our Indians, who had been a captive among them for a whole year. I asked him especially for the reason why the young women in that province went entirely naked, however cold it might be, and he told me that the virgins had to go around this way until they took a husband, and that they covered themselves after they had known man. The men here wear little shirts of tanned deerskin and their long robes over this. In all these provinces they have earthenware glazed with antimony and jars of extraordinary labor and workmanship, which were worth seeing.[8]

Chapter V

Of Cicuye and the villages in its neighborhood,
and of how some people came to conquer this country.

We have already said that the people of Tiguex and of all the provinces on the banks of that river were all alike, having the same ways of living and the same customs. It will not be necessary to say anything particular about them. I wish merely to give an account of Cicuye and some depopulated villages which the army saw on the direct road which it followed thither, and of others that were across the snowy mountains near Tiguex, which also lay in that region above the river.

Cicuye[1] is a village of nearly five hundred warriors who are feared throughout that country. It is square, situated on a rock, with a large court or yard in the middle, containing the estufas. The houses are all alike, four stories high. One can go over the top of the whole village without there being a street to hinder. There are corridors going all around it at the first two stories, by which one can go around the whole village. These are like outside balconies, and they are able to protect themselves under these. The houses do not have doors below, but they use ladders, which can be lifted up like a drawbridge, and so go up to the corridors which are on the inside of the village. As the doors of the houses open on the corridor of that story, the corridor serves as a street. The houses that open on the plain are right back of those that open on the court, and in time of war they go through those behind them. The village is inclosed by a low wall of stone. There is a spring of water inside, which they are able to divert.[2] The people of this village boast that no one has been able to conquer them and that they conquer whatever villages they wish. The people and their customs are like those of the other villages. Their virgins also go nude until they take husbands, because they say that if they do anything wrong then it will be seen, and so they do not do it. They do not need to be ashamed because they go around as they were born.

There is a village, small and strong, between Cicuye and the province of Quirix, which the Spaniards named Ximena,[3] and another village almost deserted, only one part of which is inhabited.[4] This was a large village, and judging from its condition and newness it appeared to have been destroyed. They called this the village of the granaries or silos, because large underground cellars were found here stored with corn. There was another large village farther on, entirely destroyed and pulled down, in the yards of which there were many stone balls, as big as 12-quart bowls, which seemed to have been thrown by engines or catapults, which had destroyed the village. All that I was able to find out about them was that, sixteen years before, some people called Teyas,[5] had come to this country in great numbers and had destroyed these villages. They had besieged Cicuye but had not been able to capture it, because it was strong, and when they left the region, they had made peace with the whole country. It seems as if they must have been a powerful people, and that they must have had engines to knock down the villages. The only thing they could tell about the direction these people came from was by pointing toward the north. They usually call these people Teyas or brave men, just as the Mexicans say chichimecas or braves, for the Teyas whom the army saw were brave. These knew the people in the settlements, and were friendly with them, and they (the Teyas of the plains) went there to spend the winter under the wings of the settlements. The inhabitants do not dare to let them come inside, because they can not trust them. Although they are received as friends, and trade with them, they do not stay in the villages over night, but outside under the wings. The villages are guarded by sentinels with trumpets, who call to one another just as in the fortresses of Spain.

There are seven other villages along this route, toward the snowy mountains, one of which had been half destroyed by the people already referred to. These were under the rule of Cicuye. Cicuye is in a little valley between mountain chains and mountains covered with large pine forests. There is a little stream which contains very good trout and otters, and there are very large bears and good falcons hereabouts.

Chapter VI

Which gives the number of villages
which were seen in the country of the terraced houses,
and their population.

Before I proceed to speak of the plains, with the cows and settlements and tribes there, it seems to me that it will be well for the reader to know how large the settlements were, where the houses with stories, gathered into villages, were seen, and how great an extent of country they occupied.[1] As I say, Cibola is the first:

Cibola, seven villages.

Tusayan, seven villages.

The rock of Acuco, one.

Tiguex, twelve villages.

Tutahaco, eight villages.

These villages were below the river.

Quirix,[2] seven villages.

In the snowy mountains, seven villages.

Ximena,[3] three villages.

Cicuye, one village.

Hemes,[4] seven villages.

Aguas Calientes,[4] or Boiling Springs, three villages.

Yuqueyunque,[5] in the mountains, six villages.

Valladolid, called Braba,[6] one village.

Chia,[7] one village.

In all, there are sixty-six villages. Tiguex appears to be in the center of the villages. Valladolid is the farthest up the river toward the northeast. The four villages down the river are toward the southeast, because the river turns toward the east.[8] It is 130 leagues—10 more or less—from the farthest point that was seen down the river to the farthest point up the river, and all the settlements are within this region. Including those at a distance, there are sixty-six villages in all, as I have said, and in all of them there may be some 20,000 men, which may be taken to be a fair estimate of the population of the villages. There are no houses or other buildings between one village and another, but where we went it is entirely uninhabited. These people, since they are few, and their manners, government, and habits are so different from all the nations that have been seen and discovered in these western regions, must come from that part of Greater India, the coast of which lies to the west of this country, for they could have come down from that country, crossing the mountain chains and following down the river, settling in what seemed to them the best place.[9] As they multiplied, they kept on making settlements until they lost the river when it buried itself underground, its course being in the direction of Florida. It comes down from the northeast, where they[10] could certainly have found signs of villages. He preferred, however, to follow the reports of the Turk, but it would have been better to cross the mountains where this river rises. I believe they would have found traces of riches and would have reached the lands from which these people started, which from its location is on the edge of Greater India, although the region is neither known nor understood, because from the trend of the coast it appears that the land between Norway and China is very far up. The country from sea to sea is very wide, judging from the location of both coasts, as well as from what Captain Villalobos discovered when he went in search of China by the sea to the west,[11] and from what has been discovered on the North sea concerning the trend of the coast of Florida toward the Bacallaos, up toward Norway.

To return then to the proposition with which I began, I say that the settlements and people already named were all that were seen in a region 70 leagues wide and 130 long, in the settled country along the river Tiguex. In New Spain there are not one but many establishments, containing a larger number of people. Silver metals were found in many of their villages, which they use for glazing and painting their earthenware.

Chapter VII

Which treats of the plains that were crossed,
of the cows, and of the people who inhabit them.

We have spoken of the settlements of high houses which are situated in what seems to be the most level and open part of the mountains, since it is 150 leagues across before entering the level country between the two mountain chains which I saw were near the North sea and the South sea, which might better be called the Western sea along this coast. This mountain series is the one which is near the South sea.[1] In order to show that the settlements are in the middle of the mountains, I will state that it is 80 leagues from Chichilticalli, where we began to cross this country, to Cibola; from Cibola, which is the first village, to Cicuye, which is the last on the way across, is 70 leagues; it is 30 leagues from Cicuye to where the plains begin. It may be we went across in an indirect or roundabout way, which would make it seem as if there was more country than if it had been crossed in a direct line, and it may be more difficult and rougher. This can not be known certainly, because the mountains change their directions above the bay at the mouth of the Firebrand (Tizon) river.

Now we will speak of the plains. The country is spacious and level, and is more than 400 leagues wide in the part between the two mountain ranges—one, that which Francisco Vazquez Coronado crossed, and the other that which the force under Don Fernando de Soto crossed, near the North sea, entering the country from Florida. No settlements were seen anywhere on these plains.

In traversing 250 leagues, the other mountain range was not seen, nor a hill nor a hillock which was three times as high as a man. Several lakes were found at intervals; they were round as plates, a stone's throw or more across, some fresh and some salt. The grass grows tall near these lakes; away from them it is very short, a span or less. The country is like a bowl, so that when a man sits down, the horizon surrounds him all around at the distance of a musket shot. There are no groves of trees except at the rivers, which flow at the bottom of some ravines where the trees grow so thick that they were not noticed until one was right on the edge of them. They are of dead earth. There are paths down into these, made by the cows when they go to the water, which is essential throughout these plains.

As I have related in the first part, people follow the cows, hunting them and tanning the skins to take to the settlements in the winter to sell, since they go there to pass the winter, each company going to those which are nearest, some to the settlements at Cicuye, others toward Quivira, and others to the settlements which are situated in the direction of Florida. These people are called Querechos and Teyas. They described some large settlements, and judging from what was seen of these people and from the accounts they gave of other places, there are a good many more of these people than there are of those at the settlements. They have better figures, are better warriors, and are more feared. They travel like the Arabs, with their tents and troops of dogs loaded with poles[2] and having Moorish pack saddles with girths. When the load gets disarranged, the dogs howl, calling some one to fix them right. These people eat raw flesh and drink blood. They do not eat human flesh. They are a kind people and not cruel. They are faithful friends. They are able to make themselves very well understood by means of signs. They dry the flesh in the sun, cutting it thin like a leaf, and when dry they grind it like meal to keep it and make a sort of sea soup of it to eat. A handful thrown into a pot swells up so as to increase very much. They season it with fat, which they always try to secure when they kill a cow.³ They empty a large gut and fill it with blood, and carry this around the neck to drink when they are thirsty. When they open the belly of a cow, they squeeze out the chewed grass and drink the juice that remains behind, because they say that this contains the essence of the stomach. They cut the hide open at the back and pull it off at the joints, using a flint as large as a finger, tied in a little stick, with as much ease as if working with a good iron tool. They give it an edge with their own teeth. The quickness with which they do this is something worth seeing and noting.

There are very great numbers of wolves on these plains, which go around with the cows. They have white skins. The deer are pied with white. Their skin is loose, so that when they are killed it can be pulled off with the hand while warm, coming off like pigskin. The rabbits, which are very numerous, are so foolish that those on horseback killed them with their lances. This is when they are mounted among the cows. They fly from a person on foot.

Chapter VIII

Of Quivira, of where it is and some information about it.

Quivira is to the west of those ravines, in the midst of the country, somewhat nearer the mountains toward the sea, for the country is level as far as Quivira, and there they began to see some mountain chains. The country is well settled. Judging from what was seen on the borders of it, this country is very similar to that of Spain in the varieties of vegetation and fruits. There are plums like those of Castile, grapes, nuts, mulberries, oats, pennyroyal, wild marjoram, and large quantities of flax, but this does not do them any good, because they do not know how to use it.¹ The people are of almost the same sort and appearance as the Teyas. They have villages like those in New Spain. The houses are round, without a wall, and they have one story like a loft, under the roof, where they sleep and keep their belongings. The roofs are of straw. There are other thickly settled provinces around it containing large numbers of men. A friar named Juan de Padilla remained in this province, together with a Spanish-Portuguese and a negro and a half-blood and some Indians from the province of Capothan, in New Spain. They killed the friar because he wanted to go to the province of the Guas, who were their enemies. The Spaniard escaped by taking flight on a mare, and afterward reached New Spain, coming out by way of Panuco. The Indians from New Spain who accompanied the friar were allowed by the murderers to bury him, and then they followed the Spaniard and overtook him. This Spaniard was a Portuguese, named Campo.

The great river of the Holy Spirit (Espiritu Santo),[2] which Don Fernando de Soto discovered in the country of Florida, flows through this country. It passes through a province called Arache, according to the reliable accounts which were obtained here. The sources were not visited, because, according to what they said, it comes from a very distant country in the mountains of the South sea, from the part that sheds its waters onto the plains. It flows across all the level country and breaks through the mountains of the North sea, and comes out where the people with Don Fernando de Soto navigated it. This is more than 300 leagues from where it enters the sea. On account of this, and also because it has large tributaries, it is so mighty when it enters the sea that they lost sight of the land before the water ceased to be fresh.[3]

This country of Quivira was the last that was seen, of which I am able to give any description or information. Now it is proper for me to return and speak of the army, which I left in Tiguex, resting for the winter, so that it would be able to proceed or return in search of these settlements of Quivira, which was not accomplished after all, because it was God's pleasure that these discoveries should remain for other peoples and that we who had been there should content ourselves with saying that we were the first who discovered it and obtained any information concerning it, just as Hercules knew the site where Julius Caesar was to found Seville or Hispales. May the all-powerful Lord grant that His will be done in everything. It is certain that if this had not been His will Francisco Vazquez would not have returned to New Spain without cause or reason, as he did, and that it would not have been left for those with Don Fernando de Soto to settle such a good country, as they have done, and besides settling it to increase its extent, after obtaining, as they did, information from our army.[4]

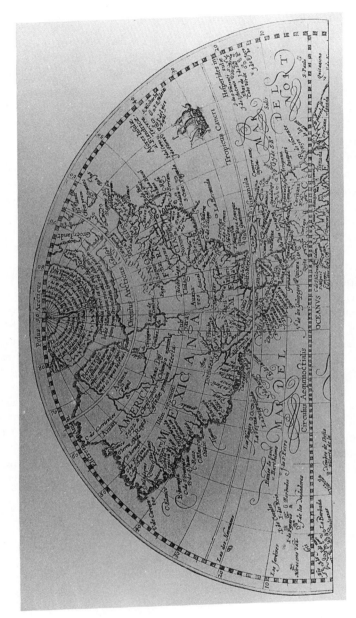

Northern Half of De Bry's America Sive Novus Orbis, 1596

THIRD PART

Which Describes What Happened to Francisco Vazquez Coronado
During the Winter, and How He Gave up the Expedition
and Returned to New Spain.

Laus Deo

Chapter I

Of how Don Pedro de Tovar came from Señora with some men,
and Don Garcia Lopez de Cardenas started back to New Spain.

At the end of the first part of this book, we told how Francisco Vazquez Coronado, when he got back from Quivira, gave orders to winter at Tiguex, in order to return, when the winter was over, with his whole army to discover all the settlements in those regions. Don Pedro de Tovar, who had gone, as we related, to conduct a force from the city of Saint Jerome (San Hieronimo), arrived in the meantime with the men whom he had brought. He had not selected the rebels and seditious men there, but the most experienced ones and the best soldiers—men whom he could trust—wisely considering that he ought to have good men in order to go in search of his general in the country of the Indian called Turk.

Although they found the army at Tiguex when they arrived there, this did not please them much, because they had come with great expectations, believing that they would find their general in the rich country of the Indian called Turk. They consoled themselves with the hope of going back there and lived in anticipation of the pleasure of undertaking this return expedition, which the army would soon make to Quivira. Don Pedro de Tovar brought letters from New Spain, both from the viceroy, Don Antonio de Mendoza, and from individuals. Among these was one from Don Garcia Lopez de Cardenas, which informed him of the death of his brother, the heir, and summoned him to Spain to receive the inheritance. On this account he was given permission, and left Tiguex with several other persons who received permission to go and settle their affairs. There were many others who would have liked to go, but did not, in order not to appear faint-hearted. During this time the general endeavored to pacify several villages in the neighborhood which were not well disposed, and to make peace with the people at Tiguex. He tried also to procure some of the cloth of the country, because the soldiers were almost naked and poorly clothed, full of lice, which they were unable to get rid of or avoid.

The general, Francisco Vazquez Coronado, had been beloved and obeyed by his captains and soldiers as heartily as any of those who have ever started out in the Indies. Necessity knows no law, and the captains who collected the cloth divided it badly, taking the best for themselves and their friends and soldiers, and leaving the rest for the soldiers, and so there began to be some angry murmuring on account of this. Others also complained because they noticed that some favored ones were spared in the work and in the watches and received better portions of what was divided, both of cloth and food. On this account it is thought that they began to say that there was nothing in the country of Quivira which was worth returning for, which was no slight cause of what afterward happened, as will be seen.

Chapter II

Of the general's fall,
and of how the return to New Spain was ordered.

After the winter was over, the return to Quivira was announced, and the men began to prepare the things needed. Since nothing in this life is at the disposition of men, but all is under the ordination of Almighty God, it was His will that we should not accomplish this, and so it happened that one feast day the general went out on horseback to amuse himself, as usual, riding with the captain Don Rodrigo Maldonado. He was on a powerful horse, and his servants had put on a new girth, which must have been rotten at the time, for it broke during the race and he fell over on the side where Don Rodrigo was, and as his horse passed over him it hit his head with its hoof, which laid him at the point of death, and his recovery was slow and doubtful.

During this time, while he was in his bed, Don Garcia Lopez de Cardenas, who had started to go to New Spain, came back in flight from Suya, because he had found that town deserted and the people and horses and cattle all dead. When he reached Tiguex and learned the sad news that the general was near his end, as already related, they did not dare to tell him until he had recovered, and when he finally got up and learned of it, it affected him so much that he had to go back to bed again. He may have done this in order to bring about what he afterward accomplished, as was believed later.

It was while he was in this condition that he recollected what a scientific friend of his in Salamanca had told him, that he would become a powerful lord in distant lands, and that he would have a fall from which he would never be able to recover. This expectation of death made him desire to return and die where he had a wife and children. As the physician and surgeon who was doctoring him, and also acted as a talebearer, suppressed the murmurings that were going about among the soldiers, he treated secretly and underhandedly with several gentlemen who agreed with him. They set the soldiers to talking about going back to New Spain, in little knots and gatherings, and induced them to hold consultations about it, and had them send papers to the general, signed by all the soldiers, through their ensigns, asking for this. They all entered into it readily, and not much time needed to be spent, since many desired it already. When they asked him, the general acted as if he did not want to do it, but all the gentlemen and captains supported them, giving him their signed opinions, and as some were in this, they could give it at once, and they even persuaded others to do the same.

Thus they made it seem as if they ought to return to New Spain, because they had not found any riches, nor had they discovered any settled country out of which estates could be formed for all the army. When he had obtained their signatures, the return to New Spain was at once announced, and since nothing can ever be concealed, the double dealing began to be understood, and many of the gentlemen found that they had been deceived and had made a mistake. They tried in every way to get their signatures back again from the general, who guarded them so carefully that he did not go out of one room, making his sickness seem very much worse, and putting guards about his person and room, and at night about the floor on which he slept. In spite of all this, they stole his chest, and it is said that they did not find their signatures in it, because he kept them in his mattress; on the other hand, it is said that they did recover them. They asked the general to give them 60 picked men, with whom they would remain and hold the country until the viceroy could send them support, or recall them, or else that the general would leave them the army and pick out 60 men to go back with him. But the soldiers did not want to remain either way, some because they had turned their prow toward New Spain, and others because they saw clearly the trouble that would arise over who should have the command. The gentlemen, I do not know whether because they had sworn fidelity or because they feared that the soldiers would not support them, did what had been decided on, although with an ill-will, and from this time on they did not obey the general as readily as formerly, and they did not show any affection for him. He made much of the soldiers and humored them, with the result that he did what he desired and secured the return of the whole army.

Chapter III

Of the rebellion at Suya and the reasons the settlers gave for it.

We have already stated in the last chapter that Don Garcia Lopez de Cardenas came back from Suya in flight, having found that country risen in rebellion. He told how and why that town was deserted, which occurred as I will relate. The entirely worthless fellows were all who had been left in that town, the mutinous and seditious men, besides a few who were honored with the charge of public affairs and who were left to govern the others. Thus the bad dispositions of the worthless secured the power, and they held daily meetings and councils and declared that they had been betrayed and were not going to be rescued, since the others had been directed to go through another part of the country, where there was a more convenient route to New Spain, which was not so because they were still almost on the direct road. This talk led some of them to revolt, and they chose one Pedro de Avila as their captain.

They went back to Culiacan, leaving the captain, Diego de Alcaraz, sick in the town of San Hieronimo, with only a small force. He did not have anyone whom he could send after them to compel them to return. They killed a number of people at several villages along the way. Finally they reached Culiacan, where Hernando Arias de Saabedra, who was waiting for Juan Gallego to come back from New Spain with a force, detained them by means of promises, so that Gallego could take them back. Some who feared what might happen to them ran away one night to New Spain. Diego de Alcaraz, who had remained at Suya with a small force, sick, was not able to hold his position, although he would have liked to, on account of the poisonous herb which the natives use. When these noticed how weak the Spaniards were, they did not continue to trade with them as they formerly had done. Veins of gold had already been discovered before this, but they were unable to work these, because the country was at war. The disturbance was so great that they did not cease to keep watch and to be more than usually careful.

The town was situated on a little river. One night all of a sudden they saw fires which they were not accustomed to, and on this account they doubled the watches, but not having noticed anything during the whole night, they grew careless along toward morning, and the enemy entered the village so silently that they were not seen until they began to kill and plunder. A number of men reached the plain as well as they could, but while they were getting out the captain was mortally wounded. Several Spaniards came back on some horses after they had recovered themselves and attacked the enemy, rescuing some, though only a few. The enemy went off with the booty, leaving three Spaniards killed, besides many of the servants and more than twenty horses.

The Spaniards who survived started off the same day on foot, not having any horses. They went toward Culiacan, keeping away from the roads, and did not find any food until they reached Corazones, where the Indians, like the good friends they have always been, provided them with food. From here they continued to Culiacan, undergoing great hardships. Hernandarias de Saabedra, the mayor, received them and entertained them as well as he could until Juan Gallego arrived with the reinforcements which he was conducting, on his way to find the army. He was not a little troubled at finding that post deserted, when he expected that the army would be in the rich country which had been described by the Indian called Turk, because he looked like one.

Chapter IV

Of how Friar Juan de Padilla and Friar Luis
remained in the country and
the army prepared to return to Mexico.

When the general, Francisco Vazquez, saw that everything was now quiet, and that his schemes had gone as he wished, he ordered that everything should be ready to start on the return to New Spain by the beginning of the month of April, in the year 1543.[1]

Seeing this, Friar Juan de Padilla, a regular brother of the lesser order,[2] and another, Friar Luis, a lay brother, told the general that they wanted to remain in that country—Friar Juan de Padilla in Quivira, because his teachings seemed to promise fruit there, and Friar Luis at Cicuye. On this account, as it was Lent at the time, the father made this the subject of his sermon to the companies one Sunday, establishing his proposition on the authority of the Holy Scriptures. He declared his zeal for the conversion of these peoples and his desire to draw them to the faith, and stated that he had received permission to do it, although this was not necessary. The general sent a company to escort them as far as Cicuye, where Friar Luis stopped, while Friar Juan went on back to Quivira with the guides who had conducted the general, taking with him the Portuguese, as we related, and the half-blood, and the Indians from New Spain. He was martyred a short time after he arrived there, as we related in the second part, chapter 8. Thus we may be sure that he died a martyr, because his zeal was holy and earnest.

Friar Luis remained at Cicuye. Nothing more has been heard about him since, but before the army left Tiguex some men who went to take him a number of sheep that were left for him to keep, met him as he was on his way to visit some other villages, which were 15 or 20 leagues from Cicuye, accompanied by some followers. He felt very hopeful that he was liked at the village and that his teaching would bear fruit, although he complained that the old men were falling away from him. I, for my part, believe that as he was a man of good and holy life, Our Lord will protect him and give him grace to convert many of those peoples, and end his days in guiding them in the faith. We do not need to believe otherwise, for the people in those parts are pious and not at all cruel, and they remain faithful and loyal friends.[3]

After the friars had gone, the general, fearing that they might be injured if people were carried away from that country to New Spain, ordered the soldiers to let any of the natives who were held as servants go free to their villages whenever they might wish. In my opinion, though I am not sure, it would have been better if they had been kept and taught among Christians.

The general was very happy and contented when the time arrived and everything needed for the journey was ready, and the army started from Tiguex on its way back to Cibola. One thing of no small note happened during this part of the trip. The horses were in good condition for their work when they started, fat and sleek, but more than thirty died during the ten days which it took to reach Cibola, and there was not a day in which two or three or more did not die. A large number of them also died afterward before reaching Culiacan, a thing that did not happen during all the rest of the journey.

After the army reached Cibola, it rested before starting across the wilderness, because this was the last of the settlements in that country. The whole country was left well disposed and at peace, and several of our Indian allies remained there.

Chapter V

Of how the army left the settlements and marched to Culiacan, and of what happened on the way.

Leaving astern, as we might say, the settlements that had been discovered in the new land, of which, as I have said, the seven villages of Cibola were the first to be seen and the last that were left, the army started off, marching across the wilderness. The natives kept following the rear of the army for two or three days, to pick up any baggage or servants, for although they were still at peace and had always been loyal friends, when they saw that we were going to leave the country entirely, they were glad to get some of our people in their power, although I do not think that they wanted to injure them, from what I was told by some who were not willing to go back with them when they teased and asked them to. Altogether, they carried off several people besides those who had remained of their own accord, among whom good interpreters could be found today.

The wilderness was crossed without opposition, and on the second day before reaching Chichilticalli Juan Gallego met the army, as he was coming from New Spain with reenforcements of men and necessary supplies for the army, expecting that he would find the army in the country of the Indian called Turk. When Juan Gallego saw that the army was returning, the first thing he said was not, "I am glad you are coming back," and he did not like it any better after he had talked with the general. After he had reached the army, or rather the quarters, there was quite a little movement among the gentlemen toward going back with the new force which had made no slight exertions in coming thus far, having encounters every day with the Indians of these regions who had risen in revolt, as will be related. There was talk of making a settlement somewhere in that region until the viceroy could receive an account of what had occurred. Those soldiers who had come from the new lands would not agree to anything except the return to New Spain, so that nothing came of the proposals made at the consultations, and although there was some opposition, they were finally quieted. Several of the mutineers who had deserted the town of Corazones came with Juan Gallego, who had given them his word as surety for their safety, and even if the general had wanted to punish them, his power was slight, for he had been disobeyed already and was not much respected. He began to be afraid again after this, and made himself sick, and kept a guard.

In several places yells were heard and Indians seen, and some of the horses were wounded and killed, before Batuco[1] was reached, where the friendly Indians from Corazones came to meet the army and see the general. They were always friendly and had treated all the Spaniards who passed through their country well, furnishing them with what food they needed, and men, if they needed these. Our men had always treated them well and repaid them for these things. During this journey the juice of the quince was proved to be a good protection against the poison of the natives, because at one place, several days before reaching Señora, the hostile Indians wounded a Spaniard called Mesa, and he did not die, although the wound of the fresh poison is fatal, and there was a delay of over two hours before curing him with the juice. The poison, however, had left its mark upon him. The skin rotted and fell off until it left the bones and sinews bare, with a horrible smell. The wound was in the wrist, and the poison had reached as far as the shoulder when he was cured. The skin on all this fell off.

The army proceeded without taking any rest, because the provisions had begun to fail by this time. These districts were in rebellion, and so there were not any victuals where the soldiers could get them until they reached Petlatlan, although they made several forays into the cross country in search of provisions. Petlatlan is in the province of Culiacan, and on this account was at peace, although they had several surprises after this. The army rested here several days to get provisions. After leaving here they were able to travel more quickly than before, for the 30 leagues of the valley of Culiacan, where they were welcomed back again as people who came with their governor, who had suffered ill treatment.

Chapter VI

Of how the general started from Culiacan
to give the viceroy an account of the army
with which he had been intrusted.

It seemed, indeed, as if the arrival in the valley of Culiacan had ended the labors of this journey, partly because the general was governor there and partly because it was inhabited by Christians. On this account some began to disregard their superiors and the authority which their captains had over them, and some captains even forgot the obedience due to their general. Each one played his own game, so that while the general was marching toward the town, which was still 10 leagues away, many of the men, or most of them, left him in order to rest in the valley, and some even proposed not to follow him. The general understood that he was not strong enough to compel them, although his position as governor gave him fresh authority. He determined to accomplish it by a better method, which was to order all the captains to provide food and meat from the stores of several villages that were under his control as governor. He pretended to be sick, keeping his bed, so that those who had any business with him could speak to him or he with them more freely, without hindrance or observation, and he kept sending for his particular friends in order to ask them to be sure to speak to the soldiers and encourage them to accompany him back to New Spain, and to tell them that he would request the viceroy, Don Antonio de Mendoza, to show them especial favor, and that he would do so himself for those who might wish to remain in his government. After this had been done, he started with his army at a very bad time, when the rains were beginning, for it was about Saint John's day, at which season it rains continuously.

In the uninhabited country which they passed through as far as Compostela there are numerous very dangerous rivers, full of large and fierce alligators. While the army was halting at one of these rivers, a soldier who was crossing from one side to the other was seized, in sight of everybody, and carried off by an alligator without it being possible to help him. The general proceeded, leaving the men who did not want to follow him all along the way, and reached Mexico with less than 100 men. He made his report to the viceroy, Don Antonio de Mendoza, who did not receive him very graciously, although he gave him his discharge. His reputation was gone from this time on. He kept the government of New Galicia, which had been entrusted to him, for only a short time, when the viceroy took it himself, until the arrival of the court, or audiencia, which still governs it. And this was the end of those discoveries and of the expedition which was made to these new lands.

It now remains for us to describe the way in which to enter the country by a more direct route, although there is never a short cut without hard work. It is always best to find out what those know who have prepared the way, who know what will be needed. This can be found elsewhere, and I will now tell where Quivira lies, what direction the army took, and the direction in which Greater India lies, which was what they pretended to be in search of, when the army started thither. Today, since Villalobos has discovered that this part of the coast of the South sea trends toward the west, it is clearly seen and acknowledged that, since we were in the north, we ought to have turned to the west instead of toward the east, as we did. With this, we will leave this subject and will proceed to finish this treatise, since there are several noteworthy things of which I must give an account, which I have left to be treated more extensively in the two following chapters.

Chapter VII

Of the adventures of Captain Juan Gallego
while he was bringing reenforcements
through the revolted country.

One might well have complained when in the last chapter I passed in silence over the exploits of Captain Juan Gallego with his 20 companions. I will relate them in the present chapter, so that in times to come those who read about it or tell of it may have a reliable authority on whom to rely. I am not writing fables, like some of the things which we read about nowadays in the books of chivalry. If it were not that those stories contained enchantments, there are some things which our Spaniards have done in our day in these parts, in their conquests and encounters with the Indians, which, for deeds worthy of admiration, surpass not only the books already mentioned, but also those which have been written about the twelve peers of France, because, if the deadly strength which the authors of those times attributed to their heroes and the brilliant and resplendent arms with which they adorned them, are fully considered, and compared with the small stature of the men of our time and the few and poor weapons which they have in these parts,[1] the remarkable things which our people have undertaken and accomplished with such weapons are more to be wondered at today than those of which the ancients write, and just because, too, they fought with barbarous naked people, as ours have with Indians, among whom there are always men who are brave and valiant and very sure bowmen, for we have seen them pierce the wings while flying, and hit hares while running after them. I have said all this in order to show that some things which we consider fables may be true, because we see greater things every day in our own times, just as in future times people will greatly wonder at the deeds of Don Fernando Cortez, who dared to go into the midst of New Spain with 300 men against the vast number of people in Mexico, and who with 500 Spaniards succeeded in subduing it, and made himself lord over it in two years.

The deeds of Don Pedro de Alvarado in the conquest of Guatemala, and those of Montejo in Tabasco, the conquests of the mainland and of Peru, were all such as to make me remain silent concerning what I now wish to relate; but since I have promised to give an account of what happened on this journey, I want the things I am now going to relate to be known as well as those others of which I have spoken.

The captain Juan Gallego, then, reached the town of Culiacan with a very small force. There he collected as many as he could of those who had escaped from the town of Hearts, or, more correctly, from Suya, which made in all 22 men, and with these he marched through all of the settled country, across which he traveled 200 leagues with the country in a state of war and the people in rebellion, although they had formerly been friendly toward the Spaniards, having encounters with the enemy almost every day. He always marched with the advance guard, leaving two-thirds of his force behind with the baggage. With six or seven Spaniards, and without any of the Indian allies whom he had with him, he forced his way into their villages, killing and destroying and setting them on fire, coming upon the enemy so suddenly and with such quickness and boldness that they did not have a chance to collect or even to do anything at all, until they became so afraid of him that there was not a town which dared wait for him, but they fled before him as from a powerful army;

so much so, that for ten days, while he was passing through the settlements, they did not have an hour's rest.

He did all this with his seven companions, so that when the rest of the force came up with the baggage there was nothing for them to do except to pillage, since the others had already killed and captured all the people they could lay their hands on and the rest had fled. They did not pause anywhere, so that although the villages ahead of him received some warning, they were upon them so quickly that they did not have a chance to collect. Especially in the region where the town of Hearts had been, he killed and hung a large number of people to punish them for their rebellion. He did not lose a companion during all this, nor was anyone wounded, except one soldier, who was wounded in the eyelid by an Indian who was almost dead, whom he was stripping. The weapon broke the skin and, as it was poisoned, he would have had to die if he had not been saved by the quince juice; he lost his eye as it was.

These deeds of theirs were such that I know those people will remember them as long as they live, and especially four or five friendly Indians who went with them from Corazones, who thought that they were so wonderful that they held them to be something divine rather than human. If he had not fallen in with our army as he did, they would have reached the country of the Indian called Turk, which they expected to march to, and they would have arrived there without danger on account of their good order and the skill with which he was leading them, and their knowledge and ample practice in war. Several of these men are still in this town of Culiacan, where I am now writing this account and narrative, where they, as well as I and the others who have remained in this province, have never lacked for labor in keeping this country quiet, in capturing rebels, and increasing in poverty and need, and more than ever at the present hour, because the country is poorer and more in debt than ever before.

Chapter VIII

Which describes some remarkable things
that were seen on the plains, with a description of the bulls.

My silence was not without mystery and dissimulation when, in chapter 7 of the second part of this book, I spoke of the plains and of the things of which I will give a detailed account in this chapter, where all these things may be found together; for these things were remarkable and something not seen in other parts. I dare to write of them because I am writing at a time when many men are still living who saw them and who will vouch for my account. Who could believe that 1,000 horses and 500 of our cows and more than 5,000 rams and ewes and more than 1,500 friendly Indians and servants, in traveling over those plains, would leave no more trace where they had passed than if nothing had been there—nothing—so that it was necessary to make piles of bones and cow dung now and then, so that the rear guard could follow the army. The grass never failed to become erect after it had been trodden down, and, although it was short, it was as fresh and straight as before.

Another thing was a heap of cow bones, a crossbow shot long, or a very little less, almost twice a man's height in places, and some 18 feet or more wide, which was found on the edge of a salt lake in the southern part, and this in a region where there are no people who could have made it. The only explanation of this which could be suggested was that the waves which the north winds must make in the lake had piled up the bones of the cattle which had died in the lake, when the old and weak ones who went into the water were unable to get out. The noticeable thing is the number of cattle that would be necessary to make such a pile of bones.

Now that I wish to describe the appearance of the bulls, it is to be noticed first that there was not one of the horses that did not take flight when he saw them first, for they have a narrow, short face, the brow two palms across from eye to eye, the eyes sticking out at the side, so that, when they are running, they can see who is following them. They have very long beards, like goats, and when they are running they throw their heads back with the beard dragging on the ground. There is a sort of girdle round the middle of the body. The hair is very woolly, like a sheep's, very fine, and in front of the girdle the hair is very long and rough like a lion's. They have a great hump, larger than a camel's. The horns are short and thick, so that they are not seen much above the hair. In May they change the hair in the middle of the body for a down, which makes perfect lions of them. They rub against the small trees in the little ravines to shed their hair, and they continue this until only the down is left, as a snake changes his skin. They have a short tail, with a bunch of hair at the end. When they run, they carry it erect like a scorpion. It is worth noticing that the little calves are red and just like ours, but they change their color and appearance with time and age.

Another strange thing was that all the bulls that were killed had their left ears slit, although these were whole when young. The reason for this was a puzzle that could not be guessed. The wool ought to make good cloth on account of its fineness, although the color is not good, because it is the color of buriel.[1]

Another thing worth noticing is that the bulls traveled without cows in such large numbers that nobody could have counted them, and so far away from the cows that it was more than 40 leagues from where we began to see the bulls to the place where we began to see the cows. The country they traveled over was so level and smooth that if one looked at them the sky could be seen between their legs, so that if some of them were at a distance they looked like smooth-trunked pines whose tops joined, and if there was only one bull it looked as if there were four pines. When one was near them, it was impossible to see the ground on the other side of them. The reason for all this was that the country seemed as round as if a man should imagine himself in a three-pint measure, and could see the sky at the end of it, about a crossbow shot from him, and even if a man only lay down on his back he lost sight of the ground.[2]

I have not written about other things which were seen nor made any mention of them, because they were not of so much importance, although it does not seem right for me to remain silent concerning the fact that they venerate the sign of the cross in the region where the settlements have high houses. For at a spring which was in the plain near Acuco they had a cross two palms high and as thick as a finger, made of wood with a square twig for its crosspiece, and many little sticks decorated with feathers around it, and numerous withered flowers, which were the offerings.[3] In a graveyard outside the village at Tutahaco there appeared to have been a recent burial. Near the head there was another cross made of two little sticks tied with cotton thread, and dry withered flowers. It certainly seems to me that in some way they must have received some light from the cross of Our Redeemer, Christ, and it may have come by way of India, from whence they proceeded.

Chapter IX

Which treats of the direction which the army took,
and of how another more direct way might be found,
if anyone was to return to that country.

I very much wish that I possessed some knowledge of cosmography or geography, so as to render what I wish to say intelligible, and so that I could reckon up or measure the advantage those people who might go in search of that country would have if they went directly through the center of the country, instead of following the road the army took. However, with the help of the favor of the Lord, I will state it as well as I can, making it as plain as possible.

It is, I think, already understood that the Portuguese, Campo, was the soldier who escaped when Friar Juan de Padilla was killed at Quivira, and that he finally reached New Spain from Panuco,[1] having traveled across the plains country until he came to cross the North Sea mountain chain, keeping the country that Don Hernando de Soto discovered all the time on his left hand, since he did not see the river of the Holy Spirit (Espiritu Santo) at all.[2] After he had crossed the North Sea mountains, he found that he was in Panuco, so that if he had not tried to go to the North sea, he would have come out in the neighborhood of the border land, or the country of the Sacatecas,[3] of which we now have some knowledge.

This way would be somewhat better and more direct for anyone going back there in search of Quivira, since some of those who came with the Portuguese are still in New Spain to serve as guides. Nevertheless, I think it would be best to go through the country of the Guachichules, keeping near the South Sea mountains all the time, for there are more settlements and a food supply, for it would be suicide to launch out on the plains country, because it is so vast and is barren of anything to eat, although, it is true, there would not be much need of this after coming to the cows.

This is only when one goes in search of Quivira, and of the villages which were described by the Indian called Turk, for the army of Francisco Vazquez Coronado went the very farthest way round to get there, since they started from Mexico and went 110 leagues to the west, and then 100 leagues to the northeast, and 250 to the north, and all this brought them as far as the ravines where the cows were, and after traveling 850 leagues they were not more than 400 leagues distant from Mexico by a direct route. If one desires to go to the country of Tiguex, so as to turn from there toward the west in search of the country of India, he ought to follow the road taken by the army, for there is no other, even if one wished to go by a different way, because the arm of the sea which reaches into this coast toward the north does not leave room for any. But what might be done is to have a fleet and cross this gulf and disembark in the neighborhood of the Island of Negroes[4] and enter the country from there, crossing the mountain chains in search of the country from which the people at Tiguex came, or other peoples of the same sort.

As for entering from the country of Florida and from the North sea, it has already been observed that the many expeditions which have been undertaken from that side have been unfortunate and not very successful, because that part of the country is full of bogs and poisonous fruits, barren, and the very worst country that is warmed by the sun. But they might disembark after passing the river of the Holy Spirit, as Don Hernando de Soto did. Nevertheless, despite the fact that I underwent much labor, I still think that the way I went to that country is the best. There ought to be river courses, because the necessary supplies can be carried on these more easily in large quantities. Horses are the most necessary things in the new countries, and they frighten the enemy most. ... Artillery is also much feared by those who do not know how to use it. A piece of heavy artillery would be very good for settlements like those which Francisco Vazquez Coronado discovered, in order to knock them down, because he had nothing but some small machines for slinging and nobody skillful enough to make a catapult or some other machine which would frighten them, which is very necessary.

I say, then, that with what we now know about the trend of the coast of the South sea, which has been followed by the ships which explored the western part, and what is known of the North sea toward Norway, the coast of which extends up from Florida, those who now go to discover the country which Francisco Vazquez entered, and reach the country of Cibola or of Tiguex, will know the direction in which they ought to go in order to discover the true direction of the country which the Marquis of the Valley, Don Hernando Cortes, tried to find, following the direction of the gulf of the Firebrand (Tizon) river. This will suffice for the conclusion of our narrative. Everything else rests on the powerful Lord of all things, God Omnipotent, who knows how and when these lands will be discovered and for whom He has guarded this good fortune.

Laus Deo

Finished copying, Saturday the 26th of October, 1596, in Seville.

Translation of the Letter from Mendoza to the King, April 17, 1540[1]

S.C.C.M.:

I wrote to Your Majesty from Compostela the last of February, giving you an account of my arrival there and of the departure of Francisco Vazquez with the force which I sent to pacify and settle in the newly discovered country, and of how the warden, Lope de Samaniego, was going as army master, both because he was a responsible person and a very good Christian, and because he has had experience in matters of this sort; as Your Majesty had desired to know. And the news which I have received since then is to the effect that after they had passed the uninhabited region of Culuacan and were approaching Chiametla, the warden went off with some horsemen to find provisions, and one of the soldiers who was with him, who had strayed from the force, called out that they were killing him. The warden hastened to his assistance, and they wounded him in the eye with an arrow, from which he died. In regard to the fortress,[2] besides the fact that it is badly built and going to pieces, it seems to me that the cost of it is excessive, and that Your Majesty could do without the most of it, because there is one man who takes charge of the munitions and artillery, and an armorer to repair it, and a gunner, and as this is the way it was under the audiencia, before the fortresses were made conformable to what I have written to Your Majesty, we can get along without the rest, because that fortress was built on account of the brigantines, and not for any other purpose.[3] And as the lagoon is so dry that it can do no good in this way for the present, I think that, for this reason, the cost is superfluous. I believe that it will have fallen in before a reply can come from Your Majesty.

Some days ago I wrote to Your Majesty that I had ordered Melchior Diaz, who was in the town of San Miguel de Culuacan, to take some horsemen and see if the account given by the father, Friar Marcos, agreed with what he could discover. He set out from Culuacan with fifteen horsemen, the 17th of November last. The 20th of this present March I received a letter from him, which he sent me by Juan de Zaldyvar and three other horsemen. In this he says that after he left Culuacan and crossed the river of Petatlan he was everywhere very well received by the Indians. The way he did was to send a cross to the place where he was going to stop, because this was a sign which the Indians received with deep veneration, making a house out of mats in which to place it, and somewhat away from this they made a lodging for the Spaniards, and drove stakes where they could tie the horses, and supplied fodder for them, and abundance of corn wherever they had it. They say that they suffered from hunger in many places, because it had been a bad year. After going 100 leagues from Culuacan, he began to find the country cold, with severe frosts, and the farther he went on the colder it became, until he reached a point where some Indians whom he had with him were frozen, and two Spaniards were in great danger. Seeing this, he decided not to go any farther until the winter was over, and to send back, by those whom I mentioned, an account of what he had learned concerning Cibola and the country beyond, which is as follows, taken literally from his letter:

"I have given your Lordship an account of what happened to me along the way; and seeing that it is impossible to cross the uninhabited region which stretches from here to Cibola, on account of the heavy snows and the cold, I will give Your Lordship an account of what I have learned about Cibola, which I have ascertained by asking many persons who have been there fifteen and twenty years; and I have secured this in many different ways, taking some Indians together and others separately, and on comparison they all seem to agree in what they say. After crossing this large wilderness, there are seven places, being a short day's march from one to another, all of which are together called Cibola. The houses are of stone and mud, coarsely worked. They are made in this way: One large wall, and at each end of this wall some rooms are built, partitioned off 20 feet square, according to the description they give, which are planked with square beams. Most of the houses are reached from the flat roofs, using their ladders to go to the streets. The houses have three and four stories. They declare that there are few having two stories. The stories are mostly half as high again as a man, except the first one, which is low, and only a little more than a man's height. One ladder is used to communicate with ten or twelve houses together. They make use of the low ones and live in the highest ones. In the lowest ones of all they have some loopholes made sideways, as in the fortresses of Spain. The Indians say that when these people are attacked, they station themselves in their houses and fight from there; and that when they go to make war, they carry shields and wear leather jackets, which are made of cows' hide, colored, and that they fight with arrows and with a sort of stone maul and with some other weapons made of sticks, which I have not been able to make out. They eat human flesh, and they keep those whom they capture in war as slaves. There are many fowls in the country, tame. They have much corn and beans and melons [squashes]. In their houses they keep some hairy animals, like the large Spanish hounds, which they shear, and they make long colored wigs from the hair, like this one which I send to Your Lordship, which they wear, and they also put this same stuff in the cloth which they make.[4] The men are of small stature [plate LXII]; the women are light colored and of gold appearance, and they wear shirts or chemises which reach down to their feet. They wear their hair on each side done up in a sort of twist [plate LXIII], which leaves the ears outside, in which they hang many turquoises, as well as on their necks and on the wrists of their arms. The clothing of the men is a cloak, and over this the skin of a cow, like the one which Cabeza de Vaca and Dorantes brought, which Your Lordship saw; they wear caps[5] on their heads; in summer they wear shoes made of painted or colored skin, and high buskins in winter.

"They were also unable to tell me of any metal, nor did they say that they had it. They have turquoises in quantity, although not so many as the father provincial said. They have some little stone crystals, like this which I send to Your Lordship, of which Your Lordship has seen many here in New Spain. They cultivate the ground in the same way as in New Spain. They carry things on their heads, as in Mexico. The men weave cloth and spin cotton. They have salt from a marshy lake, which is two days from the province of Cibola.[6] The Indians have their dances and songs, with some flutes which have holes on which to put the fingers. They make much noise. They sing in unison with those who play, and those who sing clap their hands in our fashion. One of the Indians that accompanied the negro Esteban, who had been a captive there, saw the playing as they practiced it, and others singing as I have said, although not very vigorously. They say that five or six play together, and that some of the flutes are better than others.[7] They say the country is good for corn and beans, and that they do not have any fruit trees, nor do they know what such a thing is.[8] They have very good mountains. The country lacks water. They do not raise cotton, but bring it from Totonteac.[9] They eat out of flat bowls, like the Mexicans. They raise considerable corn and beans and other similar things. They do not know what sea fish is, nor have they ever heard of it. I have not obtained any information about the cows, except that these are found beyond the province of Cibola. There is a great abundance of wild goats, of the color of bay horses; there are many of these here where I am, and although I have asked the Indians if those are like these, they tell me no. Of the seven settlements, they describe three of them as very large; four not so big. They describe them, as I understand, to be about three crossbow shots square for each place, and from what the Indians say, and their descriptions of the houses and their size, and as these are close together, and considering that there are people in each house, it ought to make a large multitude. Totonteac is declared to be seven short days from the province of Cibola, and of the same sort of houses and people, and they say that cotton grows there. I doubt this, because they tell me that it is a cold country. They say that there are twelve villages, every one of which is larger than the largest at Cibola. They also tell me that there is a village which is one day from Cibola, and that the two are at war.[10] They have the same sort of houses and people and customs. They declare this to be greater than any of those described; I take it that there is a great multitude of people there. They are very well known, on account of having these houses and abundance of food and turquoises. I have not been able to learn more than what I have related, although, as I have said, I have had with me Indians who lived there fifteen and twenty years.

"The death of Esteban the negro took place in the way the father, Friar Marcos, described it to your lordship, and so I do not make a report of it here, except that the people at Cibola sent word to those of this village and in its neighborhood that if any Christians should come, they ought not to consider them as anything peculiar, and ought to kill them, because they were mortal—saying that they had learned this because they kept the bones of the one who had come there; and that, if they did not dare to do this, they should send word so that those (at Cibola) could come and do it. I can very easily believe that all this has taken place, and that there has been some communication between these places, because of the coolness with which they received us and the sour faces they have shown us."

Melchior Diaz says that the people whom he found along the way do not have any settlements at all, except in one valley which is 150 leagues from Culuacan, which is well settled and has houses with lofts, and that there are many people along the way, but that they are not good for anything except to make them Christians, as if this was of small account. May Your Majesty remember to provide for the service of God, and keep in mind the deaths and the loss of life and of provinces which has taken place in these Indies. And, moreover, up to this present day none of the things Your Majesty has commanded, which have been very holy and good, have been attended to, nor priests provided, either for that country or for this. For I assure Your Majesty that there is no trace of Christianity where they have not yet arrived, neither little nor much, and that the poor people are ready to receive the priests and come to them even when they flee from us like deer in the mountains. And I state this because I am an eyewitness, and I have seen it clearly during this trip. I have importuned Your Majesty for friars, and yet again I can not cease doing it much more, because unless this be done I can not accomplish that which I am bound to do.

After I reach Mexico, I will give Your Majesty an account of everything concerning these provinces, for while I should like to do it today, I can not, because I am very weak from a slow fever which I caught in Colima, which attacked me very severely, although it did not last more than six days. It has pleased Our Lord to make me well already, and I have traveled here to Jacona, where I am.

May Our Lord protect the Holy Catholic Caesarian person of Your Majesty and aggrandize it with increase of better kingdoms and lordships, as we your servants desire.

From Jacona, April 17, 1540.

S.C.C.M.

Your Holy Majesty's humble servant, who salutes your royal feet and hands,
D. Antonio de Mendoza.

Translation of the Letter from Coronado to Mendoza, August 3, 1540[1]

The Account Given by Francisco Vazquez de Coronado,
Captain-General of the Force which was sent
in the Name of His Majesty to the Newly Discovered Country,
of What Happened to the Expedition after April 22 of the Year MDXL,
when He Started Forward from Culiacan,
and of What He Found in the Country through Which He Passed.

I

Francisco Vazquez starts from Culiacan with his army, and after suffering various inconveniences on account of the badness of the way, reaches the Valley of Hearts, where he failed to find any corn, to procure which he sends to the valley called Señora. He receives an account of the important Valley of Hearts and of the people there, and of some lands lying along that coast.

On the 22d of the month of April last, I set out from the province of Culiacan with a part of the army, having made the arrangements of which I wrote to Your Lordship. Judging by the outcome, I feel sure that it was fortunate that I did not start the whole of the army on this undertaking, because the labors have been so very great and the lack of food such that I do not believe this undertaking could have been completed before the end of this year, and that there would be a great loss of life if it should be accomplished. For, as I wrote to Your Lordship, I spent eighty days in traveling to Culiacan,[1] during which time I and the gentlemen of my company, who were horsemen, carried on our backs and on our horses a little food, in such wise that after leaving this place none of us carried any necessary effects weighing more than a pound. For all this, and although we took all possible care and forethought of the small supply of provisions which we carried, it gave out. And this is not to be wondered at, because the road is rough and long, and what with our harquebuses, which had to be carried up the mountains and hills and in the passage of the rivers, the greater part of the corn was lost. And since I send Your Lordship a drawing of this route, I will say no more about it here.

Thirty leagues before reaching the place which the father provincial spoke so well of in his report,[2] I sent Melchior Diaz forward with fifteen horsemen, ordering him to make but one day's journey out of two, so that he could examine everything there before I arrived. He traveled through some very rough mountains for four days, and did not find anything to live on, nor people, nor information about anything, except that he found two or three poor villages, with twenty or thirty huts apiece. From the people here he learned that there was nothing to be found in the country beyond except the mountains, which continued very rough, entirely uninhabited by people. And, because this was labor lost, I did not want to send Your Lordship an account of it. The whole company felt disturbed at this, that a thing so much praised, and about which the father had said so many things, should be found so very different; and they began to think that all the rest would be of the same sort.

When I noticed this, I tried to encourage them as well as I could, telling them that Your Lordship had always thought that this part of the trip would be a waste of effort, and that we ought to devote our attention to those Seven Cities and the other provinces about which we had information—that these should be the end of our enterprise. With this resolution and purpose, we all marched cheerfully along a very bad way, where it was impossible to pass without making a new road or repairing the one that was there, which troubled the soldiers not a little, considering that everything which the friar had said was found to be quite the reverse; because, among other things which the father had said and declared, he said that the way would be plain and good, and that there would be only one small hill of about half a league. And the truth is, that there are mountains where, however well the path might be fixed, they could not be crossed without there being great danger of the horses falling over them. And it was so bad that a large number of the animals which

Your Lordship sent as provision for the army were lost along this part of the way, on account of the roughness of the rocks. The lambs and wethers lost their hoofs along the way, and I left the greater part of those which I brought from Culiacan at the river of Lachimi,[3] because they were unable to travel, and so that they might proceed more slowly.

Four horsemen remained with them, who have just arrived. They have not brought more than 24 lambs and 4 wethers; the rest died from the toil, although they did not travel more than two leagues daily. I reached the Valley of Hearts at last, on the 26th day of the month of May, and rested there a number of days. Between Culiacan and this place I could sustain myself only by means of a large supply of corn bread, because I had to leave all the corn, as it was not yet ripe. In this Valley of Hearts we found more people than in any part of the country which we had left behind and a large extent of tilled ground. There was no corn for food among them, but as I heard that there was some in another valley called Señora, which I did not wish to disturb by force, I sent Melchior Diaz with goods to exchange for it, so as to give this to the friendly Indians whom we brought with us, and to some who had lost their animals along the way and had not been able to carry the food which they had taken from Culiacan. By the favor of Our Lord, some little corn was obtained by this trading, which relieved the friendly Indians and some Spaniards. Ten or twelve of the horses had died of overwork by the time that we reached this Valley of Hearts, because they were unable to stand the strain of carrying heavy burdens and eating little. Some of our negroes and some of the Indians also died here, which was not a slight loss for the rest of the expedition. They told me that the Valley of Hearts is a long five-days' journey from the western sea. I sent to summon Indians from the coast in order to learn about their condition, and while I was waiting for these the horses rested. I stayed there four days, during which the Indians came from the sea, who told me that there were seven or eight islands two days' journey from that seacoast, directly opposite, well populated with people, but poorly supplied with food, and the people were savages.[4] They told me they had seen a ship pass not very far from the land. I do not know whether to think that it was the one which was sent to discover the country, or perhaps some Portuguese.[5]

II

They come to Chichilticale; after having taken two days' rest, they enter a country containing very little food and hard to travel for 30 leagues, beyond which the country becomes pleasant, and there is a river called the River of the Flax (del Lino); they fight against the Indians, being attacked by these; and having by their victory secured the city, they relieve themselves of the pangs of their hunger.

I set out from the Hearts and kept near the seacoast as well as I could judge, but in fact I found myself continually farther off, so that when I reached Chichilticale I found that I was fifteen days' journey distant from the sea, although the father provincial had said that it was only 5 leagues distant and that he had seen it. We all became very distrustful, and felt great anxiety and dismay to see that everything was the reverse of what he had told Your Lordship. The Indians of Chichilticale say that when they go to the sea for fish, or for anything else that they need, they go across the country, and that it takes them ten days; and this information which I have received from the Indians appears to me to be true. The sea turns toward the west directly opposite the Hearts for 10 or 12 leagues, where I learned that the ships of Your Lordship had been seen, which had gone in search of the port of Chichilticale, which the father said was on the thirty-fifth degree.

God knows what I have suffered, because I fear that they may have met with some mishap. If they follow the coast, as they said they would, as long as the food lasts which they took with them, of which I left them a supply in Culiacan, and if they have not been overtaken by some misfortune, I maintain my trust in God that they have already discovered something good, for which the delay which they have made may be pardoned. I rested for two days at Chichilticale, and there was good reason for staying longer, because we found that the horses were becoming so tired; but there was no chance to rest longer, because the food was giving out. I entered the borders of the wilderness region on Saint John's eve, and, for a change from our past labors, we found no grass during the first days, but a worse way through mountains and more dangerous passages than we had experienced previously. The horses were so tired that they were not equal to it, so that in this last desert we lost more horses than before; and some Indian allies and a Spaniard called Spinosa, besides two negroes, died from eating some herbs because the food had given out.

I sent the army-master, Don Garcia Lopez de Cardenas, with 15 horsemen, a day's march ahead of me, in order to explore the country and prepare the way, which he accomplished like the man that he is, and agreeably to the confidence which Your Lordship has had in him. I am the more certain that he did so, because, as I have said, the way is very bad for at least 30 leagues and more, through impassable mountains. But when we had passed these 30 leagues, we found fresh rivers and grass like that of Castile, and especially one sort like what we call *Scaramoio*; many nut and mulberry trees, but the leaves of the nut trees are different from those of Spain. There was a considerable amount of flax near the banks of one river, which was called on this account El Rio del Lino. No Indians were seen during the first day's march, after which four Indians came out with signs of peace, saying that they had been sent to that desert place to say that we were welcome, and that on the next day the tribe would provide the whole force with food. The army-master gave them a cross, telling them to say to the people in their city that they need not fear, and that they should have their people stay in their own houses, because I was coming in the name of His Majesty to defend and help them.

After this was done, Ferrando Alvarado came back to tell me that some Indians had met him peaceably, and that two of them were with the army-master waiting for me. I went to them forthwith and gave them some paternosters and some little cloaks, telling them to return to their city and say to the people there that they could stay quietly in their houses and that they need not fear. After this I ordered the army-master to go and see if there were any bad passages which the Indians might be able to defend, and to seize and hold any such until the next day, when I would come up. He went, and found a very bad place in our way where we might have received much harm. He immediately established himself there with the force which he was conducting. The Indians came that very night to occupy that place so as to defend it, and finding it taken, they assaulted our men. According to what I have been told, they attacked like valiant men, although in the end they had to retreat in flight, because the army-master was on the watch and kept his men in good order. The Indians sounded a little trumpet as a sign of retreat, and did not do any injury to the Spaniards. The army-master sent me notice of this the same night, so that on the next day I started with as good order as I could, for we were in such great need of food that I thought we should all die of hunger if we continued to be without provisions for another day, especially the Indians, since altogether we did not have two bushels of corn, and so I was obliged to hasten forward without delay. The Indians lighted their fires from point to point, and these were answered from a distance with as good understanding as we could have shown. Thus notice was given concerning how we went and where we had arrived.

As soon as I came within sight of this city, I sent the army-master, Don Garcia Lopez, Friar Daniel and Friar Luis, and Ferrando Vermizzo, with some horsemen, a little way ahead, so that they might find the Indians and tell them that we were not coming to do them any harm, but to defend them in the name of our lord the Emperor. The summons, in the form which His Majesty commanded in his instructions, was made intelligible to the people of the country by an interpreter. But they, being a proud people, were little affected, because it seemed to them that we were few in number, and that they would not have any difficulty in conquering us. They pierced the gown of Friar Luis with an arrow, which, blessed be God, did him no harm. Meanwhile I arrived with all the rest of the horse and the footmen, and found a large body of the Indians on the plain, who began to shoot with their arrows. In obedience to the orders of Your Lordship and of the marquis,[1] I did not wish my company, who were begging me for permission, to attack them, telling them that they ought not to offend them, and that what the enemy was doing was nothing, and that so few people ought not to be insulted. On the other hand, when the Indians saw that we did not move, they took greater courage, and grew so bold that they came up almost to the heels of our horses to shoot their arrows. On this account I saw that it was no longer time to hesitate, and as the priests approved the action, I charged them. There was little to do, because they suddenly took to flight, part running toward the city, which was near and well fortified, and others toward the plain, wherever chance led them. Some Indians were killed, and others might have been slain if I could have allowed them to be pursued. But I saw that there would be little advantage in this, because the Indians who were outside were few, and those who had retired to the city were numerous, besides many who had remained there in the first place.

As that was where the food was, of which we stood in such great need, I assembled my whole force and divided them as seemed to me best for the attack on the city, and surrounded it. The hunger which we suffered would not permit of any delay, and so I dismounted with some of these gentlemen and soldiers. I ordered the musketeers and crossbowmen to begin the attack and drive back the enemy from the defenses, so that they could not do us any injury. I assaulted the wall on one side, where I was told that there was a scaling ladder and that there was also a gate. But the crossbowmen broke all the strings of their crossbows and the musketeers could do nothing, because they had arrived so weak and feeble that they could scarcely stand on their feet. On this account the people who were on top were not prevented at all from defending themselves and doing us whatever injury they were able. Thus, for myself, they knocked me down to the ground twice with countless great stones which they threw down from above, and if I had not been protected by the very good headpiece which I wore, I think that the outcome would have been bad for me. They picked me up from the ground, however, with two small wounds in my face and an arrow in my foot, and with many bruises on my arms and legs, and in this condition I retired from the battle, very weak. I think that if Don Garcia Lopez de Cardenas had not come to my help, like a good cavalier, the second time that they knocked me to the ground, by placing his own body above mine, I should have been in much greater danger than I was. But, by the pleasure of God, these Indians surrendered, and their city was taken with the help of Our Lord, and a sufficient supply of corn was found there to relieve our necessities.

The army-master and Don Pedro de Tovar and Ferrando de Alvarado and Paulo de Melgosa, the infantry captain, sustained some bruises, although none of them were wounded. Agoniez Quarez was hit in the arm by an arrow, and one Torres, who lived in Panuco, in the face by another, and two other footmen received slight arrow wounds. They all directed their attack against me because my armor was gilded and glittered, and on this account I was hurt more than the rest, and not because I had done more or was farther in advance than the others; for all these gentlemen and soldiers bore themselves well, as was expected of them. I praise God that I am now well, although somewhat sore from the stones. Two or three other soldiers were hurt in the battle which we had on the plain, and three horses were killed—one that of Don Lopez and another that of Vigliega and the third that of Don Alfonso Manrich—and seven or eight other horses were wounded; but the men, as well as the horses, have now recovered and are well.

III

Of the situation and condition of the Seven Cities called the kingdom of Cevola, and the sort of people and their customs, and of the animals which are found there.

It now remains for me to tell about this city and kingdom and province, of which the Father Provincial gave Your Lordship an account. In brief, I can assure you that in reality he has not told the truth in a single thing that he said, but everything is the reverse of what he said, except the name of the city and the large stone houses. For, although they are not decorated with turquoises, nor made of lime nor of good bricks, nevertheless they are very good houses, with three and four and five stories, where there are very good apartments and good rooms with corridors,[1] and some very good rooms under ground and paved, which are made for winter, and are something like a sort of hot baths.[2] The ladders which they have for their houses are all movable and portable, which are taken up and placed wherever they please. They are made of two pieces of wood, with rounds like ours.

The Seven Cities are seven little villages, all having the kind of houses I have described. They are all within a radius of 5 leagues. They are all called the kingdom of Cevola, and each has its own name and no single one is called Cevola, but all together are Cevola. This one which I have called a city I have named Granada, partly because it has some similarity to it, as well as out of regard for Your Lordship. In this place where I am now lodged there are perhaps 200 houses, all surrounded by a wall, and it seems to me that with the other houses, which are not so surrounded, there might be altogether 500 families. There is another town near by, which is one of the seven, but somewhat larger than this, and another of the same size as this, and the other four are somewhat smaller. I send them all to Your Lordship, painted with the route. The skin on which the painting is made was found here with other skins.

The people of the towns seem to me to be of ordinary size and intelligent, although I do not think that they have the judgment and intelligence which they ought to have to build these houses in the way in which they have, for most of them are entirely naked except the covering of their privy parts, and they have painted mantles like the one which I send to Your Lordship. They do not raise cotton, because the country is very cold, but they wear mantles, as may be seen by the exhibit which I send. It is also true that some cotton thread was found in their houses. They wear the hair on their heads like the Mexicans. They all have good figures, and are well bred. I think that they have a quantity of turqoises, which they had removed with the rest of their goods, except the corn, when I arrived, because I did not find any women here nor any men under 15 years or over 60, except two or three old men who remained in command of all the other men and the warriors. Two points of emerald and some little broken stones which approach the color of rather poor garnets[3] were found in a paper, besides other stone crystals, which I gave to one of my servants to keep until they could be sent to Your Lordship. He has lost them, as they tell me. We found fowls, but only a few, and yet there are some. The Indians tell me that they do not eat these in any of the seven villages, but that they keep them merely for the sake of procuring the feathers.[4] I do not believe this, because they are very good, and better than those of Mexico.

The climate of this country and the temperature of the air is almost like that of Mexico, because it is sometimes hot and sometimes it rains. I have not yet seen it rain, however, except once when there fell a little shower with wind, such as often falls in Spain. The snow and the cold are usually very great, according to what the natives of the country all say. This may very probably be so, both because of the nature of the country and the sort of houses they build and the skins and other things which these people have to protect them from the cold. There are no kinds of fruit or fruit trees. The country is all level, and is nowhere shut in by high mountains, although there are some hills and rough passages.[5] There are not many birds, probably because of the cold, and because there are no mountains near. There are no trees fit for firewood here, because they can bring enough for their needs from a clump of very small cedars 4 leagues distant.[6] Very good grass is found a quarter of a league away, where there is pasturage for our horses as well as mowing for hay, of which we had great need, because our horses were so weak and feeble when they arrived.

The food which they eat in this country is corn, of which they have a great abundance, and beans and venison, which they probably eat (although they say that they do not), because we found many skins of deer and hares and rabbits. They make the best corn cakes I have ever seen anywhere, and this is what everybody ordinarily eats. They have the very best arrangement and machinery for grinding that was ever seen [plate LXIV]. One of these Indian women here will grind as much as four of the Mexicans. They have very good salt in crystals, which they bring from a lake a day's journey distant from here. No information can be obtained among them about the North sea or that on the west, nor do I know how to tell Your Lordship which we are nearest to. I should judge that it is nearer to the western, and 150 leagues is the nearest that it seems to me it can be thither. The North sea ought to be much farther away. Your Lordship may thus see how very wide the country is. They have many animals—bears, tigers, lions, porcupines, and some sheep as big as a horse with very large horns and little tails. I have seen some of their horns the size of which was something to marvel at. There are also wild goats, whose heads I have seen, and the paws of the bears and the skins of the wild boars. For game they have deer, leopards, and very large deer,[7] and every one thinks that some of them are larger than that animal which Your Lordship favored me with, which belonged to Juan Melaz. They inhabit some plains eight days' journey toward the north. They have some of their skins here very well dressed, and they prepare and paint them where they kill the cows, according to what they tell me.

IV

Of the nature and situation of the kingdoms of Totonteac, Marata, and Acus, wholly different from the account of Friar Marcos. The conference which they had with the Indians of the city of Granada, which they had captured, who had been forewarned of the coming of Christians into their country fifty years before. The account which was obtained from them concerning seven other cities, of which Tucano is the chief, and how he sent to discover them. A present sent to Mendoza of various things found in this country by Vazquez Coronado.

These Indians say that the kingdom of Totonteac, which the father provincial praised so much, saying that it was something marvelous, and of such a very great size, and that cloth was made there, is a hot lake, on the edge of which there are five or six houses.[1] There used to be some others, but these have been destroyed by war. The kingdom of Marata can not be found, nor do these Indians know anything about it. The kingdom of Acus is a single small city, where they raise cotton, and this is called Acucu.[2] I saw that this is the country, because Acus, with or without the aspiration, is not a word in this region; and because it seems to me that Acucu may be derived from Acus, I say that it is this town which has been converted into the kingdom of Acus. They tell me that there are some other small ones not far from this settlement, which are situated on a river which I have seen and of which the Indians have told me. God knows that I wish I had better news to write to Your Lordship, but I must give you the truth, and, as I wrote you from Culiacan, I must advise you of the good as well as of the bad. But you may be assured that if there had been all the riches and treasures of the world, I could not have done more in His Majesty's service and in that of Your Lordship than I have done, in coming here where you commanded me to go, carrying, both my companions and myself, our food on our backs for 300 leagues, and traveling on foot many days, making our way over hills and rough mountains, besides other labors which I refrain from mentioning. Nor do I think of stopping until my death, if it serves His Majesty or Your Lordship to have it so.

Three days after I captured this city, some of the Indians who lived here came to offer to make peace. They brought me some turquoises and poor mantles, and I received them in His Majesty's name with as good a speech as I could, making them understand the purpose of my coming to this country, which is, in the name of His Majesty and by the commands of Your Lordship, that they and all others in this province should become Christians, and should know the true God for their Lord, and His Majesty for their king and earthly lord. After this they returned to their houses and suddenly, the next day, they packed up their goods and property, their women and children, and fled to the hills, leaving their towns deserted, with only some few remaining in them. Seeing this, I went to the town which I said was larger than this, eight or ten days later, when I had recovered from my wounds. I found a few of them there, whom I told that they ought not to feel any fear, and I asked them to summon their lord to me. By what I can find out or observe, however, none of these towns have any, since I have not seen any principal house by which any superiority over others could be shown.[3] Afterward, an old man, who said he was their lord, came with a mantle made of many pieces, with whom I argued as long as he stayed with me. He said that he would come to see me with the rest of the chiefs of the country, three days later, in order to arrange the relations which should exist between us. He did so, and they brought me some little ragged mantles and some turquoises. I said that they ought to come down from their strongholds and return to their houses with their wives and children, and that they should become Christians, and recognize His Majesty as their king and lord. But they still remain in their strongholds, with their wives and all their property.

I commanded them to have a cloth painted for me, with all the animals that they know in that country, and although they are poor painters, they quickly painted two for me, one of the animals and the other of the birds and fishes. They say that they will bring their children so that our priests may instruct them, and that they desire to know our law. They declare that it was foretold among them more than fifty years ago that a people such as we are should come, and the direction they should come from, and that the whole country would be conquered. So far as I can find out, the water is what these Indians worship, because they say that it makes the corn grow and sustains their life, and that the only other reason they know is because their ancestors did so.[4] I have tried in every way to find out from the natives of these settlements whether they know of any other peoples or provinces or cities. They tell me about seven cities which are at a considerable distance, which are like these, except that the houses there are not like these, but are made of earth [adobe], and small, and that they raise much cotton there. The first of these four places about which they know is called, they say, Tucano. They could not tell me much about the others. I do not believe that they tell me the truth, because they think that I shall soon have to depart from them and return home. But they will quickly find that they are deceived in this. I sent Don Pedro de Tobar there, with his company and some other horsemen, to see it. I would not have dispatched this packet to Your Lordship until I had learned what he found there, if I thought that I should have any news from him within twelve or fifteen days. However, as he will remain away at least thirty, and considering that this information is of little importance and that the cold and the rains are approaching, it seemed to me that I ought to do as Your Lordship commanded me in your instructions, which is, that as soon as I arrived here, I should advise you thereof, and this I do, by sending you the plain narrative of what I have seen, which is bad enough, as you may perceive. I have determined to send throughout all the surrounding regions, in order to find out whether there is anything, and to suffer every extremity before I give up this enterprise, and to serve His Majesty, if I can find any way in which to do it, and not to lack in diligence until Your Lordship directs me as to what I ought to do.

We have great need of pasture, and you should know, also, that among all those who are here there is not one pound of raisins, nor sugar, nor oil, nor wine, except barely half a quart, which is saved to say mass, since everything is consumed, and part was lost on the way. Now, you can provide us with what appears best; but if you are thinking of sending us cattle, you should know that it will be necessary for them to spend at least a year on the road, because they can not come in any other way, nor any quicker. I would have liked to send to Your Lordship, with this dispatch, many samples of the things which they have in this country, but the trip is so long and rough that it is difficult for me to do so. However, I send you twelve small mantles, such as the people of this country ordinarily wear, and a garment which seems to me to be very well made. I kept it because it seemed to me to be of very good workmanship, and because I do not think that anyone has ever seen in these Indies any work done with a needle, unless it were done since the Spaniards settled here. And I also send two cloths painted with the animals which they have in this country, although, as I said, the painting is very poorly done, because the artist did not spend more than one day in painting it. I have seen other paintings on the walls of these houses which have much better proportion and are done much better.

I send you a cow skin, some turquoises, and two earrings of the same, and fifteen of the Indian combs,[5] and some plates decorated with these turquoises, and two baskets made of wicker, of which the Indians have a large supply. I also send two rolls, such as the women usually wear on their heads when they bring water from the spring, the same way that they do in Spain. One of these Indian women, with one of these rolls on her head, will carry a jar of water up a ladder without touching it with her hands. And, lastly, I send you samples of the weapons with which the natives of this country fight, a shield, a hammer, and a bow with some arrows among which there are two with bone points, the like of which have never been seen, according to what these conquerors say. As far as I can judge, it does not appear to me that there is any hope of getting gold or silver, but I trust in God that, if there is any, we shall get our share of it, and it shall not escape us through any lack of diligence in the search.[6] I am unable to give Your Lordship any certain information about the dress of the women, because the Indians keep them guarded so carefully that I have not seen any, except two old women. These had on two long skirts reaching down to their feet and open in front, and a girdle, and they are tied together with some cotton strings. I asked the Indians to give me one of those which they wore, to send to you, since they were not willing to show me the women. They brought me two mantles, which are these that I send, almost painted over. They have two tassels, like the women of Spain, which hang somewhat over their shoulders.

The death of the negro is perfectly certain, because many of the things which he wore have been found, and the Indians say that they killed him here because the Indians of Chichilticale said that he was a bad man, and not like the Christians, because the Christians never kill women, and he killed them, and because he assaulted their women, whom the Indians love better than themselves. Therefore they determined to kill him, but they did not do it in the way that was reported, because they did not kill any of the others who came with him, nor did they kill the lad from the province of Petatlan, who was with him, but they took him and kept him in safe custody until now. When I tried to secure him, they made excuses for not giving him to me, for two or three days, saying that he was dead, and at other times that the Indians of Acucu had taken him away. But when I finally told them that I should be very angry if they did not give him to me, they gave him to me. He is an interpreter; for although he can not talk much, he understands very well.

Some gold and silver has been found in this place, which those who know about minerals say is not bad. I have not yet been able to learn from these people where they got it. I perceive that they refuse to tell me the truth in everything, because they think that I shall have to depart from here in a short time, as I have said. But I trust in God that they will not be able to avoid answering much longer. I beg Your Lordship to make a report of the success of this expedition to His Majesty, because there is nothing more than what I have already said. I shall not do so until it shall please God to grant that we find what we desire. Our Lord God protect and keep your most illustrious Lordship. From the province of Cevola, and this city of Granada, the 3d of August, 1540. Francisco Vazquez de Coronado kisses the hand of your most illustrious Lordship.

Translation of the Traslado de las Nuevas[1]

Copy of the Reports and Descriptions that Have Been Received Regarding the Discovery of a City which is called Cibola, Situated in the New Country.

His grace left the larger part of his army in the valley of Culiacan, and with only 75 companions on horseback and 30 footmen, he set out for here Thursday, April 22. The army which remained there was to start about the end of the month of May, because they could not find any sort of sustenance for the whole of the way that they had to go, as far as this province of Cibola, which is 350 long leagues, and on this account he did not dare to put the whole army on the road. As for the men he took with him, he ordered them to make provision for eighty days, which was carried on horses, each having one for himself and his followers. With very great danger of suffering hunger, and not less labor, since they had to open the way, and every day discovered waterways and rivers with bad crossings, they stood it after a fashion, and on the whole journey as far as this province there was not a peck of corn.

He reached this province on Wednesday, the 7th of July last, with all the men whom he led from the valley very well, praise be to Our Lord, except one Spaniard who died of hunger four days from here and some negroes and Indians who also died of hunger and thirst. The Spaniard was one of those on foot, and was named Espinosa. In this way his grace spent seventy-seven days on the road before reaching here, during which God knows in what sort of a way we lived, and whether we could have eaten much more than we ate the day that his grace reached this city of Granada, for so it has been named out of regard for the viceroy, and because they say it resembles the Albaicin.[2] The force he led was not received the way it should have been, because they all arrived very tired from the great labor of the journey. This, and the loading and unloading like so many muleteers, and not eating as much as they should have, left them more in need of resting several days than of fighting, although there was not a man in the army who would not have done his best in everything if the horses, who suffered the same as their masters, could have helped them.

The city was deserted by men over sixty years and under twenty, and by women and children. All who were there were the fighting men who remained to defend the city, and many of them came out, about a crossbow shot, uttering loud threats. The general himself went forward with two priests and the army-master, to urge them to surrender, as is the custom in new countries. The reply that he received was from many arrows which they let fly, and they wounded Hernando Bermejo's horse and pierced the loose flap of the frock of father Friar Luis, the former companion of the Lord Bishop of Mexico. When this was seen, taking as their advocate the Holy Saint James,[3] he rushed upon them with all his force, which he had kept in very good order, and although the Indians turned their backs and tried to reach the city, they were overtaken and many of them killed before they could reach it. They killed three horses and wounded seven or eight.

When my lord the general reached the city, he saw that it was surrounded by stone walls, and the houses very high, four and five and even six stories apiece, with their flat roofs and balconies. As the Indians had made themselves secure within it, and would not let anyone come near without shooting arrows at him, and as we could not obtain anything to eat unless we captured it, his grace decided to enter the city on foot and to surround it by men on horseback, so that the Indians who were inside could not get away. As he was distinguished among them all by his gilt arms and a plume on his headpiece, all the Indians aimed at him, because he was noticeable among all, and they knocked him down to the ground twice by chance stones thrown from the flat roofs, and stunned him in spite of his headpiece, and if this had not been so good, I doubt if he would have come out alive from that enterprise, and besides all this—praised be Our Lord that he came out on his own feet—they hit him many times with stones on his head and shoulders and legs, and he received two small wounds on his face and an arrow wound in the right foot; but despite all this his grace is as sound and well as the day he left that city. And you[4] may assure my lord of all this, and also that on the 19th of July last he went 4 leagues from this city to see a rock where they told him that the Indians of this province had fortified themselves,[5] and he returned the same day, so that he went 8 leagues in going and returning.

I think I have given you an account of everything, for it is right that I should be the authority for you and his lordship, to assure you that everything is going well with the general my lord, and without any hesitation I can assure you that he is as well and sound as the day he left the city. He is located within the city, for when the Indians saw that his grace was determined to enter the city, then they abandoned it, since they let them go with their lives. We found in it what we needed more than gold and silver, and that was much corn and beans and fowls, better than those of New Spain, and salt, the best and whitest that I have seen in all my life.

This is the Latest Account of Cibola, and of More than Four Hundred Leagues Beyond.[1]

It is more than 300 leagues from Culiacan to Cibola, uninhabited most of the way. There are very few people there; the country is sterile; the roads are very bad. The people go around entirely naked, except the women, who wear white tanned deer skins from the waist down, something like little skirts, reaching to the feet. Their houses are of mats made of reeds; the houses are round and small, so that there is hardly room inside for a man on his feet. The country is sandy where they live near together and where they plant. They raise corn, but not very much, and beans and melons, and they also live on game—rabbits, hares, and deer. They do not have sacrifices. This is between Culiacan and Cibola.

Cibola is a village of about 200 houses. They have two and three and four and five stories. The walls are about a handbreadth thick; the sticks of timber are as large as the wrist, and round; for boards, they have very small bushes, with their leaves on, covered with a sort of greenish-colored mud; the walls are of dirt and mud, the doors of the houses are like the hatchways of ships. The houses are close together, each joined to the others. Outside of the houses they have some hot-houses (or estufas) of dirt mud, where they take refuge from the cold in the winter—because this is very great, since it snows six months in the year.

Some of these people wear cloaks of cotton and of the maguey (or Mexican aloe) and of tanned deer skin, and they wear shoes made of these skins, reaching up to the knees. They also make cloaks of the skins of hares and rabbits, with which they cover themselves. The women wear cloaks of the maguey, reaching down to the feet, with girdles; they wear their hair gathered about the ears like little wheels. They raise corn and beans and melons, which is all they need to live on, because it is a small tribe. The land where they plant is entirely sandy; the water is brackish; the country is very dry. They have some fowls, although not many. They do not know what sort of a thing fish is. There are seven villages in this province of Cibola within a space of 5 leagues; the largest may have about 200 houses and two others about 200, and the others somewhere between 60 or 50 and 30 houses.

It is 60 leagues from Cibola to the river and province of Tibex [Tiguex]. The first village is 40 leagues from Cibola, and is called Acuco. This village is on top of a very strong rock; it has about 200 houses, built in the same way as at Cibola, where they speak another language. It is 20 leagues from here to the river of Tiguex. The river is almost as wide as that of Seville, although not so deep; it flows through a level country; the water is good; it contains some fish; it rises in the north. He who relates this, saw twelve villages within a certain distance of the river; others saw more, they say, up the river. Below, all the villages are small, except two that have about 200 houses. The walls of these houses are something like mud walls of dirt and sand, very rough; they are as thick as the breadth of a hand. The houses have two and three stories; the construction is like those at Cibola. The country is very cold. They have hot-houses, as in Cibola, and the river freezes so thick that load animals cross it, and it would be possible for carts to do so. They raise as much corn as they need, and beans and melons. They have some fowls, which they keep so as to make cloaks of their feathers. They raise cotton, although not much; they wear cloaks made of this, and shoes of hide, as at Cibola. These people defend themselves very well, and from within their houses, since they do not care to come out. The country is all sandy.

Four days' journey from the province and river of Tiguex four villages are found. The first has 30 houses; the second is a large village destroyed in their wars, and has about 35 houses occupied; the third about ———. These three are like those at the river in every way. The fourth is a large village which is among some mountains. It is called Cicuic, and has about 50 houses, with as many stories as those at Cibola. The walls are of dirt and mud like those at Cibola. It has plenty of corn, beans and melons, and some fowls. Four days from this village they came to a country as level as the sea, and in these plains there was such a multitude of cows that they are numberless. These cows are like those of Castile, and somewhat larger, as they have a little hump on the withers, and they are more reddish, approaching black; their hair, more than a span long, hangs down around their horns and ears and chin, and along the neck and shoulders like manes, and down from the knees; all the rest is a very fine wool, like merino; they have very good, tender meat, and much fat.

Having proceeded many days through these plains, they came to a settlement of about 200 inhabited houses. The houses were made of the skins of the cows, tanned white, like pavilions or army tents. The maintenance or sustenance of these Indians comes entirely from the cows, because they neither sow nor reap corn. With the skins they make their houses, with the skins they clothe and shoe themselves, of the skins they make rope, and also of the wool; from the sinews they make thread, with which they sew their clothes and also their houses; from the bones they make awls; the dung serves them for wood, because there is nothing else in that country; the stomachs serve them for pitchers and vessels from which they drink; they live on the flesh; they sometimes eat it half roasted and warmed over the dung, at other times raw; seizing it with their fingers, they pull it out with one hand and with a flint knife in the other they cut off mouthfuls, and thus swallow it half chewed; they eat the fat raw, without warming it; they drink the blood just as it leaves the cows, and at other times after it has run out, cold and raw; they have no other means of livelihood.

These people have dogs like those in this country, except that they are somewhat larger, and they load these dogs like beasts of burden, and make saddles for them like our pack saddles, and they fasten them with their leather thongs, and these make their backs sore on the withers like pack animals. When they go hunting, they load these with their necessities, and when they move—for these Indians are not settled in one place, since they travel wherever the cows move, to support themselves—these dogs carry their houses, and they have the sticks of their houses dragging along tied on to the pack-saddles, besides the load which they carry on top, and the load may be, according to the dog, from 35 to 50 pounds. It is 30 leagues, or even more, from Cibola to these plains where they went. The plains stretch away beyond, nobody knows how far. The captain, Francisco Vazquez, went farther across the plains, with 30 horsemen, and Friar Juan de Padilla with him; all the rest of the force returned to the settlement at the river to wait for Francisco Vazquez, because this was his command. It is not known whether he has returned.

The country is so level that men became lost when they went off half a league. One horseman was lost, who never reappeared, and two horses, all saddled and bridled, which they never saw again. No track was left of where they went, and on this account it was necessary to mark the road by which they went with cow dung, so as to return, since there were no stones or anything else.

Marco Polo, the Venetian, in his treatise, in chapter 15, relates and says that (he saw) the same cows, with the same sort of hump; and in the same chapter he says that there are sheep as big as horses.

Nicholas, the Venetian, gave an account to Micer Pogio, the Florentine, in his second book, toward the end, which says that in Ethiopia there are oxen with a hump, like camels, and they have horns 3 cubits long, and they carry their horns up over their backs, and one of these horns makes a wine pitcher.

Marco Polo, in chapter 134, says that in the country of the Tartars, toward the north, they have dogs as large or little smaller than asses. They harness these into a sort of cart and with these enter a very miry country, all a quagmire, where other animals can not enter and come out without getting submerged, and on this account they take dogs.

Translation of the Relacion del Suceso[1]

Account of what Happened on the Journey which Francisco Vazquez Made to Discover Cibola

When the army reached the valley of Culiacan, Francisco Vazquez divided the army on account of the bad news which was received regarding Cibola, and because the food supply along the way was small, according to the report of Melchor Diaz, who had just come back from seeing it. He himself took 80 horsemen and 25 foot soldiers, and a small part of the artillery, and set out from Culiacan, leaving Don Tristan de Arellano with the rest of the force, with orders to set out twenty days later, and when he reached the Valley of Hearts (Corazones) to wait there for a letter from him, which would be sent after he had reached Cibola, and had seen what was there; and this was done. The Valley of Hearts is 150 leagues from the valley of Culiacan, and the same distance from Cibola.

This whole distance, up to about 50 leagues before reaching Cibola, is inhabited, although it is away from the road in some places. The population is all of the same sort of people, since the houses are all of palm mats, and some of them have low lofts. They all have corn, although not much, and in some places very little. They have melons and beans. The best settlement of all is a valley called Señora, which is 10 leagues beyond the Hearts, where a town was afterward settled. There is some cotton among these, but deer skins are what most of them use for clothes.

Francisco Vazquez passed by all these on account of the small crops. There was no corn the whole way, except at this valley of Señora, where they collected a little, and besides this he had what he took from Culiacan, where he provided himself for eighty days. In seventy-three days we reached Cibola, although after hard labor and the loss of many horses and the death of several Indians, and after we saw it these were all doubled, although we did find corn enough. We found the natives peaceful for the whole way.

The day we reached the first village part of them came out to fight us, and the rest stayed in the village and fortified themselves. It was not possible to make peace with these, although we tried hard enough, so it was necessary to attack them and kill some of them. The rest then drew back to the village, which was then surrounded and attacked. We had to withdraw, on account of the great damage they did us from the flat roofs, and we began to assault them from a distance with the artillery and muskets, and that afternoon they surrendered. Francisco Vazquez came out of it badly hurt by some stones, and I am certain, indeed, that he would have been there yet if it had not been for the army-master, D. Garcia Lopez de Cardenas, who rescued him. When the Indians surrendered, they abandoned the village and went to the other villages, and as they left the houses we made ourselves at home in them.

Father Friar Marcos understood, or gave to understand, that the region and neighborhood in which there are seven villages was a single village which he called Cibola, but the whole of this settled region is called Cibola. The villages have from 150 to 200 and 300 houses; some have the houses of the village all together, although in some villages they are divided into two or three sections, but for the most part they are all together, and their courtyards are within, and in these are their hot rooms for winter, and they have their summer ones outside the villages. The houses have two or three stories, the walls of stone and mud, and some have mud walls. The villages have for the most part the walls of the houses; the houses are too good for Indians, especially for these, since they are brutish and have no decency in anything except in their houses.

For food they have much corn and beans and melons, and some fowls, like those of Mexico, and they keep these more for their feathers than to eat, because they make long robes of them, since they do not have any cotton; and they wear cloaks of heniquen (a fibrous plant), and of the skins of deer, and sometimes of cows.

Their rites and sacrifices are somewhat idolatrous, but water is what they worship most, to which they offer small painted sticks and feathers and yellow powder made of flowers, and usually this offering is made to springs. Sometimes, also, they offer such turquoises as they have, although poor ones.

From the valley of Culiacan to Cibola it is 240 leagues in two directions. It is north to about the thirty-fourth-and-a-half degree, and from there to Cibola, which is nearly the thirty-seventh degree, toward the northeast.

Having talked with the natives of Cibola about what was beyond, they said that there were settlements toward the west. Francisco Vazquez then sent Don Pedro de Tobar to investigate, who found seven other villages, which were called the province of Tuzan; this is 35 leagues to the west. The villages are somewhat larger than those of Cibola, and in other respects in food and everything, they are of the same sort, except that these raise cotton. While Don Pedro de Tobar had gone to see these, Francisco Vazquez dispatched messengers to the viceroy, with an account of what had happened up to this point.[2] He also prepared instructions for these to take to Don Tristan, who as I have said, was at Hearts, for him to proceed to Cibola, and to leave a town established in the valley of Señora, which he did, and in it he left 80 horsemen of the men who had but one horse and the weakest men, and Melchor Diaz with them as captain and leader, because Francisco Vazquez had so arranged for it. He ordered him to go from there with half the force to explore toward the west; and he did so, and traveled 150 leagues, to the river which Hernando de Alarcon entered from the sea, which he called the Buenaguia. The settlements and people that are in this direction are mostly like those at the Hearts, except at the river and around it, where the people have much better figures and have more corn, although the houses in which they live are hovels, like pig pens, almost under ground, with a covering of straw, and made without any skill whatever. This river is reported to be large. They reached it 30 leagues from the coast, where, and as far again above, Alarcon had come up with his boats two months before they reached it. This river runs north and south there. Melchor Diaz passed on toward the west five or six days, from which he returned for the reason that he did not find any water or vegetation, but only many stretches of sand; and he had some fighting on his return to the river and its vicinity, because they wanted to take advantage of him while crossing the river. While returning Melchor Diaz died from an accident, by which he killed himself, throwing a lance at a dog.

After Don Pedro de Tobar returned and had given an account of those villages, he then dispatched Don Garcia Lopez de Cardenas, the army-master, by the same road Don Pedro had followed, to go beyond that province of Tuzan to the west, and he allowed him eighty days in which to go and return, for the journey and to make the discoveries. He was conducted beyond Tuzan by native guides, who said there were settlements beyond, although at a distance. Having gone 50 leagues west of Tuzan, and 80 from Cibola, he found the edge of a river down which it was impossible to find a path for a horse in any direction, or even for a man on foot, except in one very difficult place, where there was a descent for almost 2 leagues. The sides were such a steep rocky precipice that it was scarcely possible to see the river, which looks like a brook from above, although it is half as large again as that of Seville, according to what they say, so that although they sought for a passage with great diligence, none was found for a long distance, during which they were for several days in great need of water, which could not be found, and they could not approach that of the river, although they could see it, and on this account Don Garcia Lopez was forced to return. This river comes from the northeast and turns toward the south-southwest at the place where they found it, so that it is without any doubt the one that Melchor Diaz reached.

Four days after Francisco Vazquez had dispatched Don Garcia Lopez to make this discovery, he dispatched Hernando de Alvarado to explore the route toward the east. He started off, and 30 leagues from Cibola found a rock with a village on top, the strongest position that ever was seen in the world, which was called Acuco[3] in their language, and father Friar Marcos called it the kingdom of Hacus. They came out to meet us peacefully, although it would have been easy to decline to do this and to have stayed on their rock, where we would not have been able to trouble them. They gave us cloaks of cotton, skins of deer and of cows, and turquoises, and fowls and other food which they had, which is the same as in Cibola.

Twenty leagues to the east of this rock we found a river which runs north and south,[4] well settled; there are in all, small and large, 70 villages near it, a few more or less, the same sort as those at Cibola, except that they are almost all of well-made mud walls. The food is neither more nor less. They raise cotton—I mean those who live near the river—the others not. There is much corn here. These people do not have markets. They are settled for 50 leagues along this river, north and south, and some villages are 15 or 20 leagues distant, in one direction and the other. This river rises where these settlements end at the north, on the slope of the mountains there, where there is a larger village different from the others, called Yuraba.[5] It is settled in this fashion: It has 18 divisions; each one has a situation as if for two ground plots; the houses are very close together, and have five or six stories, three of them with mud walls and two or three with thin wooden walls, which become smaller as they go up, and each one has its little balcony outside of the mud walls, one above the other, all around, of wood. In this village, as it is in the mountains, they do not raise cotton nor breed fowls; they wear the skins of deer and cows entirely. It is the most populous village of all that country; we estimated there were 15,000 souls in it. There is one of the other kind of villages larger than all the rest, and very strong, which is called Cicuique.⁶ It has four and five stories, has eight large courtyards, each one with its balcony, and there are fine houses in it.

They do not raise cotton, nor keep fowls, because it is 15 leagues away from the river to the east, toward the plains where the cows are. After Alvarado had sent an account of this river to Francisco Vazquez, he proceeded forward to these plains, and at the borders of these he found a little river which flows to the southwest, and after four days' march he found the cows, which are the most monstrous thing in the way of animals which has ever been seen or read about. He followed this river for 100 leagues, finding more cows every day. We provided ourselves with some of these, although at first, until we had had experience, at the risk of the horses. There is such a quantity of them that I do not know what to compare them with, except with the fish in the sea, because on this journey, as also on that which the whole army afterward made when it was going to Quivira, there were so many that many times when we started to pass through the midst of them and wanted to go through to the other side of them, we were not able to, because the country was covered with them. The flesh of these is as good as that of Castile, and some said it was even better.

The bulls are large and brave, although they do not attack very much; but they have wicked horns, and in a fight use them well, attacking fiercely; they killed several of our horses and wounded many. We found the pike to be the best weapon to use against them, and the musket for use when this misses.

When Hernando de Alvarado returned from these plains to the river which was called Tiguex, he found the army-master Don Garcia Lopez de Cardenas getting ready for the whole army, which was coming there. When it arrived, although all these people had met Hernando de Alvarado peacefully, part of them rebelled when all the force came. There were 12 villages near together, and one night they killed 40 of our horses and mules which were loose in the camp. They fortified themselves in their villages, and war was then declared against them. Don Garcia Lopez went to the first and took it and executed justice on many of them. When the rest saw this, they abandoned all except two of the villages, one of these the strongest one of all, around which the army was kept for two months. And although after we invested it, we entered it one day and occupied a part of the flat roof, we were forced to abandon this on account of the many wounds that were received and because it was so dangerous to maintain ourselves there, and although we again entered it soon afterward, in the end it was not possible to get it all, and so it was surrounded all this time. We finally captured it because of their thirst, and they held out so long because it snowed twice when they were just about to give themselves up. In the end we captured it, and many of them were killed because they tried to get away at night.

Francisco Vazquez obtained an account from some Indians who were found in this village of Cicuique, which, if it had been true, was of the richest thing that had been found in the Indies. The Indian who gave the news and the account came from a village called Harale, 300 leagues east of this river. He gave such a clear account of what he told, as if it was true and he had seen it, that it seemed plain afterward that it was the devil who was speaking in him. Francisco Vazquez and all of us placed much confidence in him, although he was advised by several gentlemen not to move the whole army, but rather to send a captain to find out what was there. He did not wish to do this, but wanted to take every one, and even to send Don Pedro de Tobar to the Hearts for half the men who were in that village. So he started with the whole army, and proceeded 150 leagues, 100 to the east and 50 to the south,[7] and the Indian failing to make good what he had said about there being a settlement there, and corn, with which to proceed farther, the other two guides were asked how that was, and one confessed that what the Indian said was a lie, except that there was a province which was called Quivira, and that there was corn and houses of straw there, but that they were very far off, because we had been led astray a distance from the road. Considering this, and the small supply of food that was left, Francisco Vazquez, after consulting with the captains, determined to proceed with 30 of the best men who were well equipped, and that the army should return to the river; and this was done at once. Two days before this, Don Garcia Lopez' horse had happened to fall with him, and he threw his arm out of joint, from which he suffered much, and so Don Tristan de Arellano returned to the river with the army. On this journey they had a very hard time, because almost all of them had nothing to eat except meat, and many suffered on this account. They killed a world of bulls and cows, for there were days when they brought 60 and 70 head into camp, and it was necessary to go hunting every day, and on this account, and from not eating any corn during all this time, the horses suffered much.

Francisco Vazquez set out across these plains in search of Quivira, more on account of the story which had been told us at the river than from the confidence which was placed in the guide here, and after proceeding many days by the needle (i.e., to the north) it pleased God that after thirty days' march we found the river Quivira, which is 30 leagues below the settlement. While going up the valley, we found people who were going hunting, who were natives of Quivira.

All that there is at Quivira is a very brutish people, without any decency whatever in their houses nor in anything. These are of straw, like the Tarascan settlements; in some villages there are as many as 200 houses; they have corn and beans and melons; they do not have cotton nor fowls, nor do they make bread which is cooked, except under the ashes. Francisco Vazquez went 25 leagues through these settlements, to where he obtained an account of what was beyond, and they said that the plains come to an end, and that down the river there are people who do not plant, but live wholly by hunting.

They also gave an account of two other large villages, one of which was called Tareque[8] and the other Arae, with straw houses at Tareque, and at Arae some of straw and some of skins. Copper was found here, and they said it came from a distance. From what the Indian had said, it is possible that this village of Arae contains more,[9] from the clear description of it which he gave. We did not find any trace or news of it here. Francisco Vazquez returned from here to the river of Tiguex, where he found the army. We went back by a more direct route, because in going by the way we went we traveled 330 leagues, and it is not more than 200 by that by which we returned. Quivira is in the fortieth degree and the river in the thirty-sixth. It was so dangerous to travel or to go away from the camp in these plains, that it is as if one was traveling on the sea, since the only roads are those of the cows, and they are so level and have no mountain or prominent landmark, that if one went out of sight of it, he was lost, and in this way we lost one man, and others who went hunting wandered around two or three days, lost.

Two kinds of people travel around these plains with the cows; one is called Querechos and the others Teyas; they are very well built, and painted, and are enemies of each other. They have no other settlement or location than comes from traveling around with the cows. They kill all of these they wish, and tan the hides, with which they clothe themselves and make their tents, and they eat the flesh, sometimes even raw, and they also even drink the blood when thirsty. The tents they make are like field tents, and they set them up over some poles they have made for this purpose, which come together and are tied at the top, and when they go from one place to another they carry them on some dogs they have, of which they have many, and they load them with the tents and poles and other things, for the country is so level, as I said, that they can make use of these, because they carry the poles dragging along on the ground. The sun is what they worship most. The skin for the tents is cured on both sides, without the hair, and they have the skins of deer and cows left over.[10] They exchange some cloaks with the natives of the river for corn.

After Francisco Vazquez reached the river, where he found the army, Don Pedro de Tobar came with half the people from the Hearts, and Don Garcia Lopez de Cardenas started off for Mexico, who, besides the fact that his arm was very bad, had permission from the viceroy on account of the death of his brother. Ten or twelve who were sick went with him, and not a man among them all who could fight. He reached the town of the Spaniards and found it burned and two Spaniards and many Indians and horses dead, and he returned to the river on this account, escaping from them by good fortune and great exertions. The cause of this misfortune was that after Don Pedro started and left 40 men there, half of these raised a mutiny and fled, and the Indians, who remembered the bad treatment they had received, attacked them one night and overpowered them because of their carelessness and weakness, and they fled to Culiacan. Francisco Vazquez fell while running a horse about this time and was sick a long time, and after the winter was over he determined to come back, and although they may say something different, he did so, because he wanted to do this more than anything, and so we all came together as far as Culiacan, and each one went where he pleased from there, and Francisco Vazquez came here to Mexico to make his report to the viceroy, who was not at all pleased with his coming, although he pretended so at first. He was pleased that Father Friar Juan de Padilla had stayed there, who went to Quivira, and a Spaniard and a negro with him, and Friar Luis, a very holy lay brother, stayed in Cicuique. We spent two very cold winters at this river, with much snow and thick ice. The river froze one night and remained so for more than a month, so that loaded horses crossed on the ice. The reason these villages are settled in this fashion is supposed to be the great cold, although it is also partly the wars which they have with one another. And this is all that was seen and found out about all that country, which is very barren of fruits and groves. Quivira is a better country, having many huts and not being so cold, although it is more to the north.

Translation of a Letter from Coronado to the King, October 20, 1541[1]

Letters from Francisco Vazquez Coronado to His Majesty, in which he gives an Account of the Discovery of the Province of Tiguex.

Holy Catholic Caesarian Majesty: On April 20 of this year I wrote to Your Majesty from this province of Tiguex, in reply to a letter from Your Majesty dated in Madrid, June 11 a year ago. I gave a detailed account of this expedition, which the viceroy of New Spain ordered me to undertake in Your Majesty's name to this country which was discovered by Friar Marcos of Nice, the provincial of the order of Holy Saint Francis. I described it all, and the sort of force I have, as Your Majesty had ordered me to relate in my letters; and stated that while I was engaged in the conquest and pacification of the natives of this province, some Indians who were natives of other provinces beyond these had told me that in their country there were much larger villages and better houses than those of the natives of this country, and that they had lords who ruled them, who were served with dishes of gold, and other very magnificent things; and although, as I wrote Your Majesty, I did not believe it before I had set eyes on it, because it was the report of Indians and given for the most part by means of signs, yet as the report appeared to me to be very fine and that it was important that it should be investigated for Your Majesty's service, I determined to go and see it with the men I have here. I started from this province on the 23d of last April, for the place where the Indians wanted to guide me.

After nine days' march I reached some plains, so vast that I did not find their limit anywhere that I went, although I traveled over them for more than 300 leagues. And I found such a quantity of cows in these, of the kind that I wrote Your Majesty about, which they have in this country, that it is impossible to number them, for while I was journeying through these plains, until I returned to where I first found them, there was not a day that I lost sight of them. And after seventeen days' march I came to a settlement of Indians who are called Querechos, who travel around with these cows, who do not plant, and who eat the raw flesh and drink the blood of the cows they kill, and they tan the skins of the cows, with which all the people of this country dress themselves here. They have little field tents made of the hides of the cows, tanned and greased, very well made, in which they live while they travel around near the cows, moving with these. They have dogs which they load, which carry their tents and poles and belongings. These people have the best figures of any that I have seen in the Indies. They could not give me any account of the country where the guides were taking me. I traveled five days more as the guides wished to lead me, until I reached some plains, with no more landmarks than as if we had been swallowed up in the sea, where they strayed about, because there was not a stone, nor a bit of rising ground, nor a tree, nor a shrub, nor anything to go by. There is much very fine pasture land, with good grass. And while we were lost in these plains, some horsemen who went off to hunt cows fell in with some Indians who also were out hunting, who are enemies of those that I had seen in the last settlement, and of another sort of people who are called Teyas; they have their bodies and faces all painted; are a large people like the others, of a very good build; they eat the raw flesh just like the Querechos, and live and travel round with the cows in the same way as these. I obtained from these an account of the country where the guides were taking me, which was not like what they had told me, because these made out that the houses there were not built of stones, with stories, as my guides had described it, but of straw and skins, and a small supply of corn there.

This news troubled me greatly, to find myself on these limitless plains, where I was in great need of water, and often had to drink it so poor that it was more mud than water. Here the guides confessed to me that they had not told the truth in regard to the size of the houses, because these were of straw, but that they had done so regarding the large number of inhabitants and the other things about their habits. The Teyas disagreed with this, and on account of this division between some of the Indians and the others, and also because many of the men I had with me had not eaten anything except meat for some days, because we had reached the end of the corn which we carried from this province, and because they made it out more than forty days' journey from where I fell in with the Teyas to the country where the guides were taking me, although I appreciated the trouble and danger there would be in the journey owing to the lack of water and corn, it seemed to me best, in order to see if there was anything there of service to Your Majesty, to go forward with only 30 horsemen until I should be able to see the country, so as to give Your Majesty a true account of what was to be found in it. I sent all the rest of the force I had with me to this province, with Don Tristan de Arellano in command, because it would have been impossible to prevent the loss of many men, if all had gone on, owing to the lack of water and because they also had to kill bulls and cows on which to sustain themselves. And with only the 30 horsemen whom I took for my escort, I traveled forty-two days after I left the force, living all this while solely on the flesh of the bulls and cows which we killed, at the cost of several of our horses which they killed, because, as I wrote Your Majesty, they are very brave and fierce animals; and going many days without water, and cooking the food with cow dung, because there is not any kind of wood in all these plains, away from the gullies and rivers, which are very few.

It was the Lord's pleasure that, after having journeyed across these deserts seventy-seven days, I arrived at the province they call Quivira, to which the guides were conducting me, and where they had described to me houses of stone, with many stories; and not only are they not of stone, but of straw, but the people in them are as barbarous as all those whom I have seen and passed before this; they do not have cloaks, nor cotton of which to make these, but use the skins of the cattle they kill, which they tan, because they are settled among these on a very large river. They eat the raw flesh like the Querechos and Teyas; they are enemies of one another, but are all of the same sort of people, and these at Quivira have the advantage in the houses they build and in planting corn. In this province of which the guides who brought me are natives, they received me peaceably, and although they told me when I set out for it that I could not succeed in seeing it all in two months, there are not more than 25 villages of straw houses there and in all the rest of the country that I saw and learned about, which gave their obedience to Your Majesty and placed themselves under your royal overlordship.

The people here are large. I had several Indians measured, and found that they were 10 palms in height; the women are well proportioned and their features are more like Moorish women than Indians. The natives here gave me a piece of copper which a chief Indian wore hung around his neck; I sent it to the viceroy of New Spain, because I have not seen any other metal in these parts except this and some little copper bells which I sent him, and a bit of metal which looks like gold. I do not know where this came from, although I believe that the Indians who gave it to me obtained it from those whom I brought here in my service, because I can not find any other origin for it nor where it came from. The diversity of languages which exists in this country and my not having anyone who understood them, because they speak their own language in each village, has hindered me, because I have been forced to send captains and men in many directions to find out whether there was anything in this country which could be of service to Your Majesty. And although I have searched with all diligence I have not found or heard of anything, unless it be these provinces, which are a very small affair.

The province of Quivira is 950 leagues from Mexico. Where I reached it, it is in the fortieth degree. The country itself is the best I have ever seen for producing all the products of Spain, for besides the land itself being very fat and black and being very well watered by the rivulets and springs and rivers, I found prunes like those of Spain [or I found everything they have in Spain] and nuts and very good sweet grapes and mulberries. I have treated the natives of this province, and all the others whom I found wherever I went, as well as was possible, agreeably to what Your Majesty had commanded, and they have received no harm in any way from me or from those who went in my company.[2] I remained twenty-five days in this province of Quivira, so as to see and explore the country and also to find out whether there was anything beyond which could be of service to Your Majesty, because the guides who had brought me had given me an account of other provinces beyond this. And what I am sure of is that there is not any gold nor any other metal in all that country, and the other things of which they had told me are nothing but little villages, and in many of these they do not plant anything and do not have any houses except of skins and sticks, and they wander around with the cows; so that the account they gave me was false, believing that as the way was through such uninhabited deserts, and from the lack of water, they would get us where we and our horses would die of hunger. And the guides confessed this, and said they had done it by the advice and orders of the natives of these provinces. At this, after having heard the account of what was beyond, which I have given above, I returned to these provinces to provide for the force I had sent back here and to give Your Majesty an account of what this country amounts to, because I wrote Your Majesty that I would do so when I went there.

I have done all that I possibly could to serve Your Majesty and to discover a country where God Our Lord might be served and the royal patrimony of Your Majesty increased, as your loyal servant and vassal. For since I reached the province of Cibola, to which the viceroy of New Spain sent me in the name of Your Majesty, seeing that there were none of the things there of which Friar Marcos had told, I have managed to explore this country for 200 leagues and more around Cibola, and the best place I have found is this river of Tiguex where I am now, and the settlements here. It would not be possible to establish a settlement here, for besides being 400 leagues from the North sea and more than 200 from the South sea, with which it is impossible to have any sort of communication, the country is so cold, as I have written to Your Majesty, that apparently the winter could not possibly be spent here, because there is no wood, nor cloth with which to protect the men, except the skins which the natives wear and some small amount of cotton cloaks. I send the viceroy of New Spain an account of everything I have seen in the countries where I have been, and as Don Garcia Lopez de Cardenas is going to kiss Your Majesty's hands, who has done much and has served Your Majesty very well on this expedition, and he will give Your Majesty an account of everything here, as one who has seen it himself, I give way to him. And may Our Lord protect the Holy Imperial Catholic person of Your Majesty, with increase of greater kingdoms and powers, as your loyal servants and vassals desire. From this province of Tiguex, October 20, in the year 1541. Your Majesty's humble servant and vassal, who would kiss the royal feet and hands:

Francisco Vazquez Coronado

Translation of the Narrative of Jaramillo

Account Given by Captain Juan Jaramillo of the Journey which he made to the New Country, on which Francisco Vazquez Coronado was the General.[1]

We started from Mexico, going directly to Compostela, the whole way populated and at peace, the direction being west, and the distance 112 leagues. From there we went to Culiacan, perhaps about 80 leagues; the road is well known and much used, because there is a town inhabited by Spaniards in the said valley of Culiacan, under the government of Compostela. The 70 horsemen who went with the general went in a northwesterly direction from this town. He left his army here, because information had been obtained that the way was uninhabited and almost the whole of it without food. He went with the said horsemen to explore the route and prepare the way for those who were to follow. He pursued this direction, though with some twisting, until we crossed a mountain chain, where they knew about New Spain, more than 300 leagues distant. To this pass we gave the name of Chichilte Calli, because we learned that this was what it was called, from some Indians whom we left behind.

Leaving the said valley of Culiacan, he crossed a river called Pateatlan (*or* Peteatlan), which was about four days distant. We found these Indians peaceful, and they gave us some few things to eat. From here we went to another river called Cinaloa, which was about three days from the other. From here the general ordered ten of us horsemen to make double marches, lightly equipped, until we reached the stream of the Cedars (arroyo de los Cedros), and from there we were to enter a break in the mountains on the right of the road and see what there was in and about this. If more time should be needed for this than we gained on him, he would wait for us at the said Cedros stream. This was done, and all that we saw there was a few poor Indians in some settled valleys like farms or estates, with sterile soil. It was about five more days from the river to this stream. From there we went to the river called Yaquemi, which took about three days. We proceeded along a dry stream, and after three days more of marching, although the dry stream lasted only for a league, we reached another stream where there were some settled Indians, who had straw huts and storehouses of corn and beans and melons. Leaving here, we went to the stream and village which is called Hearts (Corazones), the name which was given it by Dorantes and Cabeza de Vaca and Castillo and the negro Estebanillo, because they gave them a present of the hearts of animals and birds to eat.

About two days were spent in this village of the Hearts. There is an irrigation stream, and the country is warm. Their dwellings are huts made of a frame of poles, almost like an oven, only very much better, which they cover with mats. They have corn and beans and melons for food, which I believe never fail them. They dress in deerskins. This appeared to be a good place, and so orders were given the Spaniards who were behind to establish a village here, where they lived until almost the failure of the expedition. There was a poison here, the effect of which is, according to what was seen of it, the worst that could possibly be found; and from what we learned about it, it is the sap of a small tree like the mastick tree, or lentisk, and it grows in gravelly and sterile land. We went on from here, passing through a sort of gateway, to another valley very near this stream, which opens off from this same stream, which is called Señora. It is also irrigated, and the Indians are like the others and have the same sort of settlements and food. This valley continues for 6 or 7 leagues, a little more or less.

At first these Indians were peaceful; and afterward not, but instead they and those whom they were able to summon thither were our worst enemies. They have a poison with which they killed several Christians. There are mountains on both sides of them, which are not very fertile. From here we went along near this said stream, crossing it where it makes a bend, to another Indian settlement called Ispa.[2] It takes one day from the last of these others to this place. It is of the same sort as those we had passed. From here we went through deserted country for about four days to another river, which we heard called Nexpa, where some poor Indians came out to see the general, with presents of little value, with some stalks of roasted maguey and pitahayas. We went down this stream two days, and then left the stream, going toward the right to the foot of the mountain chain in two days' journey, where we heard news of what is called Chichiltic Calli. Crossing the mountains, we came to a deep and reedy river, where we found water and forage for the horses. From this river back at Nexpa, as I have said, it seems to me that the direction was nearly northeast. From here, I believe that we went in the same direction for three days to a river which we called Saint John (San Juan), because we reached it on his day. Leaving here, we went to another river, through a somewhat rough country, more toward the north, to a river which we called the Rafts (de las Balsas), because we had to cross on these, as it was rising. It seems to me that we spent two days between one river and the other, and I say this because it is so long since we went there that I may be wrong in some days, though not in the rest. From here we went to another river, which we called the Slough (de la Barranca). It is two short days from one to the other, and the direction almost northeast. From here we went to another river, which we called the Cold river (el rio Frio), on account of its water being so, in one day's journey, and from here we went by a pine mountain, where we found, almost at the top of it, a cool spring and streamlet, which was another day's march. In the neighborhood of this stream a Spaniard, who was called Espinosa, died, besides two other persons, on account of poisonous plants which they ate, owing to the great need in which they were.

From here we went to another river, which we called the Red river (Bermejo), two days' journey in the same direction, but less toward the northeast. Here we saw an Indian or two, who afterward appeared to belong to the first settlement of Cibola. From here we came in two days' journey to the said village, the first of Cibola. The houses have flat roofs and walls of stone and mud, and this was where they killed Steve (Estebanillo), the negro who had come with Dorantes from Florida and returned with Friar Marcos de Niza. In this province of Cibola there are five little villages besides this, all with flat roofs and of stone and mud, as I said. The country is cold, as is shown by their houses and hothouses (estufas). They have food enough for themselves, of corn and beans and melons. These villages are about a league or more apart from each other, within a circuit of perhaps 6 leagues. The country is somewhat sandy and not very salty (or barren of vegetation)[3], and on the mountains the trees are for the most part evergreen. The clothing of the Indians is of deerskins, very carefully tanned, and they also prepare some tanned cowhides, with which they cover themselves, which are like shawls, and a great protection. They have square cloaks of cotton, some larger than others, about a yard and a half long. The Indians wear them thrown over the shoulder like a gipsy, and fastened with one end over the other, with a girdle, also of cotton. From this first village of Cibola, looking toward the northeast and a little less, on the left hand, there is a province called Tucayan, about five days off, which has seven flat-roof villages, with a food supply as good as or better than these, and an even larger population; and they also have the skins of cows and of deer, and cloaks of cotton, as I described.

All the waterways we found as far as this one at Cibola—and I do not know but what for a day or two beyond—the rivers and streams run into the South sea, and those from here on into the North sea.

From this first village of Cibola, as I have said, we went to another in the same province, which was about a short day's journey off, on the way to Tihuex. It is nine days, of such marches as we made, from this settlement of Cibola to the river of Tihuex. Halfway between, I do not know but it may be a day more or less, there is a village of earth and dressed stone, in a very strong position, which is called Tutahaco.[4] All these Indians, except the first in the first village of Cibola, received us well. At the river of Tihuex there are 15 villages within a distance of about 20 leagues, all with flat-roof houses of earth, instead of stone, after the fashion of mud walls. There are other villages besides these on other streams which flow into this, and three of these are, for Indians, well worth seeing, especially one that is called Chia,[5] and another Uraba,[6] and another Cicuique.[7] Uraba and Cicuique have many houses two stories high. All the rest, and these also, have corn and beans and melons, skins, and some long robes of feathers which they braid, joining the feathers with a sort of thread; and they also make them of a sort of plain weaving with which they make the cloaks with which they protect themselves. They all have hot rooms underground, which, although not very clean, are very warm.[8] They raise and have a very little cotton, of which they make the cloaks which I have spoken of above. This river comes from the northwest and flows about southeast, which shows that it certainly flows into the North sea.

Leaving this settlement[9] and the said river, we passed two other villages whose names I do not know,[10] and in four days came to Cicuique, which I have already mentioned. The direction of this is toward the northeast. From there we came to another river, which the Spaniards named after Cicuique, in three days; if I remember rightly, it seems to me that we went rather toward the northeast to reach this river where we crossed it, and after crossing this, we turned more to the left hand, which would be more to the northeast, and began to enter the plains where the cows are, although we did not find them for some four or five days, after which we began to come across bulls, of which there are great numbers, and after going on in the same direction and meeting the bulls for two or three days, we began to find ourselves in the midst of very great numbers of cows, yearlings and bulls all in together. We found Indians among these first cows, who were, on this account, called Querechos by those in the flat-roof houses. They do not live in houses, but have some sets of poles which they carry with them to make some huts at the places where they stop, which serve them for houses. They tie those poles together at the top and stick the bottoms into the ground, covering them with some cowskins which they carry around, and which, as I have said, serve them for houses. From what was learned of these Indians, all their human needs are supplied by these cows, for they are fed and clothed and shod from these. They are a people who wander around here and there, wherever seems to them best. We went on for eight or ten days in the same direction, along these streams which are among the cows.

The Indian who guided us from here was the one that had given us the news about Quevira and Arache (*or* Arahei) and about its being a very rich country with much gold and other things, and he and the other one were from that country I mentioned, to which we were going, and we found these two Indians in the flat-roof villages. It seems that, as the said Indian wanted to go to his own country, he proceeded to tell us what we found was not true, and I do not know whether it was on this account or because he was counseled to take us into other regions by confusing us on the road, although there are none in all this region except those of the cows. We understood, however, that he was leading us away from the route we ought to follow and that he wanted to lead us on to those plains where he had led us, so that we would eat up the food, and both ourselves and our horses would become weak from the lack of this, because if we should go either backward or forward in this condition we could not make any resistance to whatever they might wish to do to us. From the time when, as I said, we entered the plains and from this settlement of Querechos, he led us off more to the east, until we came to be in extreme need from the lack of food, and as the other Indian, who was his companion and also from his country, saw that he was not taking us where we ought to go, since we had always followed the guidance of the Turk, for so he was called, instead of his, he threw himself down in the way, making a sign that although we cut off his head he ought not to go that way, nor was that our direction.

I believe we had been traveling twenty days or more in this direction, at the end of which we found another settlement of Indians of the same sort and way of living as those behind, among whom there was an old blind man with a beard, who gave us to understand, by signs which he made, that he had seen four others like us many days before, whom he had seen near there and rather more toward New Spain, and we so understood him, and presumed that it was Dorantes and Cabeza de Vaca and those whom I have mentioned.

At this settlement the general, seeing our difficulties, ordered the captains, and the persons whose advice he was accustomed to take, to assemble, so that we might discuss with him what was best for all. It seemed to us that all the force should go back to the region we had come from, in search of food, so that they could regain their strength, and that 30 picked horsemen should go in search of what the Indian had told about; and we decided to do this. We all went forward one day to a stream which was down in a ravine in the midst of good meadows, to agree on who should go ahead and how the rest should return. Here the Indian Isopete, as we had called the companion of the said Turk, was asked to tell us the truth, and to lead us to that country which we had come in search of. He said he would do it, and that it was not as the Turk had said, because those were certainly fine things which he had said and had given us to understand at Tihuex, about gold and how it was obtained, and the buildings, and the style of them, and their trade, and many other things told for the sake of prolixity, which had led us to go in search of them, with the advice of all who gave it and of the priests. He asked us to leave him afterward in that country, because it was his native country, as a reward for guiding us, and also, that the Turk might not go along with him, because he would quarrel and try to restrain him in everything that he wanted to do for our advantage; and the general promised him this, and said he would be with one of the thirty, and he went in this way. And when everything was ready for us to set out and for the others to remain, we pursued our way, the direction all the time after this being toward the north, for more than thirty days' march, although not long marches, not having to go without water on any one of them, and among cows all the time, some days in larger numbers than others, according to the water which we came across, so that on Saint Peter and Paul's day we reached a river which we found to be there below Quibira.

When he reached the said river, the Indian recognized it and said that was it, and that it was below the settlements. We crossed it there and went up the other side on the north, the direction turning toward the northeast, and after marching three days we found some Indians who were going hunting, killing the cows to take the meat to their village, which was about three or four days still farther away from us. Here where we found the Indians and they saw us, they began to utter yells and appeared to fly, and some even had their wives there with them. The Indian Isopete began to call them in his language, and so they came to us without any signs of fear. When we and these Indians had halted here, the general made an example of the Indian Turk, whom we had brought along, keeping him all the time out of sight among the rear guard, and having arrived where the place was prepared, it was done in such a way that the other Indian, who was called Isopete, should not see it, so as to give him the satisfaction he had asked. Some satisfaction was experienced here on seeing the good appearance of the earth, and it is certainly such among the cows, and from there on. The general wrote a letter here to the governor of Harahey and Quibira, having understood that he was a Christian from the lost army of Florida, because what the Indian had said of their manner of government and their general character had made us believe this. So the Indians went to their houses, which were at the distance mentioned, and we also proceeded at our rate of marching until we reached the settlements, which we found along good river bottoms, although without much water, and good streams which flow into another, larger than the one I have mentioned. There were, if I recall correctly, six or seven settlements, at quite a distance from one another, among which we traveled for four or five days, since it was understood to be uninhabited between one stream and the other.

We reached what they said was the end of Quibira, to which they took us, saying that the things there were of great importance.[11] Here there was a river, with more water and more inhabitants than the others. Being asked if there was anything beyond, they said that there was nothing more of Quibira, but that there was Harahey, and that it was the same sort of a place, with settlements like these, and of about the same size. The general sent to summon the lord of those parts and the other Indians who they said resided in Harahey, and he came with about 200 men—all naked—with bows, and some sort of things on their heads, and their privy parts slightly covered. He was a big Indian, with a large body and limbs, and well proportioned. After he had heard the opinion of one and another about it, the general asked them what we ought to do, reminding us of how the army had been left and that the rest of us were there, so that it seemed to all of us that as it was already almost the opening of winter, for, if I remember rightly, it was after the middle of August, and because there was little to winter there for, and we were but very little prepared for it, and the uncertainty as to the success of the army that had been left, and because the winter might close the roads with snow and rivers which we could not cross, and also in order to see what had happened to the rest of the force left behind, it seemed to us all that his grace ought to go back in search of them, and when he had found out for certain how they were, to winter there and return to that country at the opening of spring, to conquer and cultivate it.

Since, as I said, this was the last point which we reached, here the Turk saw that he had lied to us, and one night he called on all these people to attack us and kill us. We learned of it, and put him under guard and strangled him that night so that he never waked up. With the plan mentioned, we turned back it may have been two or three days, where we provided ourselves with picked fruit and dried corn for our return. The general raised a cross at this place, at the foot of which he made some letters with a chisel, which said that Francisco Vazquez de Coronado, general of that army, had arrived here.

This country presents a very fine appearance, than which I have not seen a better in all our Spain nor Italy nor a part of France, nor, indeed, in the other countries where I have traveled in His Majesty's service, for it is not a very rough country, but is made up of hillocks and plains, and very fine appearing rivers and streams, which certainly satisfied me and made me sure that it will be very fruitful in all sorts of products. Indeed, there is profit in the cattle ready to the hand, from the quantity of them, which is as great as one could imagine. We found a variety of Castilian prunes which are not all red, but some of them black and green; the tree and fruit is certainly like that of Castile, with a very excellent flavor. Among the cows we found flax, which springs up from the earth in clumps apart from one another, which are noticeable, as the cattle do not eat it, with their tops and blue flowers, and very perfect although small, resembling that of our own Spain (or and sumach like ours in Spain). There are grapes along some streams, of a fair flavor, not to be improved upon.

The houses which these Indians have were of straw, and most of them round, and the straw reached down to the ground like a wall, so that they did not have the symmetry or the style of these here; they have something like a chapel or sentry box outside and around these, with an entry, where the Indians appear seated or reclining. The Indian Isopete was left here where the cross was erected, and we took five or six of the Indians from these villages to lead and guide us to the flat-roof houses.[12] Thus they brought us back by the same road as far as where I said before that we came to a river called Saint Peter and Paul's, and here we left that by which we had come, and, taking the right hand, they led us along by watering places and among cows and by a good road, although there are none either one way or the other except those of the cows, as I have said. At last we came to where we recognized the country, where I said we found the first settlement, where the Turk led us astray from the route we should have followed. Thus, leaving the rest aside, we reached Tiguex, where we found the rest of the army, and here the general fell while running his horse, by which he received a wound on his head which gave symptoms of turning out badly, and he conceived the idea of returning, which ten or twelve of us were unable to prevent by dissuading him from it.

When this return had been ordered, the Franciscan friars who were with us—one of them a regular and the other a lay brother—who were called, the regular one Friar Juan de Padilla and the lay one Friar Luis de Escalona, were told to get ready, although they had permission from their provincial so that they could remain. Friar Luis wished to remain in these flat-roof houses, saying that he would raise crosses for those villagers with a chisel and adze they left him, and would baptize several poor creatures who could be led, on the point of death, so as to send them to heaven, for which he did not desire any other company than a little slave of mine who was called Christopher, to be his consolation, and who he said would learn the language there quickly so as to help him; and he brought up so many things in favor of this that he could not be denied, and so nothing more has been heard from him. The knowledge that this friar would remain there was the reason that many Indians from hereabouts stayed there, and also two negroes, one of them mine, who was called Sebastian, and the other one of Melchor Perez, the son of the licentiate La Torre. This negro was married and had his wife and children. I also recall that several Indians remained behind in the Quivira region, besides a Tarascan belonging to my company, who was named Andrew. Friar Juan de Padilla preferred to return to Quivira, and persuaded them to give him those Indians whom I said we had brought as guides. They gave him these, and he also took a Portuguese and a free Spanish-speaking Indian, who was the interpreter, and who passed as a Franciscan friar, and a half-blood and two Indians from Capottan (*or* Capotean) or thereabouts, I believe. He had brought these up and took them in the habits of friars, and he took some sheep and mules and a horse and ornaments and other trifles. I do not know whether it was for the sake of these or for what reason, but it seems that they killed him, and those who did it were the lay servants, or these same Indians whom he took back from Tiguex, in return for the good deeds which he had done. When he was dead, the Portuguese whom I mentioned fled, and also one of the Indians that I said he took in the habits of friars, or both of them, I believe. I mention this because they came back to this country of New Spain by another way and a shorter route than the one of which I have told, and they came out in the valley of Panico.[13] I have given Gonzalo Solis de Meras and Isidoro de Solis an account of this, because it seemed to me important, according to what I say I have understood, that His Majesty ordered Your Lordship to find or discover a way so as to unite that land to this. It is perhaps also very likely that this Indian Sebastian, during the time he was in Quivira, learned about its territory and the country round about it, and also of the sea, and the road by which he came, and what there is to it, and how many days' journey before arriving there. So that I am sure that if Your Lordship acquires this Quivira on this account, I am certain that he can confidently bring many people from Spain to settle it according to the appearance and the character of the land.

Translation of the Report of Hernando de Alvarado

Account of what Hernando de Alvarado and Friar Juan de Padilla Discovered Going in Search of the South Sea.[1]

We set out from Granada on Sunday, the day of the beheading of Saint John the Baptist, the 29th of August, in the year 1540, on the way to Coco.[2] After we had gone 2 leagues, we came to an ancient building like a fortress, and a league beyond this we found another, and yet another a little farther on, and beyond these we found an ancient city, very large, entirely destroyed, although a large part of the wall was standing, which was six times as tall as a man, the wall well made of good worked stone, with gates and gutters like a city in Castile. Half a league or more beyond this, we found another ruined city, the walls of which must have been very fine, built of very large granite blocks, as high as a man and from there up of very good quarried stone. Here two roads separate, one to Chia and the other to Coco; we took this latter, and reached that place, which is one of the strongest places that we have seen, because the city is on a very high rock, with such a rough ascent that we repented having gone up the place. The houses have three or four stories; the people are the same sort as those of the province of Cibola; they have plenty of food, of corn and beans and fowls like those of New Spain. From here we went to a very good lake or marsh, where there are trees like those of Castile, and from there we went to a river, which we named Our Lady (Nuestra Señora), because we reached it the evening before her day in the month of September.[3] We sent the cross by a guide to the villages in advance, and the next day people came from twelve villages, the chief men and the people in order, those of one village behind those of another, and they approached the tent to the sound of a pipe, and with an old man for spokesman. In this fashion they came into the tent and gave me the food and clothes and skins they had brought, and I gave them some trinkets, and with this they went off.

This river of Our Lady flows through a very wide open plain sowed with corn plants; there are several groves, and there are twelve villages, The houses are of earth, two stories high; the people have a good appearance, more like laborers than a warlike race; they have a large food supply of corn, beans, melons, and fowl in great plenty; they clothe themselves with cotton and the skins of cows and dresses of the feathers of the fowls; they wear their hair short. Those who have the most authority among them are the old men; we regarded them as witches, because they say that they go up into the sky and other things of the same sort. In this province there are seven other villages, depopulated and destroyed by those Indians who paint their eyes, of whom the guides will tell Your Grace; they say that these live in the same region as the cows, and that they have corn and houses of straw.

Here the people from the outlying provinces came to make peace with me, and as Your Grace may see in this memorandum, there are 80 villages there of the same sort as I have described, and among them one which is located on some streams; it is divided into twenty divisions, which is something remarkable; the houses have three stories of mud walls and three others made of small wooden boards, and on the outside of the three stories with the mud wall they have three balconies; it seemed to us that there were nearly 15,000 persons in this village. The country is very cold; they do not raise fowls nor cotton; they worship the sun and water. We found mounds of dirt outside of the place, where they are buried.

In the places where crosses were raised, we saw them worship these. They made offerings to these of their powder and feathers, and some left the blankets they had on. They showed so much zeal that some climbed up on the others to grasp the arms of the cross, to place feathers and flowers there; and others bringing ladders, while some held them, went up to tie strings, so as to fasten the flowers and the feathers.

Testimony Concerning Those Who Went on the Expedition with Francisco Vazquez Coronado[1]

At Compostela, on February 21, 1540, Coronado presented a petition to the viceroy Mendoza, declaring that he had observed that certain persons who were not well disposed toward the expedition which was about to start for the newly discovered country had said that many of the inhabitants of the City of Mexico and of the other cities and towns of New Spain, and also of Compostela and other places in this province of New Galicia were going on the expedition at his request or because of inducements offered by him, as a result of which the City of Mexico and New Spain were left deserted, or almost so. Therefore, he asked the viceroy to order that information be obtained, in order that the truth might be known about the citizens of New Spain and of this province who were going to accompany him. He declared that there were very few of these, and that they were not going on account of any attraction or inducement offered by him, but of their own free will, and as there were few of them, there would not be any lack of people in New Spain. And as Gonzalo de Salazar, the factor or royal agent, and Pero Almidez Cherino, the veedor or royal inspector of His Majesty for New Spain, and other citizens of Mexico who knew all the facts and had the necessary information, were present there, Coronado asked His Grace to provide and order that which would best serve His Majesty's interests and the welfare and security of New Spain.

The viceroy instructed the licentiate Maldonado, oidor of the royal audiencia,[2] to procure this information. To facilitate the hearing he provided that the said factor and veedor and the regidores, and others who were there, should attend the review of the army, which was to be held on the following day. Nine of the desired witnesses were also commanded by Maldonado to attend the review and observe those whom they knew in the army.

On February 26[3] the licentiate Maldonado took the oaths of the witnesses in proper form, and they testified to the following effect:

Hernand Perez de Bocanegra, a citizen of Mexico, stated that he had been present on the preceding Sunday, at the review of the force which the viceroy was sending for the pacification of the country recently discovered by the father provincial, Fray Marcos de Niza, and that he had taken note of the force as the men passed before him; and at his request he had also been allowed to see the list of names of those who were enrolled in the army: and he declared that in all the said force he did not recognize any other citizens of Mexico who were going except Domingo Martin, a married man, whom he had sometimes seen living in Mexico, and provided him with messengers; and one Alonso Sanchez, who was going with his wife and a son, and who was formerly a shoemaker; and a young man, son of the *bachiller* Alonso Perez, who had come only a few days before from Salamanca, and who had been sent to the war by his father on account of his restlessness; and two or three other workmen or tradespeople whom he had seen at work in Mexico, although he did not know whether they were citizens there; and on his oath he did not see in the whole army anyone else who was a citizen of Mexico, although for about fourteen years he had been a citizen and inhabitant of that city, unless it was the captain-general, Francisco Vazquez de Coronado, and Lopez de Samaniego the army-master; and, moreover, he declared that he felt certain that those above mentioned were going of their own free will, like all the rest.

Antonio Serrano de Cardona, one of the magistrates of Mexico, who was present from beginning to end of the review of the preceding Sunday, testified in similar form. He said that Alonso Sanchez had formerly been a citizen of Mexico, but that for a long time his house had been empty and he had traveled as a trader, and that he was going in search of something to live on; and one Domingo Martin was also going, who formerly lived in Mexico, and whose residence he had not known likewise for a long time, nor did he think that he had one, because he had not seen him living in Mexico. He did not think it would have been possible for any citizens of Mexico to have been there whom he did not know, because he had lived in Mexico during the twenty years since he came to Mexico, and ever since the city was established by Christians, and besides, he had been a magistrate for fifteen years. And besides, all those whom he did see who were going, were the most contented of any men he had ever seen in this country starting off for conquests. After the force left the City of Mexico, he had been there, and had noticed that it was full of people and that there did not seem to be any scarcity on account of those who had started on this expedition.

Gonzalo de Salazar, His Majesty's factor for New Spain, and also a magistrate of the City of Mexico, declared that the only person on the expedition who possessed a repartimiento or estate in New Spain was the captain-general, Vazquez de Coronado, and that he had noticed one other citizen who did not have a repartimiento. He had not seen any other citizen of Mexico, nor of New Spain, although one of the greatest benefits that could have been done New Spain would have been to draw off the young and vicious people who were in that city and all over New Spain.

Pedro Almidez Cherino, His Majesty's veedor in New Spain, had, among other things, noted the horses and arms of those who were going, during the review. He had noticed Coronado and Samaniego, and Alonso Sanchez and his wife, whom he did not know to be a citizen, and Domingo Martin, who was away from Mexico during most of the year. All the rest of the force were people without settled residences, who had recently come to the country in search of a living. It seemed to him that it was a very fortunate thing for Mexico that the people who were going were about to do so because they had been injuring the citizens there. They had been for the most part vicious young gentlemen, who did not have anything to do in the city nor in the country. They were all going of their own free will, and were very ready to help pacify the new country, and it seemed to him that if the said country had not been discovered, almost all of these people would have gone back to Castile, or would have gone to Peru or other places in search of a living.

Servan Bejarano, who had been in business among the inhabitants of Mexico ever since he came to that city, added the information that he knew Alonso Sanchez to be a provision dealer, buying at wholesale and selling at retail, and that he was in very great need, having nothing on which to live, and that he was going to that country in search of a living. He was also very sure that it was a great advantage to Mexico and to its citizens to have many of the unmarried men go away, because they had no occupation there and were bad characters, and were for the most part gentlemen and persons who did not hold any property, nor any repartimientos of Indians, without any income, and lazy, and who would have been obliged to go to Peru or some other region.

Cristobal de Oñate had been in the country about sixteen years, a trifle more or less, and was now His Majesty's veedor for New Galicia. He knew the citizens of Mexico, and also declared that not a citizen of Compostela was going on the expedition. Two citizens of Guadalajara were going, one of whom was married to an Indian, and the other was single. As for the many young gentlemen and the others who were going, who lived in Mexico and in other parts of New Spain, it seemed to him that their departure was a benefit rather than a disadvantage, because they were leading vicious lives, and had nothing with which to support themselves.

When these statements and depositions had all been duly received, signed, and attested, and had been shown to his most illustrious lordship, the viceroy, he ordered an authorized copy to be taken, which was made by Joan de Leon, clerk of Their Majesties' court and of the royal audiencia of New Spain, the 27th of February, 1540, witnessed by the secretary, Antonio de Almaguer, and sent to His Majesty, to be laid before the lords of the council, that they might provide and order that which should be most serviceable to their interests.

NOTES

Preface to Journal

1   Mendoza died in Lima, July 21, 1552.

First Part

Chapter I

1   President, or head, of the Audiencia, the administrative and judicial board which governed the province.

2   Marqués del Valle de Oaxaca y Capitan General de la Nueva España y de la Costa del Sur.

3   Guzman had presided over the trial of Cortes, who was in Spain at the time, for the murder of his first wife seven years previously (October, 1522). See Zaragoza's edition of Suarez de Peralta's Tratado, p. 315.

4   The name was changed in 1540.

5   The best discussion of the stories of the Seven Caves and the Seven Cities is in Bandelier's Contributions, p. 9, ff.

Chapter II

1   A judge appointed to investigate the accounts and administration of a royal official.

2   A full account of the licentiate de la Torre and his administration is given by Mota Padilla (ed. Icazbalceta, pp. 103–106). He was appointed juez March 17, 1536, and died during 1538.

3   They appeared in New Spain in April, 1536, before Coronado's appointment. Castañeda may be right in the rest of his statement.

4   This account has been translated by Buckingham Smith, New York, 1871.

Chapter IV

1   Bandelier (Contributions, p. 104) says this was Topia, in Durango, a locality since noted for its rich mines.

Chapter V

1   See Mendoza's letter to the King, regarding Samaniego's position.

Chapter VI

1   The correct date is 1540. Castañeda carries the error throughout the narrative.

2   See the instructions given by Mendoza to Alarcon, in Buckingham Smith's Florida, p. 1.

3   See the writings of Tello and Mota Padilla concerning Oñate. Much of the early prosperity of New Galicia—what there was of it—seems to have been due to Oñate's skillful management.

Chapter VII

1   The report of Diaz is incorporated in the letter from Mendoza to the King, translated herein. This letter seems to imply that Diaz stayed at Chichilticalli; but if such was his intention when writing the report to Mendoza, he must have changed his mind and returned with Saldivar as far as Chiametla.

Chapter IX

1   Bandelier, in his Gilded Man, identifies this with Zuñi river. The Rio Vermejo of Jaramillo is the Little Colorado or Colorado Chiquito.
2   Mota Padilla, p. 113: "They reached Tzibola, which was a village divided into two parts, which were encircled in such a way as to make the village round, and the houses adjoining three and four stories high, with doors opening on a great court or plaza, leaving one or two doors in the wall, so as to go in and out. In the middle of the plaza there is a hatchway or trapdoor, by which they go down to a subterranean hall, the roof of which was of large pine beams, and a little hearth in the floor, and the walls plastered. The Indian men stayed there days and nights playing (or gaming) and the women brought them food; and this was the way the Indians of the neighboring villages lived."
3   The war cry or "loud invocation addressed to Saint James before engaging in battle with the Infidels."—Captain John Stevens' Dictionary.
4   Compare the translation of the Traslado de las Nuevas herein. There are some striking resemblances between that account and Castañeda's narrative.
5   The persistent use of the form Señora, Madame, for the place Sonora, may be due to the copyists.
6   This should be September.

Chapter X

1   Fletcher, in The World Encompassed by Sir Francis Drake, p. 131 (ed. 1854) tells a similar story of some Indians whom Drake visited on the coast of California: "Yet are the men commonly so strong of body, that that which 2 or 3 of our men could hardly beare, one of them would take vpon his backe, and without grudging, carrie it easily away, vp hill and downe hill an English mile together." Mota Padilla, cap. xxxii, p. 158, describes an attempt to catch one of these Indians.
2   Father Sedelmair, in his Relacion, mentions this custom of the Indians. (See Bandelier, Final Report, vol. i, p. 108.)
3   Cortes.
4   The Zuñis make a similar sort of preserves from the fruit of the tuna and the yucca.

See Cushing in The Millstone, Indianapolis, July, 1884, pp. 108–109.

Chapter XI

1   Compare chapter 13. These two groups of pueblos were not the same.

2   Compare the lines which the Hopi or Moqui Indians still mark with sacred meal during their festivals, as described by Dr. Fewkes in his "Few Summer Ceremonials," in vol. ii of the Journal of American Ethnology and Archaeology.

Chapter XII

1   The report of Alvarado is probably the official account of what he accomplished.

2   In regard to the famous rock fortress of Acoma see Bandelier's Introduction, p. 14, and his Final Report, vol. i, p. 133. The Spaniards called it by a name resembling that which they heard applied to it in Zuñi-Cibola. The true Zuñi name of Acoma, on the authority of Mr. F. W. Hodge, is Hákukia; that of the Acoma people, Hákukwe.

3   An error for Tiguex, at or near the present Bernalillo. Simpson located this near the mouth of the river Puerco, southeast of Acoma, but I follow Bandelier, according to whom Alvarado pursued a northeasterly direction from Acoma. See his Introduction, p. 30, and Final Report, vol. i, p. 129.

4   Pecos. Besides his Final Report, vol. i, p. 127, see Bandelier's Report on the Pecos Ruins.

Chapter XIII

1   Coronado probably reached the Rio Grande near the present Isleta. Jaramillo applies this name to Acoma, and perhaps he is more correct, if we ought to read it Tutahaio, since the Tiguas (the inhabitants of Isleta, Sandia, Taos, and Picuris pueblos) call Acoma Tuthea-uáy, according to Bandelier, Gilded Man, p. 211.

Chapter XIV

1   This was Matsaki, at the northwestern base of Thunder mountain, about 18 miles from Hawikuh, where the advance force had encamped.

Chapter XV

1   The instructions which Mendoza gave to Alarcon show how carefully the viceroy tried to guard against any such trouble with the natives.

2   Evidently the underground, or partially underground, ceremonial chambers or kivas.

Chapter XVI

1   Wooden warclubs shaped like potato-mashers.

2   Professor Haynes corrected the error in a note in Winsor's Narrative and Critical History, vol. ii, p. 491, saying that "it is evident that the siege must have been concluded early in 1541."

Chapter XVII

1   Should be Alcaraz.

Chapter XVIII

1   Or Cervantes.

2   Coronado says, in his letter of October 20th, that he started April 23d.

Chapter XIX

1   The Rio Pecos.

2   There is an elaborate account of the sign language of the Indians, by Garrick Mallery, in the first annual report of the Bureau of Ethnology, 1879–80.

3   The reference is clearly to the district of Colima in western Mexico, where one of the earliest Spanish settlements was made.

Chapter XX

1   A manera de alixares. The margin reads Alexeres. The word means threshing floor.

2   Bandelier suggests that the name may have originated in the Indian exclamation, Texia! Texia!—friends! friends!—with which they first greeted the Spaniards.

3   Capt. John Stevens's New Dictionary says the sanbenito was "the badge put upon converted Jews brought out by the Inquisition, being in the nature of a scapula or a broad piece of cloth hanging before and behind, with a large Saint Andrews cross on it, red and yellow. The name corrupted from Saco Benito, answerable to the sackcloth worn by penitents in the primitive church." Robert Tomson, in his Voyage into Nova Hispania, 1555, in Hakluyt, iii, 536, describes his imprisonment by the Holy Office in the city of Mexico: "We were brought into the Church, euery one with a S. Benito vpon his backe, which is a halfe a yard of yellow cloth, with a hole to put in a mans head in the middest, and cast ouer a mans head: both flaps hang one before, and another behinde, and in the middest of euery flap, a S. Andrewes crosse, made of red cloth, sowed on vpon the same, and that is called S. Benito."

4   The Tiguex country is often referred to as the region where the settlements were.

Chapter XXII

1   Castañeda's date is, as usual, a year later than the actual one.

2   Yuge-uing-ge, as Bandelier spells it, is the aboriginal name of a former Tewa village, the site of which is occupied by the hamlet of Chamita, opposite San Juan. The others are near by.

3   Taos, or Te-uat-ha. See Bandelier's Final Report, vol. i, p. 123, for the identification of these places.

4   This rendering, doubtless correct, is due to Ternaux. The Guadiana, however, reappears above ground some time before it begins to mark the boundary of the Spanish province of Estremadura. The Castañeda family had its seat in quite the other end of the peninsula.

Second Part

Laus Deo

1   The Newfoundland region.

Chapter II

1   Bandelier found the Opata Indians living in houses made with "a slight foundation of cobblestones which supported a framework of posts standing in a thin wall of rough stones and mud, while a slanting roof of yucca or palm leaves covered the whole."— Final Report, pt. i, p. 58.

2   The *Opuntia tuna* or prickly pear.

3   *Prosopis juliflora.*

4   *Cereus thurberii.*

5   Sonora.

6   Bandelier, Final Report, pt. i, p. 111, quotes from the Relaciones of Zárate-Salmeron, of some Arizona Indians: "Tambien tienen para su sustento Mescali que es conserva de raiz de maguey." The strong liquor is made from the root of the Mexican or American agave.

7   These were doubtless cantaloupes. The southwestern Indians still slice and dry them in a manner similar to that here described.

8   The Pueblo Indians, particularly the Zuñi and Hopi, keep eagles for their feathers, which are highly prized because of their reputed sacred character.

Chapter III

1   Chichiltic-calli, a red object or house, according to Molina's Vocabulario Mexicano, 1555. Bandelier, Historical Introduction, p. 11, gives references to the ancient and modern descriptions.

2   These were evidently the mountain lion and the wild-cat.

3   Albert S. Gatschet, in his Zwölf Sprachen, p. 106, says that this word is now to be found only in the dialect of the pueblo of Isleta, under the form sibúlodá, buffalo.

4   Matsaki, the ruins of which are at the northwestern base of Thunder mountain. See Bandelier's Final Report, pt. i, p. 133, and Hodge, First Discovered City of Cibola.

5   The mantles of rabbit hair are still worn at Moki, but those of turkey plumes are out of use altogether. See Bandelier's Final Report, pt. i, pp. 37 and 158. They used also the fiber of the yucca and agave for making clothes.

6   J. G. Owens, Hopi Natal Ceremonies, in Journal of American Archaeology and Ethnology, vol. ii, p. 165 *n.*, says: "The dress of the Hopi [Moki, or Tusayan] women consists of a black blanket about 3 1/2 feet square, folded around the body from the left side. It passes under the left arm and over the right shoulder, being sewed together on the right side, except a hole about 3 inches long near the upper end through which the arm is thrust. This is belted in at the waist by a sash about 3 inches wide. Sometimes, though not frequently, a shirt is worn under this garment, and a piece of muslin, tied

together by two adjacent corners, is usually near by, to be thrown over the shoulders. Most of the women have moccasins, which they put on at certain times."

7   Papa in the Zuñi language signifies "elder brother" and may allude either to age or to rank.

8   Dr. J. Walter Fewkes, in his Few Summer Ceremonials at the Tusayan Pueblos, p. 7, describes the Dā´wā-wẏmp-ki-yas, a small number of priests of the sun. Among other duties, they pray to the rising sun, whose course they are said to watch, and they prepare offerings to it.

9   In his Few Summer Ceremonials at Tusayan, p. 6, Dr. Fewkes says that "with the exception of their own dances, women do not take part in the secret kibva [estufa] ceremonials; but it can not be said that they are debarred entrance as assistants in making the paraphernalia of the dances, or when they are called upon to represent dramatizations of traditions in which women figure."

10   Mr. Frank Hamilton Cushing, in the Compterendu of the Congrès International des Americanistes, Berlin, 1888, pp. 171–172, speaking of the excavations of "Los Muertos" in southern Arizona, says: "All the skeletons, especially of adults [in the intramural burials], were, with but few exceptions, disposed with the heads to the east and slightly elevated as though resting on pillows, so as to face the west; and the hands were usually placed at the sides or crossed over the breast. With nearly all were paraphernalia, household utensils, articles of adornment, etc. This paraphernalia quite invariably partook of a sacerdotal character." In the pyral mounds outside the communal dwellings, "each burial consisted of a vessel, large or small, according to the age of the person whose thoroughly cremated remains it was designed to receive, together, ordinarily, with traces of the more valued and smaller articles of personal property sacrificed at the time of cremation. Over each such vessel was placed either an inverted bowl or a cover (roughly rounded by chipping) of potsherds, which latter, in most cases, showed traces of having been firmly cemented, by means of mud plaster, to the vessels they covered. Again, around each such burial were found always from two or three to ten or a dozen broken vessels, often, indeed, a complete set; namely, eating and drinking bowls, water-jar and bottle, pitcher, spheroidal food receptacle, ladles large and small, and cooking-pot. Sometimes, however, one or another of these vessels actually designed for sacrifice with the dead, was itself used as the receptacle of his or her remains. In every such case the vessel had been either punctured at the bottom or on one side, or else violently cracked—from Zuñi customs, in the process of 'killing' it." The remains of other articles were around, burned in the same fire.

Since the above note was extracted, excavations have been conducted by Dr. J. Walter Fewkes at the prehistoric Hopi pueblo of Sikyatki, an exhaustive account of which will be published in a forthcoming report of the Bureau of Ethnology. Sikyatki is located at the base of the First Mesa of Tusayan, about 3 miles from Hano. The house structures were situated on an elongated elevation, the western extremity of the village forming a sort of acropolis. On the northern, western, and southern slopes of the height, outside the village proper, cemeteries were found, and in these most of the excavations were conducted. Many graves were uncovered at a depth varying from 1 foot to 10 feet, but the skeletons were in such condition as to be practically beyond recovery. Accompanying these remains were hundreds of food and water vessels in great variety of form and decoration, and in quality of texture far better than any earthenware previously recovered from a pueblo people. With the remains of the priests there were found, in addition to the usual utensils, terra cotta and stone pipes, beads, prayer-sticks, quartz crystals, arrowpoints, stone and shell fetiches, sacred paint, and other paraphernalia similar to that used by the Hopi of today. The house walls were constructed of small, flat stones brought from the neighboring mesa, laid in adobe mortar and plastered with the same material. The rooms were invariably small, averaging perhaps 8 feet square, and the walls were quite thin. No human remains were found in the houses, nor were any evidences of cremation observed.

Chapter IV

1. The pueblo of Picuris.

2. Bandelier gives a general account of the internal condition of the Pueblo Indians, with references to the older Spanish writers, in his Final Report, pt. i, p. 135.

3. Lewis H. Morgan, in his Ruins of a Stone Pueblo, Peabody Museum Reports, vol. xii, p. 541, says: "Adobe is a kind of pulverized clay with a bond of considerable strength by mechanical cohesion. In southern Colorado, in Arizona, and New Mexico there are immense tracts covered with what is called adobe soil. It varies somewhat in the degree of its excellence. The kind of which they make their pottery has the largest per cent of alumina, and its presence is indicated by the salt weed which grows in this particular soil. This kind also makes the best adobe mortar. The Indians use it freely in laying their walls, as freely as our masons use lime mortar; and although it never acquires the hardness of cement, it disintegrates slowly. ... This adobe mortar is adapted only to the dry climate of southern Colorado, Arizona, and New Mexico, where the precipitation is less than 5 inches per annum. ... To the presence of this adobe soil, found in such abundance in the regions named, and to the sandstone of the bluffs, where masses are often found in fragments, we must attribute the great progress made by these Indians in house building."

4. Bandelier discusses the estufas in his Final Report, pt. i, p. 144 ff., giving quotations from the Spanish writers, with his usual wealth of footnotes. Dr. Fewkes, in his Zuñi Summer Ceremonials, says: "These rooms are semisubterranean (in Zuñi), situated on the first or ground floor, never, so far as I have seen, on the second or higher stories. They are rectangular or square rooms, built of stone, with openings just large enough to admit the head serving as windows, and still preserve the old form of entrance by ladders through a sky hole in the roof. Within, the estufas have bare walls and are unfurnished, but have a raised ledge about the walls, serving as seats."

5. The American turkey cocks.

6   A custom still common at Zuñi and other pueblos. Before the introduction of manufactured dyes the Hopi used urine as a mordant.

7   Mr. Owens, in the Journal of American Ethnology and Archaeology, vol. ii, p. 163 *n.*, describes these mealing troughs: "In every house will be found a trough about 6 feet long, 2 feet wide, and 8 inches deep, divided into three or more compartments. In the older houses the sides and partitions are made of stone slabs, but in some of the newer ones they are made of boards. Within each compartment is a stone (trap rock preferred) about 18 inches long and a foot wide, set in a bed of adobe and inclined at an angle of about 35°. This is not quite in the center of the compartment, but is set about 3 inches nearer the right side than the left, and its higher edge is against the edge of the trough. This constitutes the nether stone of the mill. The upper stone is about 14 inches long, 3 inches wide, and varies in thickness according to the fineness of the meal desired. The larger stone is called a máta and the smaller one a mátaki. The woman places the corn in the trough, then kneels behind it and grasps the mátaki in both hands. This she slides, by a motion from the back, back and forth over the máta. At intervals she releases her hold with her left hand and with it places the material to be ground upon the upper end of the máta. She usually sings in time to her grinding motion."

There is a more extended account of these troughs in Mindeleff's Pueblo Architecture, in the Eighth Report of the Bureau of Ethnology, p. 208. This excellent monograph, with its wealth of illustrations, is an invaluable introduction to any study of the southwestern village Indians.

8   See W. H. Holmes, Pottery of the Ancient Pueblos, Fourth Annual Report of the Bureau of Ethnology; also his Illustrated Catalogue of a portion of the collections made during the field season of 1881, in the Third Annual Report.

Chapter V

1   Bandelier, in his Visit to Pecos, p. 114, n., states that the former name of the pueblo was Âquin, and suggests the possibility of Castañeda having originally written Acuyé. The Relacion del Suceso has Acuique.

2   The spring was "still trickling out beneath a massive ledge of rocks on the west sill" when Bandelier sketched it in 1880.

3   The former Tano pueblo of Galisteo, a mile and a half northeast of the present town of the same name, in Santa Fé county.

4   According to Mota Padilla, this was called Coquite.

5   These Indians were seen by Coronado during his journey across the plains. As Mr. Hodge has suggested, they may have been the Comanches, who on many occasions are known to have made inroads on the pueblo of Pecos.

Chapter VI

1   Bandelier, Final Report, pt. i, p. 34. "With the exception of Acoma, there is not a single pueblo standing where it was at the time of Coronado, or even sixty years later, when Juan de Oñate

accomplished the peaceable reduction 'of the New Mexican village Indians." Compare with the discussion in this part of his Final Report, Mr Bandelier's attempt to identify the various clusters of villages, in his Historical Introduction, pp. 22–24.

2   The Queres district, now represented by Santo Domingo, San Felipe, Santa Ana, Sia (Castañeda's Chia), and Cochiti. Acoma and Laguna, to the westward, belong to the same linguistic group. Laguna, however, is a modern pueblo.

3   One of these was the Tano pueblo of Galisteo, as noted on page 523.

4   The Jemes pueblo clusters in San Diego and Guadaloupe canyons. See pl. LXX.

5   The Tewa pueblo of Yugeuingge, where the village of Chamita, above Santa Fé, now stands.

6   Taos.

7   The Keres or Queres pueblo of Sia.

8   The trend of the river in the section of the pueblo settlements is really westward.

9   The Tusayan Indians belong to the same linguistic stock as the Ute, Comanche, Shoshoni, Bannock, and others. The original habitat of the main body of these tribes was in the far north, although certain clans of the Tusayan people are of southern origin. See Powell, Indian Linguistic Families, 7th Annual Report of the Bureau of Ethnology, p. 108.

10   The Spaniards under Coronado.

11   See the Carta escrita por Santisteban á Mendoza, which tells nearly everything that is known of the voyage of Villalobos. We can only surmise what Castañeda may have known about it.

Chapter VII

1   More than once Castañeda seems to be addressing those about him where he is writing in Culiacan.

2   The well known travois of the plains tribes.

3   Pemmican.

Chapter VIII

1   Mr Savage, in the Transactions of the Nebraska Historical Society, vol. i, p. 198, shows how closely the descriptions of Castañeda, Jaramillo, and the others on the expedition, harmonize with the flora and fauna of his State.

2   The Mississippi and Missouri rivers.

3   This is probably a reminiscence of Cabeza de Vaca's narrative.

4   Mota Padilla, cap. xxxiii, 4, p. 166, gives his reasons for the failure of the expedition: "It was most likely the chastisement of God that riches were not found on this expedition, because, when this ought to have been the secondary object of the expedition, and the conversion of all those heathen their first aim, they bartered with fate and struggled after the secondary; and thus the misfortune is not so much that all those labors were without fruit, but the worst is that such a number of souls have remained in their blindness."

Third Part

Chapter IV

1   The correct date is, of course, 1542.

2   A Franciscan. He was a "frayle de misa."

3   Gen. W. W. H. Davis, in his Spanish Conquest of New Mexico, p. 231, gives the following extract, translated from an old Spanish MS. at Santa Fé: "When Coronado returned to Mexico, he left behind him, among the Indians of Cibola, the father fray Francisco Juan de Padilla, the father fray Juan de la Cruz, and a Portuguese named Andres del Campo. Soon after the Spaniards departed, Padilla and the Portuguese set off in search of the country of the Grand Quivira, where the former understood there were innumerable souls to be saved. After travelling several days, they reached a large settlement in the Quivira country. The Indians came out to receive them in battle array, when the friar, knowing their intentions, told the Portuguese and his attendants to take to flight, while he would await their coming, in order that they might vent their fury on him as they ran. The former took to flight, and, placing themselves on a height within view, saw what happened to the friar. Padilla awaited their coming upon his knees, and when they arrived where he was they immediately put him to death. The same happened to Juan de la Cruz, who was left behind at Cibola, which people killed him. The Portuguese and his attendants made their escape, and ultimately arrived safely in Mexico, where he told what had occurred." In reply to a request for further information regarding this manuscript, General Davis stated that when he revisited Santa Fé, a few years ago, he learned that one of his successors in the post of governor of the territory, having despaired of disposing of the immense mass of old documents and records deposited in his office, by the slow process of using them to kindle fires, had sold the entire lot—an invaluable collection of material bearing on the history of the southwest and its early European and native inhabitants—as junk.

When the reports of these martyrdoms reached New Spain, a number of Franciscans were fired with the zeal of entering the country and carrying on the work thus begun. Several received official permission, and went to the pueblo country. One of them was killed at Tiguex, where most of them settled. A few went on to Cicuye or Pecos, where they found a cross which Padilla had set up. Proceeding to Quivira, the natives there counselled them not to proceed farther. The Indians gave them an account of the death of Fray Padilla, and said that if he had taken their advice he would not have been killed.

Chapter V

1   There were two settlements in Sonora bearing this name, one occupied by the Eudeve and the other by the Tegui division of the Opata. The former village is the one referred to by Castañeda.

Chapter VII

1 The letters of Mendoza during the early part of his administration in Mexico repeatedly call attention to the lack of arms and ammunition among the Spaniards in the New World.

Chapter VIII

1 The kersey, or coarse woollen cloth out of which the habits of the Franciscan friars were made. Hence the name, grey friars.

2 The earliest description of the American buffalo by a European is in Cabeza de Vaca's Naufragios, fol. xxvii, verso (ed. 1555).

3 Scattered through the papers of Dr. J. Walter Fewkes on the Zuñi and Tusayan Indians will be found many descriptions of the páhos or prayer sticks and other forms used as offerings at the shrines, together with exact accounts of the manner of making the offerings.

Chapter IX

1 The northeastern province of New Spain.

2 The conception of the great inland plain stretching between the great lakes at the head of the St. Lawrence and the Gulf of Mexico came to cosmographers very slowly. Almost all of the early maps show a disposition to carry the mountains which follow the Atlantic coast along the gulf coast as far as Texas, a result, doubtless, of the fact that all the expeditions which started inland from Florida found mountains. Coronado's journey to Quivira added but little to the detailed geographical knowledge of America. The name reached Europe, and it is found on the maps, along the fortieth parallel, almost everywhere from the Pacific coast to the neighborhood of a western tributary to the St. Lawrence system. See the maps reproduced herein. Castañeda could have aided them considerably, but the map makers did not know of his book.

3 Captain John Stevens' Dictionary says that this is "a northern province of North America, rich in silver mines, but ill provided with water, grain, and other substances; yet by reason of the mines there are seven or eight Spanish towns in it." Zacatecas is now one of the central states of the Mexican confederation, being south of Coahuila and southeast of Durango.

4 Apparently the location of this island gradually drifted westward with the increase of geographical knowledge, until it was finally located in the Philippine group.

Translation of the Letter from Mendoza to the King, April 17, 1540

1 From the Spanish text in Pacheco y Cardenas, Documentos de Indias, vol. ii, p. 356. The letter mentioned in the opening sentence is not known to exist.

2 Presumably the fortress of which Samaniego was warden.

3 Buckingham Smith's Florida gives many documents relating to the damage done by French brigantines to the Spanish West Indies during 1540–41.

4   In his paper on the Human Bones of the Hemenway Collection (Memoirs of the National Academy of Sciences, vi, p.156 et seq.), Dr. Washington Matthews discusses the possible former existence of a variety of the llama in certain parts of the southwest.

5   The headbands are doubtless here referred to.

6   The same salt lake from which the Zuñis obtain their salt supply to-day.

7   Compare with this hearsay description of something almost unknown to the Spaniards, the thoroughly scientific descriptions of the Hopi dances and ceremonials recorded by Dr. J. Walter Fewkes.

8   The peaches, watermelons, cantaloupes, and grapes, now so extensively cultivated by the Pueblos, were introduced early in the seventeenth century by the Spanish missionaries.

9   At first glance it seems somewhat strange that although Zuñi is considerably more than 100 miles south of Totonteac, or Tusayan, the people of the former villages did not cultivate cotton, but in this I am reminded by Mr. Hodge that part of the Tusayan people are undoubtedly of southern origin and that in all probability they introduced cotton into that group of villages. The Pimas raised cotton as late as 1850. None of the Pueblos now cultivate the plant, the introduction of cheap fabrics by traders having doubtless brought the industry to an end.

10   Doubtless the pueblo of Marata (Makyata) mentioned by Marcos de Niza. This village was situated near the salt lake and had been destroyed by the Zuñis some years before Niza visited New Mexico.

Translation of the Letter from Coronado to Mendoza, August 3, 1540

1   Translated from the Italian version, in Ramusio's Viaggi, vol. iii, fol. 359 (ed. 1556). There is another English translation in Hakluyt's Voyages, vol. iii, p. 373 (ed. 1600). Hakluyt's translation is reprinted in Old South Leaflet, general series, No. 20. The proper names, excepting such as are properly translated, are spelled as in the Italian text.

I

1   This statement is probably not correct. It may be due to a blunder by Ramusio in translating from the original text. Eighty days would be nearly the time which Coronado probably spent on the journey from Culiacan to Cibola, and this interpretation would render the rest of the sentence much more intelligible.

2   The valley into which Friar Marcos did not dare to enter.

3   Doubtless the Yaquimi or Yaqui river.

4   These were doubtless the Seri, of Yuman stock, who occupied a strip of the Gulf coast between latitude 28° and 29° and the islands Angel de la Guardia and Tiburon. The latter island, as well as the coast of the adjacent mainland, is still inhabited by this tribe.

5   As Indian news goes, there is no reason why this may not have been one of Ulloa's ships, which sailed along this coast during the previous summer. It can hardly have been a ship of Alarcon's fleet.

II

1 It is possible that this is a blunder, in Ramusio's text, for "His Majesty." The Marquis, in New Spain, is always Cortes, for whom neither Mendoza nor Coronado had any especial regard.

III

1 Hakluyt: ... "very excellent good houses of three or foure or fiue lofts high, wherein are good lodgings and faire chambers with lathers in stead of staires."

2 The kivas or ceremonial chambers.

3 Many garnets are found on the ant-hills throughout the region, especially in the Navajo country.

4 The natives doubtless told the truth. Eagle and turkey feathers are still highly prized by them for use in their ceremonies.

5 It should be noted that Coronado clearly distinguishes between hills or mesas and mountains. Zuñi valley is hemmed in by heights varying from 500 to 1,000 feet.

6 This accords perfectly with the condition of the vegetation in Zuñi valley at the present time.

7 Doubtless a slip of Ramusio's pen for cows, i.e., buffaloes.

IV

1 Coronado doubtless misinterpreted what the natives intended to communicate. The "hot lake" was in all probability the salt lake alluded to on page 157, near which Marata was situated. Totonteac was of course Tusayan, or "Tucano."

2 This is a form of the Zuñi name for Acoma—Hakukia.

3 As clear a description of the form of tribal government among the Pueblo Indians as is anywhere to be found is in Bandelier's story, The Delight Makers. Mr. Bandelier has been most successful in his effort to picture the actions and spirit of Indian life.

4 Dr. J. Walter Fewkes has conclusively shown that the snake dance, probably the most dramatic of Indian ceremonials, is essentially a prayer for rain. Coming as it does just as the natural rainy season approaches, the prayer is almost invariably answered.

5 Possibly those used in weaving.

6 The conquerors, in the literature of New Spain, are almost always those who shared with Cortes in the labors and the glory of the Spanish conquest of Mexico.

Translation of the Traslado de las Nuevas

1 Translated from Pacheco y Cardenas, Documentos de Indias, vol. xix, p. 529. This document is anonymous, but it is evidently a copy of a letter from some trusted companion, written from Granada-Hawikuh, about the time of Coronado's letter of August 3, 1540. In the title to the document as printed, the date is given as 1531, but there can be no doubt that it is an account of Coronado's journey.

2 A part of Granada, near the Alhambra. There is a curious similarity in the names Albaicin and Hawikuh, the latter being the native name of Coronado's Granada.

3   Uttering the war cry of Santiago.
4   The printed manuscript is V. M., which signifies Your Majesty.
5   Doubtless Thunder mountain.

This is the Latest Account of Cibola, and of
More than Four Hundred Leagues Beyond

1   From a manuscript in the possession of the family of the late Sr. D. Joaquin Garcia Icazbalceta, of the City of Mexico. This appears to be a transcript from letters written, probably at Tiguex, on the Rio Grande, during the late summer or early fall of 1541.

Translation of the Relacion del Suceso

1   The Spanish text of this document is printed in Buckingham Smith's Florida, p. 147, from a copy made by Muñoz, and also in Pacheco y Cardenas, Documentos de Indias, vol. xiv, p. 318, from a copy found in the Archives of the Indies at Seville. No date is given in the document, but there can be no doubt that it refers to Coronado's expedition. In the heading to the document in the Pacheco y Cardenas Coleccion, the date is given as 1531, and it is placed under that year in the chronologic index of the Coleccion.

2   See the letter of August 3, 1540.

3   The Acoma people call their pueblo Áko, while the name for themselves is Akómë, signifying "people of the white rock." The Zuñi name of Acoma, as previously stated, is Hákukia; of the Acoma people, Háku-kwe. Hacus was applied by Niza to Hawikuh, not to Acoma—*Hodge.*

4   The Rio Grande.

5   Evidently Taos, the native name of which is Tŭatá, the Picuris name being Tuopá, according to Hodge.

6   Identical with Castañeda's Cicuyc or Cicuye—the pueblo of Pecos.

7   Southeast, in Buckingham Smith's Muñoz copy.

8   Tuxeque, in the Muñoz copy.

9   Or mines, as Muñoz guesses.

10   And jerked beef dried in the sun, in the Muñoz copy only.

Translation of a Letter from Coronado to the King, October 20, 1541

1   The text of this letter is printed in Pacheco y Cardenas, Documentos de Indias, vol. iii, p. 363, from a copy made by Muñoz, and also in the same collection, vol. xiii, p. 261, from a copy in the Archives of the Indies at Seville.

2   Coronado had apparently forgotten the atrocities committed by the Spaniards at Tiguex.

Translation of the Narrative of Jaramillo

1   The text of this narrative is found in Buckingham Smith's Florida, p. 154, from a copy

made by Muñoz, and in Pacheco y Cardenas, Documentos de Indias, vol. xiv, p. 304, from the copy in the Archives of the Indies.

2   See Bandelier's Gilded Man, p. 175. This is Castañeda's "Guagarispa" as mistakenly interpreted by Ternaux-Compans, the present Arispe, or, in the Indian dialect, Hucaritz-pa. The words "Ispa, que" are not in the Pacheco y Cardenas copy.

3   Doubtless the reference is to the alkali soil and vegetation.

4   Acoma.

5   Sia.

6   Identical with Taos—the Braba of Castañeda and the Yuraba of the Relacion del Suceso.

7   Pecos. In Pacheco y Cardenas this is spelled Tienique.

8   All references to hot rooms or estufas are of course to be construed to mean the kivas or ceremonial chambers.

9   Tiguex is here doubtless referred to.

10   One of the villages whose names Jaramillo did not know was probably the Ximena (Galisteo) of Castañeda.

11   In Buckingham Smith's copy occurs the phrase, "que decian ellos para significarnoslo Teucarea." This is not in Pacheco y Cardenas.

12   The pueblos of the Rio Grande.

13   This is the spelling of Panuco in both texts.

Translation of the Report of Hernando de Alvarado

1   The text of this report is printed in Buckingham Smith's Florida, p. 65, from the Muñoz copy, and in Pacheco y Cardenas, Documentos de Indias, vol. iii, p. 511.

2   Acuco or Acoma. The route taken by Alvarado was not the same as that followed by Coronado, who went by way of Matsaki. Alvarado's course was the old Acoma trail which led directly eastward from Hawikuh or Ojo Caliente.

3   Day of the nativity of the Blessed Virgin, September 8. This was the Tiguex or present Rio Grande.

Testimony Concerning Those Who Went on the
Expedition with Francisco Vazquez Coronado

1   Translated freely and abridged from the depositions as printed in Pacheco y Cardenas, Documentos de Indias, vol. xiv, p. 373. See note on page 377. The statements of the preceding witnesses are usually repeated, in effect, in the testimony of those who follow.

2   Judge of the highest court of the province.

3   Thursday.